Critical Psychology

The International Journal of Critical Psychology

Issue 6

Political Subjects

Collection as a whole © Lawrence & Wishart 2002
Individual articles © the individual authors 2002

The authors have asserted their rights under the Copyright, Design and Patents Act, 1998 to be identified as the authors of this work. All rights reserved. Apart from fair dealing for the purpose of private study, research, criticism or review, no part of this publication may be reproduced, stored in a retrieval system, or transmitted, in any form or by any means, electronic, electrical, chemical, mechanical, optical, photocopying, recording or otherwise, without the prior permission of the copyright owner.

ISSN 1471 4167
ISBN 0 85315 964 5

Cover design Art Services
Cover image © Tim Davison
Typeset by E-Type, Liverpool, UK,
printed by Bookcraft, UK

Critical Psychology is published three times per year by
Lawrence & Wishart
99a Wallis Road
London E9 5LN
United Kingdom

Editor
Valerie Walkerdine (University of Western Sydney)
Email: v.walkerdine@uws.edu.au

Editorial Assistant
Barbara Graham
Email: ijcp@uws.edu.au

Individual subscriptions £40
Institutional subscriptions £120

For advertising information contact contact
editorial@l-w-bks.demon.co.uk

Book Reviews Editors
Dr Lisa Blackman
Dept of Media and Communications,
Goldsmith's College, University of London,
London SE14 6NW. UK
Email: coa01lb@gold.ac.uk

Professor Wendy Hollway
Head of Psychology
Faculty of Social Sciences,
The Open University
Milton Keynes
MK7 6AA, UK
Email: w.hollway@open.ac.uk

Associate Editors
Australasia
Ben Bradley (Charles Sturt University)
Ann Game (University of New South Wales)
Nicola Gavey (University of Auckland)
John Kaye (University of Adelaide)
Sue Kippax (University of New South Wales)
Isaac Prilleltensky (Victoria University)
Jane Ussher (University of Western Sydney)

UK
Lisa Blackman (Goldsmiths College, University of London)
Stephen Frosh (Birkbeck College, University of London)
Wendy Hollway (Open University)
Ian Parker (Manchester Metropolitan University)
Ann Phoenix (Open University)
Jonathan Potter (Loughborough University)
Lynne Segal (Birkbeck College, University of London)
Couze Venn (Nottingham Trent University)

North America
Tod Sloan (University of Tulsa)
John Broughton (Columbia University)
Betty Bayer (Hobart and William Smith Colleges)
Kum Kum Bhavnani (University of California, Santa Barbara)
Kareen Malone (University of West Georgia)
Michelle Fine (The City University of New York)

International Editorial Board
Erika Apfelbaum (CNRS, Paris)
Erica Burman (Manchester Metropolitan University, UK)
Teresa Cabruja (University of Girona, Spain)
Michael Cole (University of California, San Diego, USA)
Heidi Figueroa Sarriera (University of Puerto Rico)
Angel Gordo-Lopez (Universidad Complutense de Madrid)
David Ingleby (University of Utrecht, Netherlands)
Ingrid Lunt (University of London, UK)
Wolfgang Maiers (Free University of Berlin, Germany)
Amina Mama (University of Cape Town, South Africa)
Janet Sayers (University of Kent, UK)
Corinne Squire (University of East London, UK)

Contents

Editorial

Valerie Walkerdine

Features

Lorraine Johnson-Riordan, Janie Conway Herron and Pam Johnston
Decolonising the 'white' nation: 'white' psychology

Desmond Painter and Catriona Macleod
The new moral order and racism in South Africa post 11 September 2001

J. Brendan K. Maloney
September 11: trauma and American politics

Maritza Montero
Ethics and politics in psychology: twilight dimensions

Dimitris Papadopoulos
Dialectics of subjectivity: North-Atlantic certainties, neo-l rationality and liberation promises

Peter Raggatt
A plurality of selves? An illustration of polypsychism in a recovered addict

Commentary

Couze Venn
The 'globalitarian' order to come?: September 11 as event

Dennis Fox and Isaac Prilleltensky
Wading through quicksand: between the philosophically desirable and the psychologically feasible 1

Ian Parker
Personal response under attack 16

Ximena Tocornal and Isabel Piper
The other September 11: narratives and images 172

Reviews

R. Joffe Falmagne
L. Blackman, *Hearing Voices: Embodiment and Experience* — 177

T. Jefferson
L. Layton, *Who's That Girl? Who's That Boy? Clinical Practice Meets Postmodern Gender Theory* — 181

T. Strong
B. Slife, R. Williams, and S. Barlow (eds), *Critical Issues in Psychotherapy: Translating New Ideas into Practice* — 187

Notes on Contributors — 190

Editorial

Valerie Walkerdine

This issue of the journal was in the making when the shock waves of 11 September 2001 were being felt all over the world. The theme of political subjects was therefore extended, to incorporate specific responses to a call for papers and opinion pieces about critical psychology and 11 September. However, it should be borne in mind that journal issues are a long time in the making, and the Middle East conflict escalated and developed after these authors penned their pieces. Nevertheless, the complexities of the current global political situation act as a constant reminder of the need for critical psychological work to engage with the relation of the political to the making of subjectivities.

In the context of globalisation and neo-liberalism, there is a need to understand the complexities of subjectivity beyond cold war divisions, or what Venn (page 153), following Baudrillard, refers to as 'the fourth world war'. This understanding of subjectivities needs to go beyond the recourse to economics on the one hand and ideologies on the other (but without forgetting either). Since, in the Foucauldian sense, subjectification is a central plank of neo-liberal governmentalities, the engagement of critical psychologists with an understanding of the production of subjectivities is crucial.

The papers in this issue address the making of political subjects and subjectivities in relation to 11 September, and to a diverse array of political concerns, from the politics of race in Australia to the horizons of neo-liberalism. Lorraine Johnson-Riordan, Janie Conway and Pam Johnston interrogate the colonial narratives of the nation of Australia, and of psychology as 'white'. In this powerful and important paper, the authors take up a challenge they see presented by critical psychology, to rethink the place of psychology in the making of nation and national identity. In doing this they present three narratives of girl and womanhoods within Australia; narratives that are more easily told elide those which cannot so easily be spoken. Desmond Painter and Catriona Macleod also explore aspects of racism, in this case racism in South Africa after 11 September. Discussing a newspaper report about a woman wearing an Osama bin Laden T shirt, they explore the racialisation of Islam within South Africa, and think about the place of critical psychology in South Africa and other peripheral countries; they argue that dynamic responses to world events are shaped by local specificities. Those specificities help to shape thinking that presents very important directions for critical work, moving beyond a simple colonisation by Western critical psychologies of political contexts on the periphery.

Brendan Maloney explores 11 September from a different standpoint. He uses an approach to trauma from within psychoanalysis to think about political reactions to 11 September within the United States. In particular, Maloney explores the aggression of the American military response. His use of the concept of trauma is both interesting and controversial, and raises one side of an important debate for critical psychologists. In particular, discourse theorists have been very critical of the use of concepts such as trauma when attempting to understand the effectivity and impact of political events.

This debate is touched on by Tocornol and Piper in their piece, and different approaches to an understanding of subjectivity within neoliberalism are also discussed by Dimitris Papadopoulos in his exploration of different approaches to subjectivity within German critical psychology and Foucauldian-inspired work. He asks, significantly, if a critical or emancipatory moment can be identified at all within oppositions to neo-liberalism. How, he asks, can the neo-liberal subject transform him/herself to become a subject of power?

Maritza Montero discusses subjectivity and politics from the point of view of the place of ethics and politics within psychological and social research. She argues that while ethics and politics have been mentioned in discussions of psychological theorising, they have been assigned a dark and shadowy place. She explores what it would mean to retrieve ethics and politics from this place and to foreground their status in the construction of knowledge.

Pete Raggatt discusses subjectivity from the point of view of methodology. In particular he addresses the methodological issues related to the concept of the subject as multiple and fragmented. He develops and demonstrates a mode of analysis for mapping multiplicity and examining how a number of competing narratives work in the constitution of twists and turns of narrative identity.

The Opinion Section of the issue contains four commentaries on 11 September. Couze Venn explores Baudrillard's concept of a 'fourth world war', and the shaky and complex task of finding 'the soul of a transmodern and transcolonial humanity of the future'. Dennis Fox and Isaac Prilleltensky discuss what a principled response to the events might be, while also thinking about the role of psychology in the form of a response by the American Psychological Association. Ian Parker also discusses the place of psychology, by exploring the psychologisation of the sources of the conflict itself. Finally, Tocornol and Piper discuss the technologies of memory as they relate to that 'other September 11', the day in 1973 that saw the violent overthrow of the Allende government, an event etched in the popular memory and imagination. What they remark on in terms of images and rhetorical strategies gives considerable food for thought with respect to more recent events, as well as allowing us to remember that 11 September is a date which has more than one discursive and historical significance.

The issue concludes with three book reviews. Rachel Joffe Falmagne reviews Lisa Blackman's *Hearing Voices*, Tony Jefferson reviews Lynne Layton's *Who's that girl? Who's that boy?* and Tom Strong reviews Brent Slife, Richard Williams and Sally Barlow's *Critical Issues in Psychotherapy*.

Decolonising the 'white' nation: 'white' psychology

Lorraine Johnson-Riordan, Janie Conway Herron and Pam Johnston

Abstract

Drawing on Fabian's (1983) classic critique of anthropology in Time and the Other, *this paper argues that psychology too has been saturated in nineteenth-century evolutionary narratives, which, in turn, have contributed to the founding narratives and truth regimes of Australia as a 'white' modern nation, with the consequent theft of time and space from its Indigenous peoples. Within these mythological narratives and their 'camp mentality', white racialised identities and subjectivities have been produced as essentialist, frozen identities set apart from all Others, especially 'the primitive'. White Psychology, with its particular use of spatial/temporal politics and the comparative method, has added legitimacy to the projects of imperial modernity, policing the boundaries of 'whiteness' (in the name of the 'universal' self, 'natural' traits and characteristics of peoples, nations, etc), and contributing to the obliteration of difference, to epistemic (and physical) violence and to the enduring and seemingly unbridgeable gap in relations between 'whites' and Australia's Indigenous peoples. This paper suggests that a feminist (post)colonial psychology would come face-to-face with difference, engaging with what Fabian called a 'radical contemporaneity' of peoples, a re-temporalisation of its detemporalised discourse/practices, the generation of dialogue and the production of new narratives. In particular, this (post)colonial psychology would be in dialogue with Australia's reconciliation movement, that is, with contemporary de/colonising processes within the nation. Story telling and dialogue between Indigenous and non-Indigenous people about lives past, present and future will be central to the project of disrupting and reworking the unethical and immoral foundations of both the modern White Nation and White Psychology, and working towards non-racist, indeed non-racial identities and subjectivities within it. In this paper the authors offer fragments of their genealogical travelling as a 'gift of time' each to the other.*

> Because it is a systematic negation of the other person and a furious determination to deny the other person all attributes of humanity, colonialism forces the people it dominates to ask themselves the question constantly: 'In reality, who am I?' (Fanon, 1990: 200)

> We've got to be able to move the national psyche. Reconciliation is not about destroying, it's about shifting the business-as-usual mentality when it comes to Indigenous people, to a new dimension, a new relationship, a new foundation upon which new relationships can be structured and built (Dodson, 1999).[1]

New beginnings

This article attempts to take up the intellectual and political challenge opened up by the new critical psychology movement in contemporary Australian (post)colonial and (post)modern times. The authors are not practising psychologists, but as writers, artists, teachers and activists, as multiply-positioned cultural outsider/insiders, as consumers of psychology, we have an investment in engaging with a movement committed to thinking in new ways about the discipline and its practices – its teaching, curriculum, epistemological and philosophical foundations, research methods and clinical practice. In addition, our current work, in its multiple forms, is focused on questions of identity and subjectivity, race and colonialism, in the Australian nation-state. This paper links White Nation and White Psychology to postcoloniality, in a search for a morally and ethically responsible future.

As children in the 1950s, we were 'schooled' in the education institutions of the White Nation (see Story 1). The White Australia policy was not officially abandoned until the 1970s.[2] From the 1960s onwards, as students in various universities, we were the recipients of knowledge colour-coded 'white'. What we were taught in psychology courses was no exception. Not surprisingly, none of us was sufficiently politically conscious at the time to make sense of the boredom and disengagement we experienced as students. Later, as patients or 'clients' in private and community clinics, government services and elsewhere, we – as

Indigenous and non-Indigenous women, 'black' and 'white', of Irish, Romany, Jewish and Aboriginal descent – have been simultaneously its subjects and objects, spoken for and spoken about, told and untold by its 'white' colonial/modern narrative performances. Meanwhile our histories, cultures, identities, experiences, our complexly raced/gendered bodies have been misrecognised, dismissed, denied, disavowed. Take just one moment in a recent encounter of one of the authors: White male psychologist to Indigenous woman client: 'You can't be Aboriginal. You don't look like one'. This is a (post)modern instance of a white (male) professional deploying a colonising/racist mode of address. He is deeply entrenched in the racism of modernity; he sees with the raciological gaze he learned at school that 'aborigines' looked so-and-so (and no doubt that Aboriginal women were 'dirty gins'). Now, in his office in the metropolis, face-to-face with her difference, her ambiguity, the contemporary coloniser, fearful of loss of his power, deploys familiar old racist tactics. He refuses her naming of herself, her identity. He turns a blind eye, sees what he wants to see, ignores or denies her difference, transforming her, 'the Other', into someone like himself. He tries to draw her into his own comfort zone. How is an Indigenous woman, so positioned in a professional/client relationship in which his power is already weighted against hers, to speak? Can she 'talk it up' to the White Man? In other times and places, she most certainly could not. Outside the law and unprotected by it, she, the black woman, has been used and abused by white men and exploited by white women; she is likely to have had her children stolen from her (she is the dirty, neglectful, incapable mother, a threat to the health and survival of the white racist nation). She has experienced immense loss and deprivation – as yet unrecompensed by the nation – as a consequence of those acts. Yet, here, now, she, the Indigenous client, must explain herself, she must carry the burden of proof of her identity. She, an Indigenous woman client, must give him, the white male professional, a lesson in contemporary Aboriginal identity politics in order to legitimise her request for his services as an Aboriginal woman. But this is the tip of the iceberg. The full impact of Empire and colonial modernity on both coloniser and colonised, on both sides of the race divide, is yet to be confronted (Fanon, 1993). And the task becomes increasingly difficult in (post)modernity, these (new) times when global forces push against and undermine local efforts to settle the unfinished business of the past (Bauman, 1998).

In this piece, then, taking the conjuncture of blak[3]/feminist/ (post)colonial/cultural studies as our broad political/theoretical position of critique, and locating ourselves inside (but not uncritically) the contemporary Australian movement for Reconciliation[4] between Indigenous and non-Indigenous peoples, we want to pose challenging questions for a critical, politically-engaged, postcolonial psychology: How can White Psychology be transformed to be effective in the new time/space of (post)colonial, (post)modern Australia in which Indigenous and non-Indigenous peoples must live together? How can psychology contribute to the well-being of Indigenous people in this country?[5] How can psychology contribute to the reconciliation movement – to transforming the 'us' versus 'them' camp mentality which has again found expression in the contemporary race wars, and in the widespread support for Pauline Hanson's right-wing One Nation Party? How can psychology contribute to de-racialising race-d ('white' and 'black') identities and subjectivities, shaped as we have been in this country by the imperial/modern desire for affirmation of a superior European (bourgeois) body/identity, and by the subsequent foundational fictions of modern nation-state racist regimes of truth? How can a new critical psychology participate in bringing about the emergence of an alternative (anti-racist/anti-colonialist, non-racial) psychic economy in both Indigenous and non-Indigenous communities? These are very big questions, of course, questions for which we can only hope to draw a preliminary sketch toward an agenda for change. The guiding structure of this paper is the link between race and nation (White Nation) and race and discipline (White Psychology) and the implications for epistemology, ontology, curriculum and teaching.

Temporal/spatial politics and the White Nation

Historically the White Nation, Australia, began in 1901 with Federation and the White Australia policy. Floats marking the one hundredth anniversary of this event paraded through Sydney's streets on 1 January 2001, celebrating the nation's achievements. But many Indigenous people and their supporters questioned the triumphalist narrative the event told of the nation's history. Indigenous 'Dreamtime' floats led the parade, but without there ever having been a Treaty between Indigenous peoples and British settlers and their descendants, what could the inclusion of these floats mean? Who was celebrating and what were they celebrating? The scandal of Australia's 'unfinished business', and the seemingly unbridgeable gap between Indigenous and non-Indigenous peoples, remains, despite the gains over the last decades and ten years of an official national Reconciliation movement, now in visible decline.

Genocide of Indigenous peoples, mere 'primitives' to Europeans, was a founding principle of both Empire (see the notion of terra nullius in the 'discovery' narratives) and the modern nation-state, founded in eugenicist thought as it was. To understand this, and the work of temporal/spatial politics in bringing it about, it is necessary to revisit the repertoire of founding myths,[6] the 'truths' of Modernity, drawn from a constellation of nineteenth-century disciplines – Biology, History, Geography and Anthropology (Gilroy, 2000). Suffice it to say that 'the primitive' and the European bourgeois body/self (and the 'white' colonial modern body/self) were constituted within the grand narratives of Modernity, especially the evolutionary narratives of progress and civilisation, underpinned by eugenics and theories of degeneracy associated with Biology, Anthropology and Geography (see for example Fabian, 1983; Gilroy, 2000, Torgovnick, 1990). 'The primitive', long 'grist for the Western fantasy mill' (Torgovnick, 1990: 153), became the dark Other, the negative opposite of European Modernity, deemed necessary for the construction of its own self. 'We' imagined 'them' and invented 'us' by comparison. 'We' were what 'they' were not, could not be, namely fully human. 'They' were 'Stone Age Man', the 'dying race'; 'we' were 'Modern Man', inheritors of present/future time/space. As the story was told, 'primitives' and Modern Man occupied linear time, but 'primitive' Man was unchanging, while Western Man developed. The 'primitive', then, became a convenient label for the first or earliest age/stage/period of 'Mankind', the childhood of Man. The 'primitive' occupied another time and place; he was 'back then' and 'out there', not here and now.[7] He was without history, eternally past and present, always the same. History began with, and belonged to, Western Man, as did the future. He who controls time controls the future and space with it. Clearly, a Time/Space-Machine and a Mimetic Machine were brought into play to differentiate between the two peoples, to establish and legitimise temporal/spatial hierarchies between 'us' and 'them', the 'insiders' and the 'outsiders', and to determine the respective fates and futures of each in the context of Modernity. What this constituted was a monstrous crime, the sacrifice of a people and culture, the theft of the time, space and life of the 'Other'.[8]

Again, the raciological Time-Space machine supplied the logic and mechanism for the foundation of Australia not only as a Modern space legitimately 'inherited' from Indigenous peoples who were expected to 'die out', but also as a 'fortified encampment' from which all others inside and outside who were different were to be treated as enemies of the nation-state and eliminated or kept out (Gilroy, 2000: 100). Alterity within was denied; 'foreigners' from outside were excluded (see for example Hollinsworth (1998) on the White Australia policy, immigration and assimilation and integration policies and practices). To galvanise and cement the political collective, insider bodies were racialised and colour-coded 'white', 'white' being the imagined skin colour difference that marked 'us' from 'them'. The myths of essentialism – white was obviously white and you couldn't change it; and sameness (there were no differences within (see Stories 1 & 2 below)) – were deemed necessary to bind the 'white' community (Anderson's (1983) 'imagined political community'[9]). Meanwhile, Indigenous peoples, colour-coded 'black', were dispossessed, stolen from their country, spirituality, kin, culture, identity and the means of traditional existence, becoming wards of the White State, herded into artificial 'communities' and 'managed'; or 'rescued' and 'saved' by Christian missionaries; or ending up under constant surveillance in prison-like 'homes'; or used as cheap labour for whites, or left to grovel for an existence in humpies on the edge of towns (see Story 3 below). Access to Modernity, its resources and benefits, access indeed to life, necessitated denying Aboriginality. Shamefully, the 'dying race' was left to die. Nothing of benefit was done because, according to the grand narratives of Modernity, nothing could be done. They, 'the Others', were sacrificed for the sake of Modernity, Christianity, progress and civilisation. For our sake. For the life and well being of White Australia. For the life and well being of Europeans. (And who, then, were the barbarians? And why is there so much interest in Indigenous cultures in Europe at the present time? Such a strong desire, still, to hold onto the 'stuff' in the museums of Empire in London, Paris...?)

Imperialism and Modernity were both territorial and subject-constituting projects. The constitution of the subject in Modernity within a particular nation-state formation was 'accomplished through disciplinary institutions' (Hardt and Negri, 2000: 23 (following Foucault)). Schools, among other institutions (Anderson (1983) examined the museum, the census and the map), formed 'an archipelago of factories of subjectivity' in which 'the political technologies that govern our relation to ourselves, our humanity and our species' (Hardt and Negri, 2000: 196) were deployed (Gilroy, 2000: 43). These produced somatic, corporeal and ideological effects, ways of being, ways of thinking about self and others. Here were taught the mythological narratives of Modernity and White Nation; the rules and mechanisms of racial inclusion/exclusion; the rules of racialised gendered time-space ('white' and 'black' women's time and place and the racialised rules of housekeeping that permeated every nook and cranny of the Empire); a sense of home and legitimate belonging for 'whites' (in a country not your own); emotional and affective bonds to Empire, nation and family; a relation to land and the power and pleasure of citizen soldiery (see Story 1 below).

In these various (mostly racially segregated) institutions of subjectification/ subjection, both coloniser and colonised endured different forms of (epistemic) violence and different forms of alienation, through the workings of specific forms of biopower. Take the stories told in the name of History and Social Studies in primary schools in the 1940s and 1950s (see Story 1 below). In *Why Weren't We Told?* Henry Reynolds (1999) has recently noted the 'gaps' in the History he was taught at school. There was nothing about Indigenous Australians, nothing about colonial history. The conflict and violence of the frontier wars, the Aboriginal resistance to invasion and, later, their contribution to the development of the cattle industry, for instance, were completely left out, Reynolds claims. In the version of History he was taught, the colonial past was forgotten. But why did this happen? In his analysis of narratives of nation, Homi Bhabha (1990) argued that, once the mass migration of the nineteenth century was over, the idea of 'the Nation' was deployed to bring disparate communities together. Making the Nation demanded narratives that secured the new home. It demanded 'potent symbolic and affective sources of cultural identity' (Bhabha, 1990: 292). Consequently, Bhabha argued, a temporal spatial displacement took place in narrating the new Nation, its history and culture. The past of the present place (in the case of Australia, the history of colonial settlement, of frontier conflict and violence, Indigenous resistance, massacres and so on) was displaced, and substituted with a 'true' National past, namely English history, heritage and culture. The colonial past could then become a site of forgetting and repression, sustained by (and perpetuating) the myth of the 'dying race' – the end of the 'primitive' and the beginning of modern man and the progressive nation-state. This 'double-time' ('disjunctive time') of the nation and its corresponding spatial displacements, in turn, produced a 'knowledge disjunct'. Bhabha argued that forms of alienation in processes of self-identification emerged from these temporal/spatial disjunctures.

Imagine the dislocations for a 'white' girl in the 1950s classroom – living in Australia but learning English History, learning mythological stories of Australian white male heroes, and limited racialised notions of white women's time/place (e.g. in home 'science' learning how to keep an unpolluted dust/dirt free home, utilising a variety of brooms and other cleaning devices, how to use her 'white goods' to keep a healthy, hygienic, clean, germ-free family), and only racist ideas about Aborigines, 'the dying race' (see Story 1). Imagine the dislocations for an Aboriginal girl (if she was indeed allowed into the same or any classroom given that she was more than likely to have been either deemed a 'full-blood' and left in the 'blacks' camp', or deemed a 'half-caste' and stolen by the state (as in the film *Rabbit-Proof Fence* (2002)) – a child who must repress her Aboriginal identity and learn that her people are the 'dying race' (her grandmother, her mother) and that she must be 'white' to live, to be free.[10] For both 'black' and 'white' Australians, coloniser and colonised, the 'true' stories of our shared histories were never told, could never be told, in a nation founded in unethical race-based narratives. Instead, for the sake of the White Nation and the Empire we were transported by a Time-Space Machine, and taught a mythological and triumphalist version of History with which we were supposed to identify, and within which we were to become good 'white' citizen soldiers. Indigenous and non-Indigenous Australians are yet to know 'our' true history. It is still being rewritten, and only recently taught. It is a site of intense ongoing public debate and contention. But until we do know what happened, until we can restore the time that has been stolen, understand that a debt is owed and pay the rent, we will neither know ourselves nor how to walk and talk together in the future.

Temporal/spatial politics and White Psychology

Disciplines have a history, and psychology, along with other disciplines in the Social and Natural Sciences – biology, anthropology, history, sociology, and geography – is saturated in the grand master narratives of Modernity. That includes the privileging of rationality, genealogies of origins, universalising and homogenising narratives of 'the individual' and selfhood, narratives of identity formation, human progress and development, assumptions of sameness of culture and community, and the deployment of historical amnesia and horizontal, homogenous empty time/space (see, for example, Venn, 2000). As historically and culturally produced discourse, psychology is also embedded in the project of Empire in a specific nation-state, in this case in the cultural imaginary of the White Nation, Australia, its race-d, gendered and class-ed projects. Following feminist poststructuralists (see, for example, Harraway, 1989) and the work of cultural studies, the science of psychology can be usefully thought of as a narrative, a discourse caught up in the local historical and cultural imaginary of the nation-state and harnessed and put to work by it in its own ('white' bourgeois) interests.

Psychology is productive, too. It produces discourses about reality and it produces identities and subjectivities. As a political technology of the self and relations with others, 'White' Psychology has served as an apparatus of the nation-state, constituting, promoting and policing the borders and boundaries of the 'universal' self (read: the modern 'white' self that takes cover in transcendent discourses). 'White' Psychology has worked to provide the border maintenance of the assumed, invisible, 'white' inside and the visible 'primitive' and other Others outside. This assumption of 'invisibility', the sign of the universal self, has always been a tactic deployed in the Australian context of imperial modernity to produce the political collective of seemingly non-racialised 'individuals', a community of 'equal' insiders, with its own morality and rules for civic behaviour. 'Individualism' covers over the whiteness of insiderism.

'White' Psychology's border work is performed through its decontextualised and detemporalised discourses, its location in universal time and space. How does the Time-Space Machine work in this discipline and with what effects? Johannes Fabian's (1983) critique of anthropology makes an interesting and persuasive argument about temporal spatial politics in anthropology, which is also useful, he says, in critiquing sociology and psychology. All science, he argues, involves temporalisation. Indeed, whatever knowledge we have is expressed in terms of temporal categorisation. That Time is used to create an object is a central tenet of his argument (Fabian 1983:78). Moreover, temporality is deployed strategically to create space/distance and, thereby, to reinscribe hegemonic power relations in communicative practices such as science (and, we would stress, in the community more generally). 'White' Psychology's comparative method is caught up in this Time-Space Machine. Ontological in its imperative, it focuses on the classification of entities and traits, taxonomies and developmental sequences, in its search for what 'Man' 'is'. It produces and conserves frozen identities for possession and display, for pleasure and power. One outcome is the re-centring of the unmarked 'white' self, but not without cost – an unbridgeable chasm between self and other, and a distancing, a disengagement, a removal, from lived cultures, 'ours' and 'theirs'.

It is not too big a leap to argue that the discourse and practice of White Psychology has contributed over the decades to the scandal of the petrified relation between 'whites' and Indigenous peoples in this country. 'White' Psychology, underpinned by an epistemology of sameness following Anthropology, has studied (cultural) isolates, without historical explanation. The outcome is a kind of mapping of spatially distributed traits. Distancing is the condition of possibility and the outcome of this sort of psychological discourse/practice – distancing from contemporary reality, cultural differences and past history. A flat dead field, an allochronic landscape, abstracted from life, from history, from experience, has been a game played by the rules of a Time-less frame – a response, Fabian (1983: 68) has argued, significantly, to its own historical and cultural context. In Australia, only the official White History or a mythological 'historicality' could be taught; differences were negated and excluded, and alienated selves were the outcome. The irony and tragedy of 'White' Psychology is that it, too, can only produce alienated selves. It can neither give an account nor offer a critique of the psychic impact of colonisation, particularly on Indigenous men and women; nor can it contribute to decolonisation in the present. Its narratives are morally, ethically and intellectually bankrupt. Its practices are offensive and racist (see 'New Beginnings' above).

Time, space and decolonising the White Nation

'Decolonising' implies the possibility of 'self and collective transformation' (Alexander and Mohanty, 1997: xlii), through critical consciousness, and, in turn, the mobilisation of opposition forces within and against the racialised nation and its racist effects. Decolonising implies the necessity of a challenge to, and transformation of, the founding fictions of the modern nation-state, and a de-racialising of the racialised 'us' versus 'them' camp mentality at their core. Time returns in the re-temporalisation of the relationship between the 'white' coloniser and the 'primitive' Other. To return to Fabian's critique of Anthropology: in attempting to overcome the time-space problem generated by Anthropology and its epistemology of identity (put into practice in the modern White nation), he turned to a different politics of temporality, to what he called 'coevalness' or a 'radical contemporaneity of mankind' (Fabian, 1983: xi). He suggested that two peoples who coexist, who live in the same time and place, could come together face-to-face and engage in dialogue. Following Fabian's line of argument, one could say that here, now, together, I/you/we can tell stories which could become the occasion for Time, place, memory, history, experience, language and power to be reclaimed, and the relationship between us renegotiated. Such a process would involve reciprocity (if not exchange); the story would be a gift given freely (unlike the story given to the Anthropologist by the native, possessed and retold by him), but carrying with it the weight of responsibility and the expectation of ethical action (see the three stories told below).

Political activism, separately and in coalition, by Indigenous and non-Indigenous Australians (with the support of international networks and organisations) dates back, in this century, to the 1930s and 1940s, and was growing stronger, and more united, over the decades until the recent lull in action. There has been Aboriginal resistance in the Wavehill strikes for equal pay, the Freedom Rides of the 1960s (influenced by the Civil Rights movement in the United States), the Bark petition for Land Rights, the 1967 Referendum, the Tent Embassy for Land Rights, the protest march at the 1988 bicentenary celebrations and, over the past decade, the High Court's Mabo and Wik decisions, the Deaths in Custody Inquiry, the Stolen Generations Inquiry, the Council for Reconciliation, and assorted, grass roots pro-Indigenous movements such as ANTaR, which has collected hundreds of thousands of signatures nation-wide supporting Native Title and Reconciliation. A million people have signed Sorry Books. The year 2000 saw hundreds of thousands of people, Indigenous and non-Indigenous, walking across the nation's bridges to signal their support for Reconciliation. Even the opening ceremony of the Olympic Games has been hailed as pro-Reconciliation, not to mention Indigenous athlete Cathy Freeman's successful run for gold in the 400 metres.

Through this complex and ongoing 'race war' (Foucault, 1980), counter-memories and counter-narratives have emerged to contest the old regime of truths of imperial modernity, and to reinscribe and reconstitute Indigenous and non-Indigenous identities and subjectivities, largely outside the familiar identity-constituting apparatuses of modernity. Indigenous voices, long silenced, are telling stories that have not been heard before in white public space. Over the past two decades, there has been a Blak cultural renaissance, an explosion of Indigenous art, writing, performance, dance, music, photography and film (see, for instance, the controversial 2002 Adelaide Festival). This proliferation of Indigenous cultural expression constitutes a 'subjective explosion' (Foucault, 1980) bursting into the historically white public arena – art galleries, performance spaces, bookstores, music festivals, and city squares. A new space for writing b(l)ak, talking b(l)ak, and a new space for engagement and dialogue between Indigenous and non-Indigenous peoples has opened up. Whatever its form, it is in-your-face praxis, produced and performed from the speaking position of 'I'/'we' – Indigenous voices speaking for and about themselves, their memories, their histories. A central message is WE HAVE SURVIVED – we are here, now, in this time and in OUR place. You are on OUR land, so PAY THE RENT. Cultural festivals such as Adelaide's and Sydney's *Festival of the Dreaming* (1997) have provided many examples of this confronting reversal. The *Wimmin's Business* series at The Playhouse (in Sydney's pre-eminent Opera House) was a significant event featuring Deborah Cheetham's *White Baptist Abba Fan*, Ningali Lawford's story of herself (*Ningali*) and Deborah Mailman's *Seven Stages of Grieving*. Staged around the lives, loves, grief and pain of blak women, they played to mostly white middle-class audiences (and our Indigenous students who loved every minute of it!).

'Witnessing' has become a new mode of Indigenous story-telling in public spaces in Australia. Stories, once told only in Indigenous families and communities, are now told (undoubtedly in edited versions) to white audiences around the country. In support of the Wik people's Native Title claim[11], and following the harrowing stories witnesses told to the Stolen Generations Inquiry,[12] non-Indigenous activists called political meetings in halls, Leagues Clubs and other venues in and around Sydney and invited Indigenous people to address large crowds of non-Indigenous supporters. Again they gave of their time, but this time was in their hands. They came and told their stories, the most precious of gifts. And for many non-Indigenous people in the audience it was a profoundly disturbing, even shocking, face-to-face encounter, the first they had had with an Indigenous person in their whole lifetime.

If the reconciliation movement and all the other events have gone some considerable way to defrost the frozen, empty, distant and hostile relationship between most Indigenous and non-Indigenous peoples, if the story-telling from one side of the divide to the other has at least brought people face-to-face, each in the presence of the other, given recognition, shown a desire to welcome and to be told 'first hand' what has happened – what we have done to them and what have been and remain ongoing consequences of those actions – still the process of undoing what was done continues down a hard road. Jack Beetson, interviewed on Radio National Breakfast Show in January 2000, commented on the apartheid-like distance that still remains between the two groups of peoples. Despite calls for leadership at the Federal government level, it seems that many in the ruling conservative Coalition Party continue to circulate old raciological narratives; these seem out of time and out of place in a (post)modern and (post)colonial Australia,[13] and in the context of a globalising world, yet they still hold sway amongst large numbers of people, including those disaffected by the effects of globalisation and economic rationalism (e.g. Pauline Hanson's One Nation Party attracted a million votes in the last Federal election of the twentieth century). Moreover, racism continues to be deployed by the Coalition as a weapon in the game of wedge politics, effectively blocking changes favourable to Indigenous peoples, in order to maintain the nation as a white space and to win the populist vote. Caught in the net of globalisation, the Howard government, having little to offer those negatively affected by it, wields the weapon of racism for its own survival. It refuses to say Sorry to Indigenous peoples, refuses both Treaty and compensation for past wrongs.[14] It cannot give the ethical, moral, intellectual leadership demanded of it. Indeed, it must continue to wage race wars, in defence of white hegemony, its political constituency and its own power.

And while the presence of Indigenous people and their counter-narratives has begun to break down the tired old racist myths of 'the dying race', and the old reified stereotypes about what Indigenous people look like and live like (see section 'New Beginnings' above), the question remains whether this new phenomenon of Indigenous story-telling to mostly white audiences places too much of the burden for change on Indigenous peoples. Is it enough that 'whites' learn about them, the Others who are strangers to us? Is it enough that *we* learn about their past and present lives and cultures[15] even though we are deeply implicated in the time of those stories, the horror of what happened (and continues to happen) and the privileges that resulted. Or might this run the risk of a mere feel-good redemptive exercise? As Leslie Roman (1993) has pointed out, discourses of redemption have a limited transformative potential. There's no clear-cut easy answer about how to go about such a national agenda of transformation. We don't know much about the changes in 'white' subjectivities that have come about from listening to the stories of the Stolen Generations delivered first hand. (We did watch the Leader of the Opposition on television as he wept in Parliament after reading the *Bringing Them Home* Report.) We don't know much about the 'inside' details of why people walked across the bridges in their hundreds of thousands to express their support for Indigenous people and their plight. Some media commentators said it didn't matter so long as they walked. But it does matter when it comes to moral responsibility. Under the conditions of imperial modernity, moral responsibility was taken over by the State. Now is the time, in postmodernity, to reclaim it, to act on it. Further, the Indigenous leadership frequently says 'whites' must work on themselves; 'whites' should not expect Indigenous people to explain themselves all the time, to carry all the burden of representing what happened in the past or to tell them what to do. So what 'work' can 'whites' do, what stories can 'whites', who have been made strangers to themselves in/by the modern racist state, made unconscious of, or not responsible for, the conditions of our privileged existence in this land, know and tell? How can and must we pay the rent?

Time, space and decolonising White Psychology

'Decolonising White Psychology' will necessarily involve a multiplicity of projects and strategies within and without the critical psychology movement. We would situate the work in universities as well as communities and, more broadly, within the national Reconciliation movement, recognising that education is a key strategy in decolonisation, as indeed it has been in colonisation, and that it takes place both inside and outside education institutions. Education institutions and their associated disciplines, which historically have functioned to (re)produce the 'white' cultural imaginary and the dominant white regime of power, have a significant role to play in decolonising their own practices and in providing intellectual leadership in the Reconciliation movement in the wider society. Undoubtedly, the effect of not challenging the hegemony of whiteness and white knowledge is likely, as Alexander and Mohanty (1997) have argued, to bolster 'inherited regimes of race and Eurocentrism' (xvi).

So far the pattern has tended to be that Indigenous people have taken the time to tell their stories to 'whites'. But this paper argues that non-Indigenous people, 'white' and not white, must also participate in doing work to 'demystify'[16] and 'demythify'[17] their/our pasts, our 'knotted histories' (see Stories 1 & 2 below). This is particularly the case if non-Indigenous people (especially white Australians who grew up here in times like the 1950s, as two of the authors did) understand the idea, argued in various ways by Barthes, Fanon and Foucault, that both coloniser and colonised are caught in the web of power of colonial modernity; each is 'colonised' by the racist state, albeit in different ways and with very different effects. Both coloniser and colonised live with 'wounded forms of consciousness'. Decolonisation therefore necessitates the transformation of both groups, 'white' and 'black' (Indigenous and non-Indigenous), since each has been ideologically circumscribed within mythological speech. Fanon's notion of 'the open door of every consciousness' (Fanon, 1993: 232) suggests such transformation is indeed possible. There is hope. What is needed, he argues, is a 'bursting apart' of colonised consciousness, an eruption and fragmentation of selves constituted in colonialism. Similarly, specifically in relation to white (bourgeois) consciousness, Barthes advocated a demythologisation of the production of identity, subjectivity and consciousness, and a demythologisation of the 'psychosocial forms around which consciousness becomes constituted as "white"' (Sandoval, 1997: 86); and of the 'rhetoric of supremacy ... that structures and naturalises the unjust relations of exchange that arise within and between coloniser and colonised communities' (Sandoval, 1997: 86) (see Story 1 below).

Decolonising necessitates a new 'anti-racist', non-racial economy (Gilroy, 2000), a transformation of the temporal/spatial relations of the 'us' versus 'them' camp mentality, and of the racist grammar of colonial/imperial modernity, the gendered, sexualised and always racialised narratives of White Nation that most of us have had instilled in us (see Story 1 below). The point is to reinvent and reinscribe 'White' and

'Black' bodies with alternative non-racial narratives of identity and subjectivity. To this end, this paper argues for a politics of coalition that can sustain ongoing critical engagement between Indigenous and non-Indigenous people, no matter how difficult the process may be.

This engagement will, it is hoped, transform the philosophical and epistemological foundations of the knowledge of White Psychology, as well as challenge the traditional positioning of the typically white teacher/psychologist, the agent of white psychological knowledge. How many psychology lecturers teach from a position of critique of their own 'whiteness' and the 'whiteness' of the knowledge they disseminate? Yet 'whiteness' has been integral to the production and performance of academic knowledge in the West, and certainly in Australia. The 'body' of knowledge has been taught without attention to the cultural differences and minority positioning of many students (Johnson-Riordan, 1997). The 'culture wars' waged in the 1980s and 1990s in the United States were symptomatic of resistance to dominant Whiteness and Eurocentrism. In Australia this struggle has been couched in terms of an advocacy of 'multicultural' curricula (Women's Studies and Indigenous Studies amongst others). But little attention has been given to the transformation of 'white' knowledge in disciplines in education institutions. In fact, to date, universities have done little to critique their own practices at the level of curriculum and pedagogy, specifically in relation to their implication in imperial modernity. Universities have not made a solid commitment to participating in the national reconciliation and anti-racist movements, yet they are surely central to those processes. This was an issue raised at the National Anti-Racism Conference at the Sydney Opera House in March 2002. Increasing participation in Indigenous studies is commendable but not enough. Like Women's Studies in the Australian context, it too easily becomes another area of study, an enclave for Indigenous students and lecturers, leaving the rest of the offerings untouched. This is not to argue that a 'White' Psychology be dis/replaced by a 'Black' Psychology. Some Indigenous educators and activists may indeed argue for this. But this paper suggests the necessity of going beyond coloured or racialised epistemologies, 'White' or 'Black', and indeed beyond race-based ways of knowing. Moreover, in relation to 'mainstream' knowledges like White Psychology, the point is not merely to add-on[18] Indigenous narratives (and other non-white, non-Indigenous 'multicultural' narratives) as appendages to white scenes (as often happens with the now problematic notion of 'Aboriginal perspectives'); the aim is to disrupt 'white' knowledge by juxtaposing it with alternative narratives, putting each into dialogue with the other, in order to engage the foundational assumptions and premises of the discipline. Confronted with the narratives of the Stolen Generations,[19] for instance, Developmental Psychology, one branch of White Psychology, could never be the same!

Decolonising psychology works against essentialist ontological notions of identity, understanding identity and subjectivity as historically, culturally and politically constituted. It works towards a demystification and demythification of the production of synthetic modern identities ('white' and 'black') in specific contexts (see Story 1) and towards an understanding of the complex tensions in their unravelling and transformation (see Stories 2 & 3).

Finally, in arguing for the need 'to address decolonisation as a fundamental aspect of feminist struggle', and as 'central to self and collective transformation', Alexander and Mohanty (1997) have stressed the importance of 'individual' and collective genealogies, narratives told within the specificities of particular histories of colonialism and nation formation (xv). Such counter-narratives bring together the nexus of race-gender-sexuality-nation and enable an explication of how each is co-articulated and co-constituted (e.g. Stoler, 1995; McClintock, 1995). The formation of racialised, gendered identities in specific historical contexts of modern colonial nation-states has mostly been omitted by 'white' feminists writing in different disciplines in the Australian context (see for example, Supriya, 1998). A postcolonial feminism would ask how Janie Conway Herron and Lorraine Johnson-Riordan were mythologically constituted as 'GOOD' LITTLE WHITE GIRLS within the White Nation, while Pam Johnston was made to be a 'BAD' LITTLE BLACK GIRL. We need to understand the effects of this programming on each of our life-trajectories, in order to understand how we can reinvent ourselves and talk to one another. We need to understand how to create the conditions in which we can work in coalition to re-imagine the nation-state and remove its current unethical foundations. Because we have been so differently positioned within/by the colonising discourse and practices of the White Nation state, because we have been so divided by a state of apartheid, the process of reconciliation of 'white' and 'black' women has still a long hard road ahead. The truth of women's relationships across the divide (and the truth of our historically complex relationships with Indigenous and non-Indigenous men) has yet to be put into the public arena for open and honest discussion.

Three new stories

What follows are three stories, extracts from longer works-in-progress by each of the authors, friends and colleagues, two of whom grew up 'white' and one 'Aboriginal'. Readers are reminded that the latter is a label Europeans gave to Indigenous people. Imagine these stories, in a different form and style, being told around the kitchen table, as part of an ongoing conversation. The first two stories by the two women who grew up as 'good little white girls' make a start on the 'work' 'whites' need to do on/for ourselves – to critically investigate the hidden ethical/political/economic agenda of the production of white racist identities and subjectivities in/by/for imperial modernity. The first story suggests a way of doing critical demythologising work through remembering schooldays and through a critique of old school textbooks, one storage place of the official narratives of the prison-houses of Empire and Modernity. The second story tells of the gradual unravelling of a synthetic, frozen 'white' identity, of the unveiling of what lies beneath that artificial 'whiteness', and of Janie Conway Herron's complex personal journey (from a taxi cab, to a train journey, to raves with activist friends) as she persistently seeks an answer to the question: 'Who am I?' The third story, titled *Kipaympili* (meaning 'to give in return', 'give back', 'throw back', 'exchange away'), presents a counter-scene to 'whiteness', the story of an Indigenous woman, who, in contemporary times, can speak the differences and similarities of her story to both Indigenous and non-Indigenous communities. Pam Johnston claims her Aboriginality, her voice and her power as an Indigenous woman living in the city and working as an artist/activist/teacher with Indigenous women in the prison system in Sydney's West. Taken together as 'gifts of time', and put into dialogue, these are the kinds of stories in all their complexity and ambiguity needed to (in)form new narratives of identity and nation, narratives based not in racist mythologies as they have been in the past, but in truths which will enable morally responsible, transformative political action.

Story 1 Breaking out of 'whiteness'

Towards a (de)mythological reading of 1950s Social Studies textbooks

Written on the occasion of the one-hundredth anniversary of Littlehampton Primary School, November 2000, by Lorraine Johnson-Riordan, an old scholar

It's always fun to look back at your old schoolbooks, the texts you were taught from and the workbooks you wrote and drew in. Since I was the sort of child who kept everything, I have plenty of personal antiques around – my first grade reader, my arithmetic book and several of my primary school social studies textbooks and workbooks, as well as my report books are amongst my collection. I've become passionately involved in revisiting these childhood pedagogical texts to help me think more systematically about identity formation – not just what we learned about but who we were learning to become in Australia in the 1950s. Whiteness was just not something we'd ever really talked about. Girl talk, yes. But beside the odd comment about being 'lily white' – meaning you hadn't got enough sun – whiteness was something you took for granted. You had white skin, or skin you thought was 'white', and that was that.

I grew up in a tiny country town in the Adelaide hills in South Australia. We lived on the outskirts of town, in an old settlers' cottage, which had a mixture of timber and dirt floors, calcimined walls, no running water or sewage, a wood stove for cooking and a tin bath which, to conserve water, everybody took turns to use on bath day. We did have electricity. Despite its shortcomings 'Rose Cottage' was home to us. It nestled behind a very large tangled bush (a typical windbreak) on the downside of a smallish hill (well, not so small when you were riding your bike home from school on a hot summer's afternoon). St James Church, Rectory and Sunday School were perched on top of the hill. So was the cemetery with its fascinating old graves, nineteenth-century tea roses and tall gums teeming with native birds. This hill, and its tiny settlement, was called Blakiston. When we were primary school age my stepfather acquired land adjoining the old cottage and built 'the new house' as we called it, a modern house with a proper bathroom and shower, hot and cold running water, sewage, electricity and, of course, a TV. Rose Cottage remained standing, a symbol of the past, while the new pale brick house marked our family's progress into the future of Modernity. That was 1955.

We rode our bikes to school in Littlehampton. The primary school was a two-roomed stone building. The 'little room' was for grades one to three, 'the big room' for four to seven. Mr Prater, my Headmaster, would teach grades four to seven simultaneously. Each grade had its own row of wooden desks with their inkwells and telltale signatures. Talkers sat at the front, quiet achievers at the back, but that changed weekly depending on how well you did in Friday's test and how well you behaved each week. A photo of a young Queen Elizabeth II hung prominently on the wall. When the old iron bell rang, we lined up outside in straight lines, sang 'God Save the Queen', saluted her flag and marched inside to the beat of her drum. We chanted loudly in unison: 'I am an Australian, I love my country, I salute her flag, I honour her Queen, I promise to obey her laws.' We studied her English, sang our times tables, learned everything 'by heart'.

What did we learn in Social Studies? We learned about, or just as importantly, we learned to desire everything that went into building 'our' Modern White Nation. We learned our place in the nation – gendered and race-d but apparently classless – as unquestioning citizen soldiers. Looking at the Social Studies texts again after all these years, I found myself, to my astonishment, clearly remembering specific pages that I had learned 'by heart' or drawings I had copied with tracing paper.[20] I asked myself what was the message of the images on the textbook covers? On one was a drawing of the statue of Colonel Light up on Montefiore Hill, pointing to the city of Adelaide founded by him. Two white children, a boy and girl, stand before him, pointing upwards in admiration while an aeroplane passed overhead, over the modern city buildings in the background. Modernity – a picture of peace, progress, civilization, the way forward. Coloured white. On another was a drawing of the river of Time. Upstream, in the past, stood the figure of an aborigine, in noble savage pose. As Time moved downstream, the riverbanks become cluttered with the artefacts of modernity and the aborigine was no more.

In Social Studies we learned the symbols of Empire and of 'our nation' within it – 'our flags', the Union Jack, the symbol of England, Scotland and Ireland 'joined together' and 'our own flag'. We coloured in maps ('Your teacher will tell you which colours to use', said the textbook), always carefully keeping inside the line ('Don't go over the line', the teacher said), the borders of territory, 'theirs' and 'ours', red for 'our' Commonwealth, yellow, brown, purple for the others. I remember how I loved to 'colour in', always drawing a heavy black line around every body and every thing. And, of course, we always made that bright blue frill around Australia's coastline to represent the sea and its summer pleasures, and the safety and security of 'our' island home from 'foreigners'.

We celebrated National days – the Queen's Birthday, Anzac Day, Commonwealth Day ('On May 24th we should remember that we are members of a big family of countries which make up the British Commonwealth of Nations. These countries are very friendly and have been grouped together to help each other,' said the textbook), Pioneers Day, Arbor Day.

We learned about a succession of historical events ('Timeline: When we write or tell a story we relate the incidents in the order that they occur'; students must 'write down in correct order the main events in the progress of the state', said the textbook). History was linear, a list of events, a narrative of progress, a story of social evolution. We learned about the English village and the Chief's house 'of long ago'. 'In those days houses did not have glass windows, or any windows, and dogs came in and out as they pleased' ... 'Each man cut off his meat with a dagger'; whereas, now, 'we use knives, forks and spoons'. Then, a minstrel played on a harp, now we have radio and TV. Then the storyline changed to how it was 'in the early days' of colonial settlement and 'the many wonderful things that have happened in South Australia' since the first settlers arrived in 1836. Another story of progress.

We learned about famous men – and the odd women like Joan of Arc and Florence Nightingale, as well as a few pioneering women. (Much more of what it meant to be a white girl/woman we learned in specific ways in Home Science.) We learned about the legendary journeys of our heroes, the brave, courageous white men who were the 'discoverers' and 'first explorers' of this difficult land. (I remember the *Men of Stamina* cards you found in the pockets of your school uniform.) On the other hand, we learned about 'the trouble with the natives'. The 'trouble' was, of course, always to do with their supposed 'nature', not the facts of invasion and dispossession of their lands and their attempts to defend it. There was the story of Edmund Kennedy and his 'brave and faithful' 'Jackie Jackie' (a familiar racist term), who helped him find his way, and to deal with 'the unfriendly natives' who were 'after them all the time'. There was Charles Sturt's trip down the River Murray and the 'crowd of angry natives ... in war-paint ... yelling and dancing and shaking their spears'. We read how 'Sturt did not wish to harm them, but he saw that he might have to fight if he wished to go on'. (The 'primitive' will give way to 'progress' and the future.) We read of the 'sad death' of Captain Collett Barker (after whom the mount near our place was named), who was 'speared by natives' at the mouth of the Murray, and of the 'wonderful journeys' of Eyre and his native guide Wylie (probably pronounced Wily suggesting he couldn't be trusted). Eyre's 'poor overseer' died at the hands of treacherous natives, 'two murderers', 'who had plundered the camp and made off with all they could carry'. What happened to Wylie at journey's end? 'For his faithfulness', 'he was given a weekly allowance of food, so that he was never in want'.

Christianity was the one true religion. (In Pope Gregory's story in the section on 'famous men', we read how 'Angle children were fair, with golden hair and blue eyes. The other slaves in the market place were dark, and their hair was black.' Later, Pope Gregory says 'Angles, did you say? No, no. They should be called angels, they look so fair.')

House and home were at the centre of the discourse of colonial modernity and the racist nation-state. In grade three we learned to identify with 'our country', 'our own land', 'our home', 'our food', 'our own lands', 'our clothing', 'our houses'. Other people were different. Each 'kind' had 'their own lands', 'their own flags', 'their houses', and 'their foods'. (Note the pervasive 'us'/ 'them' racial grammar – 'our pastoral country', 'our grainlands', 'our mallee lands', 'our wheat'.) 'If we made a trip to different parts of the world we would find that many lands would have something strange to show us' ... 'Food is not everywhere the same' ... 'Clothes are also different' ... 'It is the same with houses' ... 'At one time people even lived in caves'. 'Our homes', 'the home of today' is 'much nicer' than the homes of the early settlers, and much nicer than the homes of other people elsewhere. (Turning on a tap is better than carting water and 'nearly every home has a refrigerator', the textbook assured its readers.)

We were told that people from ethnic groups other than English (that is 'foreigners') were sometimes granted permission to settle. German settlers, for instance, were 'the first migrants from a foreign country'. They 'became good South Australians and have done much to help our country become rich and prosperous'. They were good market gardeners. (As indeed was my mother's father, but no mention was ever made of his German ancestry within the family.) But, we were told, their difference remained identifiable. 'It is easy for us to tell where many of them settled because they built little villages like those in Germany, each with its pretty little Lutheran Church'. And the Irish? Well, according to my textbooks, they had already 'joined together' with the English, and that was the end of that story. (Except it wasn't when you knew your father was Irish Catholic and you heard stories about your old gran, your great grandmother, taking a boat from Wexford to Australia a long time ago, and she a single mother with three small children in tow ... and you wondered why she never spoke, sitting as she always did in what seemed to me as a child a dark corner of a dark house ...)

In the discourse on home, every reference to Aborigines (and there weren't many) was in the past tense (and lower case). They 'used to live' here. 'When white people came to make their homes in Australia they found a dark-skinned people living in many parts of the land. We call these people "aborigines". The word "aborigine" means "people who were here first". The aborigines did not grow crops, or keep sheep and cows (not like us)!: 'They got their living by hunting and fishing. They made spears and boomerangs for hunting, and spears and nets for fishing' ... 'Their Food: With these weapons they killed kangaroos, emus, possums, and other animals. Sometimes they ate grubs and lizards and frogs, and even snakes. To cook their food they made a fire' ... ('Ooooh!! How could you eat such things!' we all thought.) 'Their houses: The aborigines had no real houses. There was little need for houses because they were always moving on from one place to another ...'

I became a good little white girl, at least in so far as I believed the racial myths I was taught. There were other ideas about women's place I completely rejected from an early age (like marriage and motherhood), but I believed the myth of the 'dying race', down to the abominable notion that white genes were superior and any intermarriage would be for the better in that 'whiteness' of skin and 'ways' would emerge superior and 'blackness' would fade away. I thought, with every other 'white' person at the time it seemed, that if any Aboriginal people remained, they were 'out there' on reserves living traditional lives. I collected pictures of 'the noble savage' and stuck them on my maps, in the middle of the desert with the flora and fauna. I had no idea what we had done to them. I had not been told. But if 'they' weren't around, if I couldn't see them, then that must confirm both our presence and our superiority. There was nothing to be responsible for, nothing to be done. I was so inoculated, so 'whitewashed', so separated from 'others' (and so alienated from the complex politics of my own multiple ethnic inheritances), that I had no other reference point from which to judge these outrageous eugenicist myths, The Facts that we were tested on every Friday. It wasn't until I was nineteen and a student at the University of Adelaide on a field trip that I met Aboriginal people for the first time. That was the late 1960s. It took another twenty years and a long time living outside of Australia before I was jolted out of my white daze.

Story 2

Keeping it in the family

Janie Conway Herron

My identity is written on me from the outside. Meaning is inscribed on my body like a tattoo, giving definition to its size and shape, its colour and sex. In search of understanding I gather meaning into myself. I collect stories and arrange the narratives according to my own satisfaction. But as I gather them together, the meaning changes. Like a river my identity is fluid, always just out of reach, waiting to change once again.

I decided to use the history of my own family as the basis for my novel *Stories and Secrets*, and to concentrate on the lives of selected women, starting prior to the invasion of Australia in each of the countries that they had come from. I wanted to weave the cloth of my narrative from the many unravelled threads left dangling in the gaps of public and historical records, as well as the smaller narratives that came from family anecdotes and a variety of collected community histories and stories.

Stories and Secrets begins with five women in separate parts of the globe prior to the invasion of Australia. Between them they speak eight languages. There's a young Cadigal girl looking out from the shores of Tubberwole or Sydney Cove. Another is living in the port town of Folkestone in Southern England. Yet another is looking out at the crest of Ben Nevis in the Scottish Highlands. There is a Polish woman watching her son from the window of her house in the Jewish district of Cracow, and a young girl of twelve years on her first day's apprenticeship as a dressmaker in east London. This young girl will meet up with the young Cadigal girl within a year of when the story starts. There's a present-day narrator too. She's searching for her identity and gradually, over the course of the novel, it comes to her.

Hidden identities

I stand on the pavement, edging closer to the curb as waves of water fan out from under the tyres that hiss through the puddles of rain. Headlights glisten in the moist night air and I raise my arm a dozen or more times before a taxi dares to stop.

'Where you going to?' the driver asks brusquely.

'Balmain,' I answer.

'OK, I'll take you there,' he says, as if he's doing me a favour rather than accepting a customer. Feeling grateful just to get out of the drizzling rain, I relax into the warmth of the cab.

'Cold outside?' the driver asks, swinging deftly into the middle of the traffic. He looks into the rear view mirror and grins. A row of neat white teeth is reflected and contained within the steel frame of the mirror. I nod in answer to his question. I don't feel like conversation.

'You going home from work?' he persists.

'Sort of,' I answer curtly.

He turns around.

'What have you been doing today?'

'I've been at the library,' I say impatiently.

'You are a librarian?'

'No, I've been doing research.'

'Oh, you're a student. What do you study?'

'Life.' I laugh, but it sounds hollow as if I'm being smart instead of funny. Thankfully the driver's laugh is round and warm in return.

'Ha, ha, so you are a student of life.' He pauses, and then his Cheshire grin disappears. 'But you don't get life out of books, that's not life,' he says contemplatively.

'Some people do,' I say.

'Old people maybe,' he answers, 'but you are young, you should enjoy life. Living, that's the way to study life.'

I look out the window. We drive in silence for a few minutes. The driver begins to hum. He doesn't like the silence. He fires another question over his shoulder.

'Where you from?'

'Sydney.'

'No, where were you born?' He says the last four words slowly, making sure I understand.

'I was born in Sydney,' I reply firmly.

'But your parents, they weren't born in Sydney,' he chuckles.

'They were actually.'

'No! I don't believe it!' he yells. 'You look like a Lebanese girl or maybe Spanish. Or Turkish. That's it, you're a Turkish girl. Your grandparents, they were Turkish, like me!' He bangs the steering wheel in triumph, then angles his forehead at the rear vision mirror making sure I can see his frown. 'You should be proud of who you are. I am Turkish and proud of it. All my family are Australian citizens, but my children know where they come from, they're not ashamed, like some people.'

I try to explain as honestly as I can. 'On my mother's side, eight generations have been born in Australia. On my father's side, at least four generations, except for my grandmother, we don't know where she came from.'

'So your grandmother was Turkish,' the driver answers emphatically.

'My grandmother said she was French.'

'Oh French, yes, you could be French,' he sounds disappointed.

'My grandfather was Jewish but he was born in Australia,' I add confidently, 'but I don't think my grandmother was French.'

'No, why not?'

'She didn't have a French accent, she couldn't even speak French.'

'So, she is a mystery.'

'Yes, she is,' I answer happily, indicating to the driver to pull over. I hand him the fare. 'My grandmother had a secret,' I add. 'She didn't want anyone to know who she really was.'

The driver counts out the change carefully.

'And now you don't know who you are.'

I smile, looking straight at him for the first time in this short but intimate journey.

'Sometimes I wonder if it matters,' I say and back out of the cab.

'Perhaps your grandmother is Turkish after all!' the taxi driver yells after me.

'Perhaps,' I yell back and a small tight laugh escapes my lips. The driver shakes his head and moves out into the glinting headlights of the night traffic.

(*Stories and Secrets*, 68-69).

New belongings

I grew up feeling 'Australian'. As a young girl I never questioned this, but over the years my sense of identity and belonging has changed. A feeling of 'outsiderness' began to grow inside of me, passed from the outside to the inside, to the core of my being, so that as I grew older my sense of foreignness increased. At least this is my perception of my growing realisation of my own alienation.

It took thirty years of living on the east coast of Australia before I came into contact with Indigenous Australians, and these meetings influenced me, in turn, to look at where I had come from, of what cultures I was made up and how they had, in turn, been part of the historical and cultural construction of my own life. And in a journey that looks inwards, outwards and backwards in an historical, cultural, genealogical and spatial sense, I have discovered a sense of otherness inside my 'white' Australian self.

I knew I had an ancestor who was a woman convict who came out on the First Fleet and that I had a mysterious grandmother whose identity I was convinced, when I began my work, was Indigenous Australian. But as the journey continued I found that she was a Romany or Gypsy woman from the south of England. This discovery was to have enormous ramifications both on my sense of self and my work.

I cannot return to the disparate parts of the globe where my family came from and say, yes, this is where I belong, because I do not belong in any holistic sense to any of these places even if a part of my sensibilities feels as if it does. And yet through my growing awareness of Indigenous Australian history I have had to acknowledge that my existence has come as a result of others' displacement, be they Cadigal on the shores of Sydney Cove, Wangal from Parramatta and Rosehill, Werundjeri and Kurnaje from what is now the suburbs of Melbourne, or the Buandik people of eastern South Australia.

Is it any wonder, given the weight of responsibility that comes with an awareness of the fact that Australia does have a black history, that I would grasp with relief an identity that does not rely on place as much as it does on culture. That in the process of discovering my grandmother's Romany background, which is only one part of who I am, I would say with pride and relief I am a Romany chai.

And yet this identification has not been a simple one. Here is a letter I wrote to Romany musician and historian Jimmie Storey just after meeting up with him and discussing the possibilities of my grandmother's origins.

Dear Jimmie,

I would like to share with you some of my feelings so far, about my possible Romany grandmother and how this has impacted on my sense of identity.

First of all I think you should know that my search for my grandmother's identity has been going on for some years, although she had been dead for some time before I even questioned who she was. The reason I'm saying this is a nervousness about being seen as having some sort of romantic idealism about her identity and therefore my own. You mentioned how many people claim they have a Gypsy grandmother in order to jump on the Gypsy bandwagon. My nervousness about being seen in this way was really strong in me when I met you and other Roma at the conference. I found myself longing to belong and being scared of not belonging because I didn't have any proven Romany identity.

I have also felt totally overwhelmed by the world that has been opening up to me as a result of these discoveries. The knowledge I would need to have of the culture, the languages and the political situation in the various countries Roma live in, plus their histories. And on top of that there is my grandmother's own story to contend with and the mystery of why she hid her identity.

You mentioned the way people of Romany descent often become involved with Indigenous people or with political causes around other marginalised people in a search for their own identity. For the last fifteen years I have been involved with Aboriginal people's battle for equality, equity, land rights and I have formed many strong friendships as a result of this work.

In the beginning, I was an angry table-bashing gubba with a loud voice who was on a crusade to right the injustices of white Australia's black history. Then, after hearing many stories of Indigenous Australians who had hidden their Aboriginal identity, or refused to hand down the culture for fear of their children suffering the same prejudice they had, I began to wonder about my grandmother and the rumours I had heard about her 'black' brother. Although she said she was French, she never spoke French nor did she have an accent. Then a young indigenous man from Alice Springs said to me, 'You have to find out. It's a piece of lost history, another lost voice that needs to be heard.'

I tried for more than ten years to fit an indigenous identity to my grandmother, and met lots of Murris, Kooris and Nungas who were convinced that I was one of them. But I couldn't make the facts fit. At the same time I enrolled in university and people there began to question my right to speak about indigenous issues. I made a radio documentary about Black Deaths in Custody based on my long-time contact with Eddie Murray's family. With their approval I had written a song about Eddie's death in custody which I had sung all round Australia, but at university, my right to speak was questioned.

I began to feel increasingly like an outsider. I understood the dilemma and didn't want to be seen as 'speaking for' anyone. My search for my grandmother's identity intensified alongside my need to find a sense of belonging. But I found myself wondering things like, what if she is Aboriginal? I can't just suddenly go around claiming my Aboriginality. I haven't grown up in the culture. I observed awkwardness between those people who'd grown up knowing their culture and those who had just recently found out about their identity. I began to step back from it all. I kept my friendships but I stopped being so involved.

Out of the blue my brother rings and tells me about meeting you and how you had suggested our grandmother might be a Romany woman from the south of England. I don't know what made you say that, but after talking with you a number of pieces of the puzzle have begun to fall into place. My contact with Ruth McDonald has been marvellous. Between us we have found the birth, death and marriage certificates of the woman listed as the mother of Elsie Marsh (my grandmother) in Elham near Folkestone, England. The stories have begun to fit, but a Romany identity has made her secret seem all the more poignant.

As I have begun to feel increasingly nervous about wrongly identifying as Romany, my otherness has become more confusing. What about my father changing his name from Aarons to Conway after the war, because some fascist in the company he worked for wanted to know what a Jew was doing in the firm! I don't know my Jewishness either. I didn't grow up in the culture. You talked about it being fashionable now to have convict ancestry. You said it rather derisively.

Again I cringed. One of the other women I have been researching was the youngest woman convict to come out on the First Fleet. (Yes, I could claim First Fleet status and join the appropriate society but I haven't.) It's not the heroics I'm looking for, but the underbelly of history. My convict ancestor's story is so sad and awful; it's hardly something to celebrate. She was thirteen when she was imported from England, at fourteen she received forty lashes for insolence and was then shipped to Norfolk Island which was a hell on earth for most convicts, but far worse for the few women who were sent there.

After meeting you I had a five-hour trip home and plenty of time to think. The angst around 'what if I'm not Romany' began to dissipate. I have had a long-standing interest in things from Rajasthan. I went home and showered and changed, put on all my rings and my collection of multi-coloured bracelets and went to a book launch clinking with jewellery. I looked ostentatious and out of place, but it no longer mattered. I think that what I am at the moment is some kind of boundary rider, riding the edges of all these different cultures, looking for who I am. Is this a metaphor for being Romany? What do you think?

Love and regards,
Janie C

Story 3
Kipaympili[21]

Pam Johnston

I grew up in the 1940s and 1950s, in the era of Hasluck's assimilation policies and the Protection Acts, without a sense of what it meant to be who I was.[22] At least I knew I was Aboriginal, but the image I internalised of being Aboriginal was one of shame, of being less human than everyone else.

Because I was Aboriginal I experienced many different foster homes and institutions, with times in between with my biological family. We were in and out of each other's lives to the point where we did not know how we should relate to each other.

As a consequence of my 'background', I was defined by social workers, medical practitioners and psychologists of the day as 'disturbed' and 'at risk'. Also as a consequence of my 'background', I experienced very many instances of abuse that ensured that, in the 'normal' course of events, I would have a long-time relationship with psychology.

I had, in common with many Aboriginal people, the recognition that it wasn't us that was creating the problems we were experiencing. It was the world around us that was creating the problems. Aboriginal magistrate Pat O'Shane (1995) has written:

> I recognised all the things that happened to me through my grandparents and their parents, their brothers and sisters, through my mother and her siblings, through my cousins and my siblings, the things that happened to thousands of other Aboriginal families, and I marvelled, THAT WE ALL WEREN'T STARK RAVING MAD! (p25).

Make no mistake. Psychology has not healed me. Psychology played a major role in my continuing injury, as it did to many other Aboriginal children. I was just one. Our own observations of the damage being done, and our own confirmation of these experiences, are what contributed to any coping or recovery skills over the years. Psychology, and the theories underpinning it, was one of our enemies and we united in fear against it.

Bundjalung Elder, author and historian Ruby Langford Ginibi (1999) says:

> When a Koori person has a breakdown, it's very easy for people to blame that person alone, because they do not understand that that person's breakdown is part of a bigger historical picture. They never look at the dispossession, the having to conform to other people's laws, rules, and standards. Koori people have never been able to be themselves (p48).

The damage was done through underlying assumptions, stereotyping, and race and class assertions of superiority. There was no knowledge/acknowledgement of Aboriginality, and the historical, social, cultural issues related to it. Any so-called 'treatment' inevitably involved a confirmation of particular views already professed by white teachers, doctors and politicians. Their reality was that our 'breed' was less than 'pure' and that we had less intelligence, less hope, less ability, than those who did not have the 'stain' of Aboriginality. Aboriginality had to be hidden as a source of huge shame. There was no encouragement to a brighter future: there WAS NO future if you were an Aboriginal child raised in the time that I was raised in.

As a result of my childhood experiences I became exactly what I was told I was. I was angry and unreliable and my relationship with the world was a constant battle. However, there was always a dichotomy between the outside world (the European world) and the inside world (the Aboriginal world) and understanding this gave me my knowledge of the world and my compassion.

As an adult, I sought out the meaning to me of Aboriginality and this search led to an ongoing deconstruction and reconstruction of my very core. To be Aboriginal required a number of constructions that were already defined by the non-Aboriginal world. At times I would be suicidally empty and at other times maniacally full. On the one hand, the definition of an Aboriginal was, first of all, that we were 'black', with a tendency to wander which made us unreliable ('gone walkabout'), and an inability to be social in any way without getting shamefully drunk. We were presumed inevitably to be forever on the fringes of intelligent academic and cultural life. We had within us a constant questioning of those things that made us human and functional, as we understood these attributes to be a facade, an assumed mantle, which we would surely lose if we exposed our Aboriginality.

Darwinism was rife, and the dominant belief was that Aboriginality was, if not the so-called 'missing link' between human and ape, closer to animal than to man. For this reason, we internalised a concept of ourselves that we did not have the ability to maintain any humanity – we had to work on it with the assistance of those 'professionals' who were our non-indigenous superiors.

On the other hand, thanks to Rousseau and his discourse on the 'noble savage', we were perceived to have an almost inhuman psychic and spiritual understanding of the world, an incredible ability to survive in almost any setting untouched by 'civilisation', a clairvoyant relationship to each other, a child-like and endearing nature; we also had the ability to both understand and answer any question about Aboriginality. This last confirms how issues of Aboriginality are regarded as simple and accessible by non-Aboriginals, and how both privacy and ownership are devalued by professionals, in that any questions could be asked with impunity.

Aboriginal people are forever observed, defined, studied, dug up and analysed. We are like ants under the microscope. Indigenous antiquity is invisible and, by implication, has no value. We are subject and object, patient and client. We are 'told' by professionals, and we believe. We are, after all, Aboriginal. We have all seen the film *Jedda* (1955) – she inevitably turns 'wild/savage' and dies as a consequence. We internalised that we would eventually revert to wild native/animal ways if we weren't constantly on our guard.

My extended family has spent most of its life hiding its Aboriginality, for a number of reasons. This has meant that I have been rejected by both Aboriginal and non-Aboriginal people when trying to claim my identity. Without those cornerstones of confirmation of 'self' that are linked with identity and hope, I was very vulnerable in a number of ways. Thus when I was referred in the direction of psychological 'help', it was a process of further injury rather than of healing. I realised quite early on that I was very much on my own. I found I could not rely on external knowledge or professional help as it worked to destroy who I was and who I could be. So I embarked on a course of education that culminated in post-graduate research projects which documented, in visual and written texts, the course of my self-discovery. I explored my dysfunctional personal life experience and professional expertise by building a *Song Cycle*.

A *Song Cycle* in traditional Aboriginal ways is a series of ceremonies that incorporate concepts of birth, life and death. The whole is made up in sections representing these three progressions, and each part of these progressions incorporates elements within it of birth, life and death.

In making the *Song Cycle* contemporary, I acknowledge my culture and my heritage as a living, breathing entity of which my experience is very much a part. This act of placing 'personal' narrative inside 'academic' research is a powerful tool for/by Indigenous people, given that Aboriginal lives and knowledge have been and continue to be unrecorded.

In the first section of my *Song Cycle* I explore the birth of my identity through a narrative text of a childhood experience with sun, rocks, water and snakes. I expand this narrative visually with a series of thirty-six artworks. I follow the visual work through by researching the development of an aspect of contemporary Aboriginal identity. This research on identity observes institutional, social and political policies that impact only on Aboriginal lives, and shape a way of looking at the world and fitting into it that is uniquely Aboriginal. This part of my work is called *conception BIRTH (identity)*.

In the second section of my *Song Cycle* I speak of what gave me life and an understanding of land. I am forever seeking a mother figure in order to nurture and be nurtured. As luck would have it, I fell into the arms of my adopted mother many years ago. She is a profound and knowledgeable woman who led me back to many older women who, in turn, gave me an understanding of land as mother and nurturer.[23] This image of life, through these old women, is full of strength and connection.

My own experience of parenting was virtually nil. I had no reference in life to what mothering, caring, and nurturing meant. Any information that was available to me was based on the nuclear family unit as defined by the American-based advertising campaigns of the 1950s – not exactly a mine of information that I could relate to my day-to-day experience of life. As a result of this, and of the extreme brutality I experienced as a child, my parenting skills, when I had children, were very consciously performed. I could not trust my 'instinctive' reactions to guide me through, as I knew them to be a danger to both my children and myself. My experiences with my Elders and my understanding of the Aboriginal relationship to land gave me an emotional key. This part of my work is called *transition LIFE (land)*.

In the final section of my *Song Cycle* I speak of appropriation and genocide, which continue to this day and which cause the death, both physically, spiritually and psychically, of Aboriginal people. I choose the word 'appropriation' to explore the difference between the use of this term in post-modern theory, and its use in describing actions that destroy Aboriginal people. The Aboriginal discussion speaks of 'appropriation' starting with the taking of our land without our permission, the taking of our lives and identity, the taking of our children, and our language, the redefinition of our tribal selves, the use of our culture and spirituality to represent this country. I speak of the many deaths in custody, and specifically refer to Malcolm Charles Smith one of the first cases dealt with by the Inquiry Into Deaths In Custody.[24] This section of my work is titled *transformation DEATH (appropriation)*.

By building this *Song Cycle* I have reclaimed my right to define myself and my right to confirm and document my own history in relation to both my internal and external life. By owning every aspect in this way, I settled much that was problematic for me. By asserting both my right to my own story and embedding it into history as a subjective/objective narrative, I became the expert of myself – I owned myself.

During this process of building the *Song Cycle* I speak of, I started teaching in the New South Wales Corrective Service system. First of all I taught at Long Bay Gaol. Within a year of starting at Long Bay, I was teaching at Mulawa Women's Correctional Centre, as well as at the Norma Parker Centre and at Emu Plains Women's Prison. The work I had done through my *Song Cycle* stood me in good stead in this environment.

Although I have taught diverse groups of prisoners, the bulk of my classes were specifically for Aboriginal inmates. I have been a successful Koori teacher over the period I taught within these institutions for a number of reasons. The most important reason was that I knew many of the inmates' families and communities. Most importantly, I knew they were in there because they were Aboriginal. Whatever they had done, they were there because they were Aboriginal. Their addiction, their theft, their violence, and finally their arrest, guilty or not, was because they were Aboriginal. There were very many issues where my Aboriginal students and I were one. There was no argument. I also knew of the alienation, and the dispossession, the lack of education and hope, the abuse and the despair, the issues about Aboriginality, and I knew that I had to surround them with positive aspects of self. I felt that my Aboriginal students had to be profoundly surrounded with their Aboriginal being, with themselves, so they could have tools to heal themselves.

Interestingly, in one way their Aboriginality was both a curse and a blessing. Aboriginal inmates generally chose to paint in the particular dot style that is now so familiar. Any viewer would observe the painting, recognise it as 'Aboriginal', and thus the artist's identity was confirmed. She became not a 'criminal' but an 'Aboriginal artist' with a particular and unique skill. I set up a number of processes whereby inmates not only developed skills in the area of Fine Art, including drawing, painting, collage, mural making, design and application of technology, but also experienced an end process that had both a personal meaning and a public face.

Given the recidivism rate, many of my students became quite skilled and started to look for other language to assert their being. Starting at Norma Parker Centre for three hours a week initially, eight women I had known for many years started meeting and talking. This talking started with working out what were common experiences and where those experiences and Aboriginality met. In owning our history and ourselves we became quite powerful in our culture. When we started this process we had a varying rate of illiteracy from profoundly illiterate to barely literate.

Once we started these meetings, I installed myself as the scribe by writing down particular narratives that came out. I did this with the group's permission and with the understanding that we would, first of all, learn to read and write, and secondly, aim towards a book of some sort. I would read my text back to the group at the end of our time and the women would observe spelling, structure, and so on. Over a period of time the role of scribe broadened as each woman became both confident and competent in this area. My focus was still on the idea of surrounding them with their Aboriginality. With this in mind I taught them to write and to listen for the integrity of voice and language of each person. Correct writing structure would come later, I decided. The bigger test was to read individual texts to women who weren't part of the group, to see if they identified the voice of the writer. If there was the response, 'oh that's so and so – it sounds just like her!' then I felt we had succeeded.

By owning their own language and their own stories in this way, the skills base was expanded rapidly to the point where we had a number of stories that they felt were publishable. It had taken over a year to get from illiteracy to this point. But I was concerned about the impact some of the stories might have. For one thing, these stories spoke of incredible pain, suffering, and brutality, which, in the 'normal' course of events, would be considered private. In exposing these stories the women were very vulnerable, I felt. I also felt concerned that in articulating these events as they had happened to the women, it seemed that there should be a follow-up process – perhaps counselling or psychological long-term support.

By this time I had obtained funding to publish. As a group, we talked through the issues that I raised, as well as other issues as they came up. The final decision from the group was a resounding publish. The title was to be *Free Spirit*. I discussed with many professionals what I should do as a consequence of the revelations in the book. I was advised again and again by social workers, counsellors and psychologists, that I was on dangerous ground and that, professionally, I needed to put supports into place for those who might need them. However, within my own community, the discussion was very different. Sorrow was expressed but also admiration that the women had achieved so much for themselves. I came to understand, as I already knew, that there were no supports for these women that weren't ultimately more damaging. They were still in and out of jails and the basic fact that they were Aboriginal would never change. The language of healing was a white language, not an Aboriginal one in the context of prison and Aboriginality. The healing language was already in the book and was already in the community. In naming their pain they owned it and that in itself was empowering in a life that had had no power up to that point. Learning the skill of naming made visible what was invisible.

The practice of psychology can help heal the ongoing effects of colonisation within Aboriginal communities, but it must be relevant. It must look both inward and outward, to its language, to its methodology, to its history, and to its understanding of both theory and knowledge. It has to look at the implications of the practice of professional power on Aboriginal people and take responsibility for the effects of that power. In Australia, perhaps those who speak on the side of critical psychology will come to speak the word the current Prime Minister can't speak on behalf of the nation, and that is to say **SORRY**. That might be a good place to make a new beginning.

This paper is woven together from the presentations at the roundtable 'Decolonising White Psychology' at the World Conference in Critical Psychology, University of Western Sydney, Nepean, Sydney, Australia, 30 April-2 May, 1999. Lorraine Johnson-Riordan takes responsibility for any limitations in the introductory theoretical framework.

'Keeping it in the Family' is an extract from Janie Conway Herron's current major writing project, Stories and Secrets.

Notes
1. This is an extract from Indigenous leader Pat Dodson's speech to an ANTaR meeting in Sydney in July 1999. ANTaR is the acronym for 'Australians for Native Title and Reconciliation'.
2. The White Australia policy was codified in the Commonwealth Immigration Restriction Act of 1901, the year of Federation.
3. 'Blak', coined by Aboriginal artist Destiny Deacon ('Kudjeris' exhibition, Boomalli, Sydney, 1991), subverts 'black', the racial/racist labelling of Indigenous Australians. It also subverts the notion that Aboriginal identity can be read off the body.

4. The Council for Reconciliation was established with bipartisan support in 1991 following the demise of the idea of a Treaty with Indigenous peoples to that point. The Council had a ten-year term. An independent body, Reconciliation Australia, was set up at the beginning of 2001. Reconciliation has been a controversial process consistently provoking resistance from segments of both Indigenous and non-Indigenous communities for different reasons. Indigenous leader Pat Dodson has approached reconciliation from the point of view of real transformation (rather than the production of documents that has characterised much of the past ten years). The truth about the past (colonial) history, a national apology, compensation to the Stolen Generations, the evolution of Native Title law, a referendum on constitutional reform in addition to attention to poor housing, health care, unemployment, education, deaths in custody, etc, were all necessary elements of the reconciliation process (Pat Dodson, 'Healing beyond the grassroots', *The Australian*, 13.7.99, p15). By May 2000 Dodson and others had put the Treaty back on the table.
5. According to a 1999 report released by the Australian Bureau of Statistics and the Australian Institute of Health and Welfare, Indigenous peoples are disadvantaged on a wide range of measures. Life expectancy for indigenous people is currently where it was for whites at the turn of the twentieth century, that is, a hundred years ago. Babies born to Indigenous mothers are more likely to die around the time of birth, are more likely than other Australians to live in poor conditions, to be unemployed, to suffer from violence, to be imprisoned, to develop a range of chronic diseases and to be hospitalised. See also Debra Jopson, 'Black violence and sex assault "is an epidemic"', *Sydney Morning Herald*, 1.3.02: News 2; Debra Jopson, 'Black communities in a mess, warns Aboriginal minister', *Sydney Morning Herald*, 8.3.02: News 9. See, too, *Bringing Them Home, Report of the National Inquiry into the Separation of Aboriginal and Torres Strait Islander Children from Their Families, Human Rights and Equal Opportunity Commission*, April, 1997.
6. Myth, wrote Barthes (1990), is a mechanism that produces a distorted, deformed knowledge, a knowledge 'deprived of memory', 'half-amputated' but still alive (122). This knowledge is presented as 'the real', as fact, as certain. But while it may have an element of truth, it is also a 'dream'. Mythical speech is 'frozen speech', a 'magical object' from which history has been emptied out (125).
7. Paul Gilroy (2000) cites McGrane: 'Beyond Europe was henceforth before Europe ... differences residing in geographical space ... became differences residing in developmental historical time ... the simultaneity of geographical space was transformed into the successive linearity of evolutionary time'(329). What and who was out there beyond Europe was prior to Europe, before, not of or in, Europe's time.
8. See, for example, Couze Venn, *Occidentalism: Modernity and Subjectivity*, Sage, London, 2000.
9. Benedict Anderson, *Imagined Communities: Reflections on the Origin and Spread of Nationalism*, Verso, London & New York, 1983, p6.

10. See, for example, Kris Johnson, 'Learning to be White', in *Travelling Tracks: a collection of writing by Indigenous students of Goolangullia*, University of Western Sydney, Macarthur, 1998, pp29-32.
11. See, for instance, meetings organised by 'Women for WIK'. The High Court's decision (December 1996) in favour of the Wik peoples that the granting of a pastoral lease did not necessarily extinguish Native Title provoked the Howard government to draw up a 10-point plan to extinguish Native Title which, in turn, mobilised pro-Indigenous supporters such as 'Women for WIK'.
12. See the Human Rights and Equal Opportunity Commission's *Bringing Them Home* report. The term 'Stolen Generations', initially coined by the historian Peter Read in 1981, refers to so-called 'half-caste' children taken from their Aboriginal mothers to be raised as wards of the state in 'homes', etc. The term has been the site of considerable public contention because it contests the official history of White Australia and is disruptive of white hegemony. The conservative Coalition government and their supporters (e.g. *Quadrant* magazine) refuse both the words 'stolen' and 'generation', preferring 'separated' or 'rescued'.
13. For instance, it was reported in the Australian press prior to the Olympic Games (September 2000) that Phillip Ruddock, as Minister for Immigration and Reconciliation (and also Minister for Aboriginal Affairs), had told *Le Monde* that the reason why Australia's Indigenous people were 'behind' in living standards, etc, was because contact with the Western world had been recent relative to other countries.
14. For a critique of contemporary racism in Australia see L. Johnson-Riordan, 'Time, space and the race wars', in *Beyond the Race Wars: Narrating Postcoloniality*, chapter 2, forthcoming.
15. This tends to be the pedagogical line taken in reconciliation circles around the country. See *Whiteys Like Us*, directed by Rachel Landers, 1999, a documentary of one such circle.
16. On 'demystification' see, for example, Cornel West, 'The New Cultural Politics of Difference', in Russell Ferguson et al (eds), *Out There: Marginalisation and Contemporary Cultures*, New Museum of Contemporary Art, New York, 1990, pp19-36.
17. Barthes (1990), writing of 'demythification', suggests the critical reader of myth must 'connect a mythical schema' to history and to the interests of a particular society in order to re-politicise depoliticised speech.
18. Alexander and Mohanty (1997), reflecting on the tokenistic tendency to 'include' texts by women of colour in the United States, argue that the effect is to absorb and silence minority voices unless there is a reconceptualising of the whole knowledge base. 'This says, in effect, that our theories … carry explanatory weight only in relation to our *specific* experiences, but they have no use value in relation to the rest of the world' (xvii).
19. See *Bringing Them Home, op. cit.* and Phillip Noyce's recently released film *Rabbit-Proof Fence* (2002).
20. References to Social Studies texts are from C. Eakins & A.E. Williams,

Social Studies Through Activities (Grade 3, 4, 5, 6, 7), Carroll's Pty. Ltd., Printers and Publishers, Perth, n.d.
21. From the Ngiyampaa word (northwest New South Wales) meaning 'to give in return', 'give back', 'throw back' (literally 'exchange-away').
22. At the third Native Welfare conference (1951) Paul Hasluck, then Federal Minister for Territories, introduced the supposed benefits of assimilation to Aboriginal people. The conference agreed it was the aim of 'Native Welfare Measures'. 'Assimilation means, in practical terms, that, in the course of time, it is expected that all persons of Aboriginal blood or mixed blood in Australia will live like other Australians do' (Hasluck, 1953:16). The Protection Act had its roots in the Aboriginal Protection Act (N.S.W. Parliament, December 1909) as an answer to extending the powers of the Aborigines Protection Board. This Board had only two pieces of legislation it could apply to Aborigines – the Supply of Liquor to Aborigines Protection Act (1867), and Clause 4 of the Vagrant Act of 1851 which prevented white people wandering in the company of Aboriginal people.
23. I refer here to well-known Bundjalung elder, author, lecturer, historian and activist, Dr Ruby Langford Ginibi. She writes in her books of our adventures together.
24. Malcolm Charles Smith was the first of the deaths in custody before the Royal Commission into Aboriginal Deaths in Custody. The Inquiry acknowledges the effects of the Protection Act as a major contributing factor in Malcolm Smith's incarceration and untimely death. The Royal Commission into Aboriginal Deaths in Custody was convened in 1987 before a full bench. The final report was handed down in 1992.

References

Alexander, M. J. & Mohanty, C. T. (eds) (1997), *Feminist Genealogies, Colonial Legacies, Democratic Futures*, New York & London: Routledge.
Anderson, B. (1983) *Imagined Communities*, London & New York: Verso.
Barthes, R. (1977) *Images, Music, Text*, Glasgow: Fontana.
Barthes, R. (1990) *Mythologies*, New York: Noonday Press.
Bauman, Z. (1998) *Globalization: The Human Consequences*, Cambridge: Polity Press.
Bhabha, H. (ed.) (1990) *Nation and Narration*, New York: Routledge.
Bhabba, H. (1990) 'DissemiNation: time, narrative, and the margins of the modern nation', in *Nation and Narration*, New York: Routledge: 291-322.
Bhavnani, K. K. & Phoenix, A. (eds) (1994) *Shifting Identities, Shifting Racisms: A Feminism and Psychology Reader*, London: Sage.
Conway Herron, J. (2000) *Stories and Secrets*, unpublished doctoral dissertation, University of Western Sydney.
Dodson, P. (1999) 'Healing beyond the grassroots', *The Australian*, 13 July 1999, p5.
Eakins, C. & Williams A.E, (n.d.) *Social Studies Through Activities* (Grade 3,4,5,6,7). Perth: Carroll's Pty. Ltd, Printers & Publishers.

Fabian, J. (1983) *Time and the Other: How Anthropology makes its object*, New York: Columbia University Press.
Fanon, F. (1990[1961]) *The Wretched of the Earth*, London: Penguin.
Fanon, F. (1993[1967]) *Black Skins, White Masks*, London: Pluto Press.
Fine, M., Weis, L., Powell, L.C. & Mun Wong, L. (eds) (1997) *Off White: Readings on Race, Power, and Society*, New York & London: Routledge.
Foucault, M. (1980) *The History of Sexuality: Volume1: An Introduction*, New York: Vintage.
Frankenburg, R. (ed) (1997) *Displacing Whiteness: Essays in Social and Cultural Criticism* Durham & London: Duke University Press.
Ginibi, R. L. (1999) *Haunted By The Past*, Sydney: Allen & Unwin.
Gilroy, P. (2000) *Against Race: Imagining Political Culture beyond the Color Line*, Cambridge: Harvard University Press.
Hardt, M. & Negri, A. (2000) *Empire*, Cambridge: Harvard University Press.
Harraway, D. (1989) *Primate Visions: Gender, Race, and Nature in the World of Modern Science*, New York: Routledge.
Hasluck, P. (1953) *Native Welfare in Australia*, Patterson Brokenshaw.
Hollinsworth, D. (1998) *Race and Racism in Australia*, Katoomba: Social Sciences Press.
Human Rights and Equal Opportunity Commission. (1997) *Bringing Them Home: National Inquiry into the Separation of Aboriginal and Torres Strait Islander Children from Their Families*, Canberra: Australian Government Printing Press.
Jedda (1955), Charles Chauvel Productions.
Johnson, K. (1998) 'Learning to be White', in *Travelling Tracks: a collection of writing by Indigenous students of Goolangullia*, Campbelltown: University of Western Sydney, Macarthur: 117-130.
Johnson-Riordan, L. (1997) 'Teaching/Cultural Studies (or Pedagogy for "World- Travellers"/ "World-Travelling" pedagogy', in J. Canaan & D. Epstein (eds), *A Question of Discipline: Pedagogy, Power and the Teaching of Cultural Studies*. Boulder, Colorado: Westview Press: 117-130.
Johnson-Riordan, L. (forthcoming) *Beyond the Race Wars: Narrating Postcoloniality*.
Johnston, P. (ed) (1996) *Free Spirit: a collection of work by female inmates*, Norma Parker Centre, Sydney: Contemporary Women Artists Gallery Press.
Jopson, Debra. (2002) 'Black violence and sex assault "is an epidemic"', *Sydney Morning Herald*, 1 March: News 2.
Jopson, Debra. (2002) 'Black communities in a mess, warns Aboriginal minister', *Sydney Morning Herald*, 8 March: News 9.
McClintock, A. (1995) *Imperial Leather: Race, Gender and Sexuality in the Colonial Conquest*, Routledge: New York & London.
O'Shane, P. (1995) *Aboriginal and Islander Health Worker Journal*, Vol. 19, May/June.
Rabbit-Proof Fence (2002) Dir. Phillip Noyce, Australia.
Reynolds, H. (1999) *Why Weren't We Told?: A Personal Search for the Truth About Our History*, Sydney: Viking.

Roman, L. (1993) 'White is a Color! White Defensiveness, Postmodernism, and Anti-Racist Pedagogy', in C. McCarthy & W. Crichlow (eds), *Race, Identity and Representation in Education*, New York & London: Routledge: 71-88.

Roman L. (1997) 'Denying (White) Racial Privilege: Redemption Discourses and the Uses of Fantasy', in M. Fine et al (eds) *op. cit.*

Sandoval, C. (1997) 'Theorising White Consciousness for a Post-Empire World: Barthes, Fanon, and the Rhetoric of Love', in R. Frankenburg (ed), *Displacing Whiteness: Essays in Social and Cultural Criticism*, Durham & London: Duke University Press: 86-106.

Stoler, A. L. (1995) *Race and the Education of Desire: Foucault's History of Sexuality and the Colonial Order of Things*, Durham & London: Duke University Press.

Supriya, K.E. (1999) 'White difference: Cultural Constructions of White Identity', in T. K. Nakayama & J. N. Martin (eds.), *Whiteness: The Communication of Social Identity*, London: Sage: 129-148.

Torgovnick, M. (1990) *Gone Primitive: Savage Intellects, Modern Lives*, Chicago: The University of Chicago Press.

Venn, C. (2000) *Occidentalism: Modernity and Subjectivity*, London: Sage.

Wong, M. (1994) 'Dis(s)-ecting and Dis(s)- closing "Whiteness": Two Tales about Psychology', in K. K. Bhavnani & A. Phoenix (eds), *op. cit.*

West, C. (1990) 'The New Cultural Politics of Difference', in R. Ferguson et al (eds) *op. cit.* 19-36.

Whiteys Like Us (1999) Dir./writer R. Landers, Ronin Films, (orders@ronin-films.com.au).

The new moral order and racism in South Africa post 11 September 2001

Desmond Painter and Catriona Macleod

Abstract
In this paper we briefly analyse a newspaper article reporting on the disciplining of a white Muslim woman in South Africa for wearing an Osama bin Laden t-shirt to work, arguing that the moral representation of the 11 September events as a clash between Western and Islamic values have unique local effects. The outrage depicted in the newspaper article about a white woman identifying with a fundamentalist Islamic cause shows how the global discourse of Islamic threat creates yet another possibility for racialising practices to continue in South Africa without being framed in explicitly racial terms. Based on this analysis we also reflect on the implications of these events, and the complex interplay of the global and the local they demonstrate, for critical psychology in South Africa. We argue that critical psychologists in peripheral places like South Africa are well positioned to critique the moral and political dilemmas created by processes of globalisation.

11 September will no longer be merely a date. More than signifying the attacks on the two towers of the World Trade Centre in New York and the Pentagon in Washington DC, this date signifies a series of events that have been globalised by media coverage on an unprecedented scale. It was little less than uncanny the way people around the globe could literally watch on their screens the unfolding of the attacks, the search for bodies, the fear, the devastation. The coverage, of course, was

also biased. Since the world media is dominated by the US, an attack on the latter was easily transformed into an attack on the West. Even worse, as the constraints of post-colonial political correctness gave way to national pride, it became an attack on civilisation.

Critical psychologists and other researchers of discourse processes will have a field day in years to come studying the representations and rhetorical strategies of the major Western role players in the aftermath of 11 September. More interesting to us, however, is the way countries on the peripheries of these events, but still more and more dependent on the global economy, are forced into positions that will affect in unforeseen ways their internal politics in addition to their foreign relations. In this paper, then, we briefly examine how 11 September happened and continues to happen in one such country, South Africa. Through a brief discussion of the possible racialising effects of the construction of the Islamic world as Other, we will make some suggestions on the challenges facing critical psychologists in this country.

Despite being geographically and ideologically peripheral to the conflicts played out by 11 September, South Africans are not simply drawn into it as mere consumers of American news broadcasts. One of the concrete repercussions for South Africa of the 11 September events and its aftermath was a decline in our economy, with our currency consistently reaching new lows against the dominant Dollar for the past six months. Our apparent marginality is therefore, in many respects, misleading. One could even go further, and say that in Derridean terms peripheral countries like South Africa form an absent trace essential to the functioning and meaning of the centre (Derrida, 1974). What happens here, and how South Africa and the many other marginal countries in the world respond to this conflict, will be essential to the maintenance or challenging of hegemonic representations of what is occurring.

In this regard we argue that South Africa, as a 'developing country', is not drawn into an economic order only. We are at the same time drawn into a moral order. In the wake of the collapse of the Soviet Union, communism and the Cold War, this moral order sets the West as the epitome of what is civilised and good, up against a new Other, primarily Islamic fundamentalists epitomising barbarity and evil. One of the great problems of this ideological development is that it shifts the focus away from issues around post-colonial exploitation of Third World countries and the reality of Western economic interests, making these issues secondary to the more pressing defence of civilisation and the good.

Being drawn into this new moral order, however, means more than *economic* woes for South Africa. Apart from struggling against the West around the place of Third World countries and African debt in the global economy, South Africa is still struggling with a past of colonialism, racial oppression, and specifically apartheid policies. While the change from institutionalised racism to a democratic South Africa owed a lot to sustained moral critique from inside as well as outside the country, we argue that the moral order we have been describing above now may facilitate the casting of practices of racism in new frameworks. These frameworks are hard to detect and critique, precisely because they are bolstered by a seemingly legitimate global outrage against certain categories of people.

Religion and the racialisation of Islam in South Africa

South Africa's history, as is well known, has been fractured in many ways, including along religious lines. The apartheid government treated Christianity as the state religion. For example, Christian National Education was the official pedagogic strategy and all learners in state schools were obliged to take Religious Instruction (based on the *Bible* only). Only those whose parents posted strong (religious) objections were exempted. In post-apartheid South Africa the constitution enshrines the right of individuals to practise religious freedom. The practice of (Christian) Religious Education appears to continue in most state schools, but, positively, public broadcasters are required to give equal airtime to all the dominant religions in South Africa.

Despite religious diversity and some conflicts around religion, race took precedence both in defining the Other and in struggling for freedom during the apartheid era. In the light of this, the position of the minority Muslim population is noteworthy. Concentrated mostly in the Western Cape province, Muslims have usually been classified as 'coloured'. This is in keeping with the racial nature of South African society under the apartheid government, and it is only in recent years that their faith has given Muslim people a special, and growingly problematic, position in society. While mainly due to militant Islamic groups who, after being involved in the fight against apartheid, started embracing more explicitly religious and theocratic ideologies during the 1990s, the development of Islamic identity is also symptomatic of a feeling of continued political marginalisation among 'coloured' people in South Africa. As a result, Muslim people are increasingly distinguished in public discourse from Christian 'coloured' people.

That Islamic militancy in the Western Cape is restricted to a minority within the Muslim community made no difference to a growing public awareness of and concern about Islam as a religious identity. This accelerated during the mid- to late-1990s, especially in response to the founding of the People Against Gangsterism and Drugs (PAGAD). This group, founded by Muslim leaders but enjoying wider support initially, proclaimed itself as a community-based response to crime (especially drug and gangster-related activities) in the Western Cape. Soon, however, PAGAD became suspected of fundamentalist religious agendas and blamed for various acts of vigilantism and terror attacks in the city of Cape Town. These terror attacks were often focused on targets associated with the United States of America (eg the bombing of Planet Hollywood in August 1998). Not unlike the situation in the West generally, the Othering of Islam had thus already begun in South Africa well before 11 September 2001.

What 11 September has done is to make possible a new discursive link between religion and old racial divisions in South Africa, creating a situation where religious and racial Othering can feed off one another's logic. An intricate discursive space where practices of oppression can take on a seemingly moral posture takes shape, and racism, experienced and understood as immoral in the new South Africa, becomes hidden from view. To illustrate this we analyse an incident reported in the *Sunday Times*, 21 October 2001, in which a 'white' Muslim secretary was disciplined by her employer for wearing an Osama bin Laden T-shirt to work (Eshak, 2001).

Racial and religious Othering

The *Sunday Times* is a weekly paper that, though it bills itself as providing serious political analysis and commentary, is mostly known for its sensationalist stories. For example, the famous back page contains, *inter alia*, the latest Hollywood scandals. The incident referred to above was not reported in the *Mail & Guardian* (a South African weekly affiliated to the UK *Guardian*), which does in fact provide incisive political and social analyses. The article's appearance in the *Sunday Times* is related, we would suggest, to the exotic nature of the event and its potential to tantalise and/or infuriate the reader. Many people would have read the article, as the *Sunday Times* has a large circulation nationwide, owing partially to its style and partially to its containing the largest Advertisements for Employment section in the country.

The following are extracts from the article:

Extract 1
Osama bin Laden T-shirt lands Muslim secretary in hot water (Title)

Extract 2
A South African Muslim woman who wore an Osama bin Laden T-shirt to work was hauled before a disciplinary hearing this week because her boss said she had been inciting her colleagues. (First sentence of the article)

Extract 3
'He shouted at me, "You're a white Afrikaner. How can you wear this shirt?

How can you support these people?" And he walked out.' (Emboldened excerpt in the body of the article – quote from Sumaya, the woman in question)

Extract 4
'It is company policy that political, racist or religious propaganda or material not be displayed at work.' (Quote from Sumaya's 'boss')

Extract 5
'That she supports one of the warring parties is neither here nor there because Osama bin Laden is innocent until proven guilty' (Quote from spokesperson from the Freedom of Expression Institute).

In neither of Extract 1 or 2 (the first two bits of information made available to the reader) is the racial identity of the secretary revealed. The racialising nature of the incident (the reason why, we would argue, the events are considered newsworthy) is obscured in the interests of 'objective reporting'. In Extract 3, however, localised South African racial politics reveals itself. The signifiers 'white', 'Afrikaner' and 'these people' are mixed in ways fully understood by South Africans trained through years of racialised personal and public politics to read their significance: 'Afrikaner' traditionally excludes all but white Afrikaans speakers, and 'these people' is a euphemism for various racial others. However, in the past, 'these people' would have signified the Other in terms of race only. Here (in the light of the new moral order in place before 11 September but solidified by the events of that day) the reader is in no doubt that 'these people' intersects race and religion.

Various South African academics have traced how racialised politics take on new forms in post-apartheid South Africa (eg Dixon & Durrheim, in press; Durrheim & Dixon, 2000; Foster, 1999; Macleod & Durrheim, in press). For example, rather than defending practices of segregation in racial terms, people use the more acceptable or politically correct categories of culture and tradition. These categories derive their apparent legitimacy from the high value placed on multi-culturalism and minority rights, but are often rhetorically used in ways that facilitate the maintenance of divisions and exclusions created by racial distinctions in the past. What 11 September has added to racialised politics is religion, fuelled by the globalised threat of Islamic terror. The outrage expressed in Extract 4, where Sumaya's employer expresses his disbelief about a white Afrikaner woman with Muslim sympathies and who has adopted Islam as a religion, captures the new inter-weaving of racialised, religious and linguistic boundaries very well.

During apartheid, Afrikaner nationalism mobilised cultural, linguistic, and Christian ideologies in a racialised form. The fact that 'coloured' people in general shared cultural, linguistic and religious identifications with white Afrikaners still left them excluded and discriminated against on the basis of their 'race'. There has been a move in recent years in more progressive Afrikaner circles to extend Afrikaner identity beyond racialised boundaries, including people formally called 'coloured' into the Afrikaner identity. This in turn fits in with the post-apartheid South African vision of multi-culturalism, liberal-humanism and economic and political Westernisation. 11 September and its aftermath has, however, created multiple fissures along race and religious grounds. While 'coloured' Christians remain within the progressive Afrikaner and new South African visions, 'coloured' Muslims are in danger of slipping across the divide to the darkness of the Other.

These fissures, although in some senses new, are also old, drawing as they do on established racialised boundaries. Thus the lines drawn around the intersection of race and religion gain solidity rapidly. It is this that allows for the shock of the employer (as well as for the newsworthiness of the article). A 'white' Muslim woman breaks racialised and religious boundaries and becomes the marginalised and silenced Other.

There are numerous other stories to tell about this incident. There is the gendered story. Sumaya is a secretary, a position virtually always held by women, a position with little formalised power in organisations. Furthermore, she has fractured the patriarchal Afrikaner ideal of the obedient daughter. There is also the corporate story. Consider, for example, Extract 4, where 'company policy' is said to prohibit the display of religious, political or racist 'propaganda'. This statement implies that the social is privatised with the individual turning into a neutral corporate worker. However, this neutrality is misleading. It disguises the Westernised, capitalist values that saturate corporate business in South Africa. It is only Islamic Otherness (along with other forms of marginality) that is forced into the private. When this form of the private intrudes on the corporate, it renders it open to disciplining.

The writer of the newspaper article takes a human rights perspective on the incident. She calls on various experts to comment, including spokespeople from the Lawyers for Human Rights and the Freedom of Expression Institute. They agree that Sumaya's right to freedom of expression has been infringed. The 'rights' discourse is a relatively new one in South Africa, given our brutal past. It has been taken up in many, sometimes contradictory, ways. It is intended in the newspaper article to provide an anti-bias stance. However, it also feeds off the same liberal-humanist base as the one that saw Sumaya being disciplined. Consider, for example, Extract 5. This statement implies that there is no space for Sumaya to express solidarity with Osama bin Laden if he is guilty. In other words, her freedom of expression or right of political choice is governed by the guilt (or not) of an individual. The privatisation of certain forms of the social and the saturation of the public with Westernised capitalist values (equated as they are, post 11 September, with 'civilisation') means that it is not possible to see the West as evil, or to see bin Laden's cause as righteous or justified.

Critical psychology in South Africa post 11 September

We turn finally to some of the roles of and challenges to critical psychology in South Africa with reference to the events and aftermath of 11 September. For critical psychology 11 September is important because it demonstrated so dramatically that globalisation is not simply a benign and natural development in an independent realm of economic regularities. Globalisation forces one into moral choices and implies real and symbolic violence on those who won't define themselves in Western terms. This is true for psychology as well, where our (as South Africans) participation in global discussions and debates will also be structured and constrained by the hidden locations of methods, theories and concepts.

We contend that critical psychology in South Africa should, as a first step, locate itself strongly against the hidden hands of history, the market or science. Not only traditional, but also critical psychology should not be imported in reified ways. It has to be brought into dialogue with local concerns and insights, as has indeed been happening in South Africa (Durrheim, 2001; Painter & Theron 2001; Terre Blanche, 1998; Van Staden, 1998). However, taking our locality seriously doesn't mean we should isolate ourselves within nationalist or purely regional agendas. 11 September has demonstrated, in fact, that such isolation is not feasible.

Secondly, we have argued that events in the Third World or 'developing' countries are more than mere effects of those that happen in the West. They are dynamic responses that take on unique local forms. More than this, we have suggested that the 'developing' world functions as 'absent trace' permeating Western reason and feeding Western privilege (and, nowadays, Western fear). The task of critical psychology is, at the very least, to make these absent traces visible. For this task, critical psychologists in peripheral places like South Africa are uniquely positioned.

The authors would like to thank two anonymous reviewers for their critical and very helpful comments on earlier versions of this paper.

References

Derrida, J. (1974) *Of grammatology* Baltimore: Johns Hopkins University Press.
Dixon, J. & Durrheim, K. (in press) 'Contact and the ecology of racial division: Some varieties of informal segregation', *British Journal of Social Psychology*.
Durrheim, K. (2001) 'A defence of an "immanentist" account of social form and experience', *South African Journal of Psychology* 31(1): 9-11.
Durrheim, K. & Dixon, J. (2000) 'Theories of culture in racist discourse', *Race and Society*, 3(2), 93-109.
Eshak, B. (2001) 'Osama bin Laden T-shirt lands Muslim secretary in hot water', *Sunday Times*, 21 October 2001.

http://www.sundaytimes.co.za/2001/10/21/news/news08.aspFoster, D. (1999).
Macleod, C. & Durrheim, K. (in press) 'Racializing teenage pregnancy: "culture" and "tradition" in the South African scientific literature', *Ethnic and Racial Studies*.
Painter, D. & Theron, W. (2001) 'Heading South! Importing discourse analysis', *South African Journal of Psychology* 31(1): 1-8.
Terre Blanche, M. (1998) 'This is war. A reply to Fred van Staden', *South African Journal of Psychology* 28(1): 44-46.
Van Staden, F. (1998) 'The "new discursive paradigm": as yet an elitist European import? Comment of special edition of the SAJP', *South African Journal of Psychology* 28(1): 44.

September 11: trauma and American politics

J. Brendan K. Maloney

Abstract
This essay attempts to understand the American political reaction to 11 September in terms of the psychoanalytic concept of trauma. The analysis proceeds as follows. First, I demonstrate the two major factors at work in neurotic trauma: Nachträglichkeit (or 'deferred action') and the repression of libidinal fantasy. Secondly, I demonstrate how this political reaction, if viewed in this light, cannot be understood as a neurotic structure. It is distinct in two ways: as a projection of aggression and an uncompromising and uniform rhetoric. I explore the Imaginary function of identification and the function of projection in order to show how the reaction cannot be based on a repression. Instead, I come to recognise the psychotic mechanism of foreclosure at its base. In this way, thirdly, the aggression of war and the refusal of dialogue with the perpetrators are shown to be complementary aspects of a purely egological dimension that eschews genuine communication with autonomous Others.

Introduction
After the shock of the 11 September World Trade Centre (WTC) terrorist attacks, the Western world, led by America, finds itself in a 'war against terror' that is defined in the iteration of vague but determined ideology: the defence of freedom, bringing the guilty to justice. This article attempts to read the events of 11 September and the American political reaction to it in terms of the psychoanalytic structure of trauma. It is not being suggested that this was a literal trauma, but the concept can serve as a tool for understanding the major elements at work.

The description of the trauma

A recent documentary featured the emblematic story of a woman who, like so many others, had the opportunity to speak to her husband trapped in one of the towers. After he had heard the explosion, he telephoned her. His voice was calm, she said. He had heard the explosion, but assumed it was a bomb. He reassured her that people were not panicking, the evacuation was proceeding and he would be home, safe and sound, within the hour. She trembled, helpless and frightened, waiting by the phone. He called two further times before the building collapsed. The next time he phoned, she said that she could hear noises in the background that were not present before: screaming, shouts of panic, the rumble and clattering of displaced furniture. His voice was starting to quiver. Nonetheless, he still attempted to placate her. The evacuation was continuing, floor by floor, and he would not delay one second in taking his turn down the stairs. It was after this second call that the news first featured images of the airplanes striking the side of the buildings. The wife was now petrified. She had realised that the disaster was far beyond the scale of even her husband's proximate understanding. The situation was critical. There was no time remaining. It was then that he called the third – and last – time. At this stage, she recounted to the camera between gasping sobs, the sounds of the environment around him were of a hellish pandemonium. Fierce and anguished cries were heard piercing the air around him. The sound of smashing glass, bellowing roars of fury and deep, miserable hopelessness could be distinguished. The husband was weeping uncontrollably, she said, worse than she had ever known during their decades of marriage. People had gone mad, he said. Bodies were falling from the windows; people were hurling themselves into oblivion. Smaller explosions and sudden tongues of flame were rising from the stairwell, scorching the now wild escapees. Corpses littered the floor, disfiguration and the smell of burning flesh. Men had lost their reason. 'Help me,' he had bewailed. The line was cut. It was then that the first of the two towers imploded, disintegrating into a heap of unidentifiable rubble.

This story reveals the emotional horror brought about by this event. But if we are to examine it according to the criteria of psychoanalytic trauma, we should not be overhasty, by ascribing its traumatic impact solely to the presence of intense emotions. The three-part phone call helps illustrate the temporality of the experience that is more structurally significant. The shock of the WTC disaster was not a specific, momentary puncture in these people's everyday world. It lasted a certain time, it had a duration. At first there was the initial explosion. This was the impact of American Airlines Flight 11 that hit the tower at 8:45am EDT. But we can only identify the event in this way after the fact. At the time, no one knew why, or how, this explosion had taken place. Then there was slow but gradual realisation. Information started coming through the news media. At this moment, the fire in the building seemed the largest danger. The Fire Department was on its way ... It was only in the second moment – when the edifice itself heaved under its own weight, and the high rise world of the WTC collapsed into nothingness – that all these hopes, fears and aspirations were taken up and swallowed by the full ferocity of the traumatic realisation.

In a recent article re-written and re-distributed after 11 September, Slavoj Zizek uses the word trauma. 'Now, in the days immediately following the bombings,' he writes, 'it is as if we dwell in the unique time between a traumatic event and its symbolic impact, like in those brief moments after we are deeply cut, and before the full extent of the pain strikes us' (Zizek, 2001). The power of a trauma can only be revealed after-the-fact. The pain of the trauma is not the consequence of an initial and singular concussion of intense emotion. The pain is post-factual. It is as if the moment we call the trauma – the first moment – could only become a trauma on the basis of a second moment that came after it. The strange double structure of this event places all the intervening moments in a sort of suspension. But that is not realised until the second moment. In our current example, we hoped that people would escape unharmed, that the Fire Department would save the day ... But it all turned out to be delusive as the irrevocable magnitude of the damage became apparent. We now know that there was no hope of anyone ever getting out of that particular building alive. And it is this realisation – that all our hope and efforts were doomed from the start – that takes this normally brave and meaningful action and inverts it.

Neurotic trauma and psychoanalysis
The technical term for this psychological and temporal structure of the trauma is *Nachträglichkeit* or 'deferred action'. It refers to that inverted causality by which an element, second in time, confers upon the chronologically prior one the aetiology of causation. From the begin-

ning, Freud associated it with the domain of neurotic sexual trauma (cf Emma in Freud, 1895). But Freud's encounter with trauma in the First World War – what he misleadingly called the 'war neuroses' – forced him to include violent traumas in his libidinal theory as well (Freud, 1919, p208). However, despite his efforts to retain a neurotic structure, traumas related to violent shock cannot be exhaustively explained by a neurotic mechanism.

Freud tried to describe the war neuroses as a libidinal conflict between two ego tendencies, between the desire of one and the social, moral or even aesthetic demands of the other that would not tolerate it. This desire, Freud argued, was not one that the person, as a conscious subject, would claim as his or her own, or actually feel as desirable. On the contrary, it was a sort of desire 'in us in spite of us'. It would retain its dogged determination in our minds in complete opposition to any reasonable or generally permissible course of action. In terms of the war neuroses, 'the conflict is between the soldier's old peaceful ego and his new warlike one' (Freud, 1919, p209). There is a desire for a happy and safe existence, with no war, no violence. But there is also a 'war ego', coveting a desire for revenge, retribution against enemies, and the sheer pleasure in blowing things up and causing general destruction. When the peaceful ego finds itself in conflict with its own inner, more violent predisposition, 'the human ego is defending itself from a danger ... in a shape assumed by the ego itself' (Freud, 1919, p210). Even if it is the explosions, the pain, and the suffering that sets the trauma off, 'what is feared is nevertheless an internal enemy': the enemy within that, in spite of our better selves and better judgement, nonetheless seems to want this destruction (Freud, 1919, p210).

In so far as Freud was developing a neurotic understanding of this traumatic and violent shock, he maintained that libidinal desire was essential to introduce conflict into the structure of deferred action. Thus *Nachträglichkeit*, while necessary, was not a sufficient condition for trauma. Libidinal conflict had to be present too.

Freud's libido is the realm of infantile sexuality and fantasy (*Phantasie*). It stretches from the earliest of infancy and extends into every sphere of thought and action. It is the realm of desire before it is the realm of 'sexuality', if one equates sexuality with adulthood, genital sexuality. As an imaginative scenario, libidinal fantasy cannot but imply a relationship to the identity of the person fantasizing, even if he or she does not explicitly occupy a role in it. In this sense, both the 'peacetime' and 'wartime' egos would have their own active fantasy life, the former fantasizing about tranquillity, the latter about barbarity. If we employ this neurotic structure to try and understand the experience of 11 September, it would suggest that it was the confrontation of these two divergent impulses, through a deferred temporal structure, that instantiated the conflict. The libidinal fantasies would have introduced mental conflict by infiltrating thought and action with irreconcilable inclinations. This is the generally accepted power of the libido: it sets memories against one another, or otherwise establishes libidinal relations that are unsustainable (cf Freud, 1906, p274).

As Zizek pointed out in the above-mentioned article, America also enjoys its good dose of fantasy once in a while: in the movie theatre. And often, the key to the fantasy is a cruel devastation of the American landscape. This does not mean that everyone who goes to the movies actually wants to see America levelled by explosions and warfare. But desire often occurs in us in spite of us, a kind of fantasy pleasure that revels in everything that our social and moral selves would deny with vehemence.

The 11 September attacks have revealed to us a special form of this insipid desire. If we use the neurotic structure of libidinal and fantastic conflict as our criterion, certain aspects of the day in question become comprehensible. After the first moment, when there was news, but no one knew what it was about, there was at least a fascination with the events as they unfolded on television. The overwhelming power of the images played, at least in part, the role of bewitchment. In a certain way, we were enjoying what we watched. This is because, in that moment, we did not know it would be such a massacre caused by terrorists. All we had before us was a fascinating scene. In short, it was allowing the images on the live news report to be the optical objects of our fantasy, allowing an indulgence of optical fantasy life.

The second moment came later, when the building came crashing down. When suddenly faced with the full import of this event, all the feelings and intentions of that intermediate period were quashed by a new and far more oppressive sensation. Yet, in spite of that, no matter how intense the second moment of realisation may have been, it did not obliterate those earlier moments from existence.

Nonetheless, while some elements of the event resemble the libidinal conflict of neurosis, 11 September ultimately cannot be understood as a neurotic structure.

The prototypical neurotic defence against a trauma described by Freud is that of repression (*Verdrängung*), whereby irreconcilable tendencies are forced out of the ego only to return via a symptom in a displaced form. This is a question of the ego versus something else. It is the basic structure of a neurotic pathology. But, there are two aspects of the post-traumatic American reaction that, as a whole, cannot be reduced to a neurotic structure. The first is that the mechanism of projection (*Projektion*) – not repression – has qualified the American response. I will examine this entirely on the level of the American political reaction, taking the statements of the American governmental Administration, and those of George W. Bush in particular, as representative of this response. This projection takes on the character of an exteriorisation of aggression. The centrality of this aggression is what is distinct from a neurotic process. Though Freud attempted to contain the description of war trauma within neurotic boundaries, he found himself obliged to describe the conflict entirely on the level of the ego. Or, that is, between a diametrically opposite pair of egos. This introduction of two kinds of ego formation, not an ego versus something outside of it, is already an indication that the neurotic explanation does not go far enough. There is a reflection of the ego's relationship to itself through the outside world that suggests a different mechanism. Secondly, and most importantly, there is the peculiar fact that the American reaction to 11 September has always retained the character of a sort of megalomaniacal discourse. It refers to nothing but itself and therefore evades any form of intersubjective dialogue. With the combination of these two characteristics, I feel that the American response resembles a generally psychotic structure, versus a neurotic one. To demonstrate this, I will rely on the work of Jacques Lacan. It will be the conjunction of projection and egological aggression that will lead us to the concept of foreclosure – a refusal of dialogue.

Identification and political projection

In the question of projection, what is at stake is the demonstration that irreconcilable fantastic desires are separated from one another, but not necessarily as a consequence of repression. Projection is therefore not necessarily the result of the conflict between these impulses. (My use of the term 'projection' in what follows is primarily in the Freudian sense.)

The immense outpouring of sympathy for the victims of 11

September was based in a process of identification. For those of us not actually on the scene that day, or close to it, we cannot have been traumatised in any literal, psychological sense. Safe in my home, I did not feel the encroachment of oppressive death brought about by the tumbling concrete. I saw the explosions on television. Later, I saw the planes impact with devastating force. Because of this, however, I could perform the act of imagination that would put me at the scene of this crime. It is on this basis that I can share – in an infinitesimally small way – the horrors that were experienced on 11 September. Importantly, mutual possession of a common feeling or emotion is not the basis of the identification. It is not because I personally felt the horror of the attacks that I could identify with the victims. Rather, it was because I could see the position of those other people, and recognise in it a potential for my own experience, that the feeling of sympathy became possible.

The first stage of political reaction is based in this experience of sympathy through identification. Through it, we can see how the site-specific trauma of that day can pass, at least in some way, from the particular to the general. We all identified with the victims of the tragedy and therefore related to them on the level of our egos, defining ourselves on the basis of the image provided by an other. In this, 'we are faced by the process which psychology calls "empathy" and which plays the largest part in our understanding of what is inherently foreign to our ego in other people' (Freud 1921, p108).

In Lacanian terminology, such identification takes place entirely on the level of the Imaginary (cf Lacan, 1977). It is the realm of narcissism. The image of the other provides the basis upon which our own egos achieve their character and unity. This is the peculiar feature of the human ego, says Lacan, in that it requires the introjection of a foreign image in order to achieve its own unification. It is the means whereby the infantile auto-erotic body, born ill-prepared and utterly without co-ordination, reaches a level of self-sufficiency through reliance on mimicry. The fragmented body is caught up in the Imaginary captivation of the promise of a lived totality. But, Lacan also argues, human identification is so fragile and unstable that it must also be inserted into and sustained by the regulative order of the human social and linguistic Symbolic universe. Otherwise, the ego will not have the ability to maintain its identifications and will deteriorate back into its decomposed and fragmented state. It is in the name of this social order, internalised by the subject, eventually postulated as the superego, that the ego performs neurotic repressions. All of this is found directly in Freud and is only made more explicit in Lacan's work. 'Repression', Freud writes in his paper on narcissism, is not simply the act of the ego; 'it proceeds from the self-respect of the ego' (Freud 1914, p93). The transition from the formation of an ego as alienated identity to the socialised adult of moral conscience is the transition from Imaginary identification with an 'ideal ego' in childhood to the internalisation of cultural values in the form of cultural ideals, the agency of which Freud calls an 'ego ideal'. 'The subject's narcissism makes its appearance displaced on to this new ideal ego', but 'as he grows up, he is disturbed by the admonitions of others and by the awakening of his own critical judgement, so that he can no longer retain that perfection, [and] he seeks to recover it in the new form of an ego ideal' (Freud 1914, p94). The failure to instil this socialised ego ideal as a regulatory principle for the ego's identifications would result in the regressive collapse into the original disorganised fragmentation.

The process of identification is not isolated to individual egos, however. It also extends from individuals to group psychology. Groups are formed, Freud claimed, in the same way as any singular ego is formed: an identification submits to the authority of an idealised image. The ego is henceforth dominated and guided by its example. Any group, Freud argues, 'is a number of individuals who have put one and the same object in the place of their ego ideal and have consequently identified themselves with one another in their ego' (Freud 1921, p116). In the case of the United States, it is the President who is the grand leader that occupies this unifying social position and represents the American reaction to the crisis.[1]

The leader, therefore, as ego ideal, is the embodiment of the social stratification by which the general populace will judge themselves and the identity of their nation. The way he or she speaks, the positions he or she takes, the actions performed, provide the model, not for individual emulation, but for the evaluation of the moral and social accomplishments of the group as a whole. It is the leader who determines the position of the State, for example, on the international stage. It is his accomplishments and failures that reflect on the State's 'self respect'. This is idyllic, however. Analogous to the individual, a deterioration of the leader's Symbolic function would also lead to an equivalent regression of the group to the Imaginary order.

With this in mind, let us continue with 11 September. The popular reaction to the WTC attacks in the USA was a call to war (polled at over 90%). It is this reaction that will characterise the function of projection.

The American 'war against terror' is a projection in so far as the aggressive libidinal desires uncovered in the fascination of 11 September were assigned to external individuals. In this case, it is a rhetorical expulsion of malignant and unpalatable tendencies present in the Western world by ascribing their meanest intensity, without distinction, onto others.

When one imagines the horrible fate for those within the Twin Towers, it seems a natural and immediate reaction to seek justice. In many ways, this means seeking retaliation, though it should be the pursuance of legal justice before retribution. The military action pursues the perpetrators (and those that harbour them) in order to put them to trial, not to exact revenge upon innocents. Yet we must remember that, concerning war and violence, we are discussing desires that are present yet are not appropriated by the people enacting them. They persist alongside and in spite of our better tendencies and judgements. In other words, the psychical vicissitudes beneath the trauma find their unconscious expression in the policy of the State. As Freud himself wrote, 'when human beings are incited to war they may have a whole number of motives for assenting – some noble and some base, some which are openly declared and others which are never mentioned ... A lust for aggression and destruction is certainly among them: the countless cruelties in history and in our everyday lives vouch for its existence and its strength' (Freud, 1933, p210). We know that any act of war will cause the suffering and death of innocent civilians. This may be labelled 'collateral damage' and, as such, may be necessary in the light of staunch and just action. Nonetheless, the experience of the WTC extends and perpetuates – on the other side of the globe, through the other – the self-same images that fuelled our fantasy.

In this way, the peacetime ego of free, democratic and enterprising New York (along with the rest of the Western world) can be preserved. It is preserved through a reciprocal identification with the other: he is now in the place where we were. We are not the aggressors, they are. The explosions will not take place here anymore. But the explosions still take place. Now, however, they happen safely (and somewhat entertainingly) on our television screens.

But even though projection is present in the American political reaction to 11 September, this does not mean that it is the consequence of a neurotic repression. And certain aspects of the American reaction do not fit the general neurotic description. I will list three of these. Firstly, when an experience or fantasy causes a libidinal neurotic conflict, repression is the result. The fantasy or memory is removed from consciousness and placed in a state of amnesia. Most certainly, America has not forgotten about its trauma. Secondly, if it was merely a matter of rejecting the inner tendencies to aggression, then it would be quite inconsistent for the ensuing American position to be precisely that: an aggressive attitude of war. If this was the case, America should have emerged from the shock as docile and conciliatory. This was far from being the case. Rejection would have simply led to repression that, in turn, would have produced an opposite reaction formation (such as extreme pacifism, for example). Thirdly, the American political reaction to 11 September was far more protracted than what one would expect from the struggle with unacceptable desires. The American reaction was so prodigious that it could only be manifest in a reorganisation of the political world order as a whole. The very reality of international politics has altered. Every country's position within that new order has now been redefined according to the struggle against terrorism. According to America's political position, the world is now polarised between peace-seeking, civilised, America-supporting democrats and violent, murderous terrorists. According to President Bush, 'the freedom-loving nations of the world stand by our side' (Sept11) against 'the barbaric criminals who profane a great religion by committing murder in its name' (Oct7). There is now a category of 'human life, liberty, elemental rights and peaceful co-existence' that is violently opposed by the 'black list' of all terrorist groups – each one, from Islamic zealotry to ETA separatism, held together by a collective menacing 'connection' – according to Vice-President and Interior Spanish Minister Mariano Rajoy, speaking after his meeting with Dick Cheney in Washington (*El Mundo*, Oct 16). 'The North American government also understands it in this way', he explained. If the only factor at work was an internal struggle against certain aggressive tendencies, it seems inexplicable that the trauma of 11 September should have produced such a tremendous alteration of America's view of international politics and its place within it.

Non-neurotic projection

Freud encountered a similar problem in the case of Daniel Paul Schreber (Freud, 1911). Schreber was presumably also struggling against divergent internal tendencies: heterosexuality and homosexuality. Yet his symptoms were far more excessive than anything neurosis could produce. Dora, for example, was a female hysteric whose relatively minor symptoms (including a nervous cough and dyspnoea) were also based in conflictual and bisexual libidinal fantasies (Freud 1905, p60). Schreber, on the contrary, was persecuted by voices and hallucinations, believed the world was coming to an end, that everyone around him was 'false' and 'improvised' (i.e. cadavers), and that he was the chosen mate of God Himself, whose interventions were slowly transforming him into a woman and the future mainspring of all future humanity. Even more, whereas the neurotic retains the ability to speak normally and represses the elements of his or her unconscious that henceforth evade verbal expression, the psychotic consciously and quite verbally retains all the elements of the unconscious and never ceases to speak of them. '[I]n schizophrenia a great deal is expressed as being conscious which in the transference neuroses can only be shown to be present in the *Ucs.* by psycho-analysis' (Freud 1915, p197). Schreber speaks openly about his sexual struggle with God; Dora is not even aware that she is in love with Frau K.

What Freud did not doubt was that the majority of psychotic symptoms could be explained as proceeding from projection. Schreber's love for previous men (his father and brother) was reversed in the unconscious ('I do not love him, I hate him') and then projected outside himself and assigned to his persecutors ('I hate him, because he persecutes me'). The symptoms of torment and hallucination, seemingly coming from the outside world, were therefore traceable to Schreber's own internal tendencies. Yet this very process of projection was so distinct from neurosis in both its mechanism and its effects, that Freud could not permit himself to describe it in the same terms. Speaking of Schreber's internal experience of his own conflicting fantastical desires, Freud remarked, 'it was incorrect to say that the perception which was suppressed internally is projected outwards; the truth is rather, as we now see, that what was abolished internally returns from without' (Freud 1911, p71). The implication is that, when internal tendencies are first encountered by the subject as symptoms from the outside, in his or her interaction with the world, then something else is required to explain it, other than the familiar repressive defence.

The reason Freud had so many difficulties with Schreber is that he was a paranoid psychotic, not a neurotic. And Freud's psychoanalytic metapsychology was ill equipped to explain such acute symptoms. Nonetheless, Freud was perspicacious enough to see that narcissism was the issue at stake in the pathology. The sudden and complete withdrawal of Schreber's libidinal investment in the world, resulting for him in the eclipse of the reality of the world and its inhabitants, was described by Freud as a retreat of that libido back onto the narcissism of the ego (Freud 1911, pp 60-2 and 73-5). Schreber's tormented relation with his divine persecutor was nothing less than a bifurcation of his struggle with his own identity as ego. Yet this explanation did not go far enough as, in 1915, Freud was forced to admit that this psychotic retreat back to narcissism could not be the origin of the problem, as it appeared to be more of an attempt at a cure than a direct consequence of a pathology. This is also why, in tandem, the psychotic's language seems to be so much more affected than that of the neurotic: the retreat to narcissism also effects a greater libidinal cathexis of language itself. 'It turns out that the cathexis of the word-presentation is not part of the act of repression, but represents the first attempts at recovery or cure which so conspicuously dominate the clinical picture of schizophrenia' (Freud 1915, pp203-4). Freud was able to perceive that psychosis has an intimate relationship with language, the ego and narcissism, and that it could not be explained by normal repression, but he could go no further in untangling the phenomenon.

Freud's doubts are perfectly visible in his discussion of the 'war neuroses'. Retaining his belief that repression – as a neurotic defence – would be present in some fashion in it, he nonetheless postulated a conflict between two kinds of ego, not between the ego and unconscious desire. This is a direct indication that what is at issue is on the level of the ego itself. Taking 11 September as a model, one can see that the American response to the trauma does not resemble neurosis, but rather, it manifests itself as a relationship to the outside world (in a complete alteration of the international political scene) and is directly observable in the language and rhetoric of the American Administration.

Socialisation, the specular ego and the dialectic of aggression

Part of the reason why 'war neuroses' occupy such an important place in Freudian theory is that they provide the first example in which the famous 'pleasure principle' is no longer dominant. While dreams epitomise that principle, always fulfilling a wish, those suffering from war traumas display a remarkable tendency: to repeat the scene of the trauma over and over again in their nightmares. Rather than seek to alter the memory into something pleasant, for example, the subject is tormented by the recurrence of what terrifies them. In this case, 'the function of dreaming,' Freud has to admit, 'is upset in this condition and diverted from its purposes' (Freud 1920, p13). This was so perplexing for Freud that it lead him 'to reflect on the mysterious masochistic trends of the ego', which ultimately culminated in his final metapsychological postulate of Eros and the death drive (Freud 1920, p14).

In Freud's later metapsychology, the struggle between Eros and the death drive (or conflict as such – cf Freud's reference to Emedocles in Freud, 1937, pp244-6) is mapped out in a distinction between an internal and external aggression. The ego becomes the seat not only of identification but also of rivalry. This is most clearly seen in his discussions about conscience, the realm of the aforementioned 'masochism of the ego'. Conscience exhibits an internalisation of aggression by turning earlier aggressive feelings inward as guilt: it is an aggression against one's own self-image (the ideal ego) in so far as it does not converge with the ideal it has established for itself (the ego ideal). 'Aggressiveness is introjected, internalised; it is, in point of fact, sent back to where it came from – that is, it is directed towards his own ego. There it is taken over by a portion of the ego, which sets itself over against the rest of the ego as super-ego, and which now, in the form of "conscience," is ready to put into action against the ego the same harsh aggressiveness that the ego would have liked to satisfy upon other, extraneous individuals' (Freud 1930, p123). The coherent and peaceful fabric of society is maintained through an assumption of morality by its members, generating in them a sense of duty, rather than permitting them to exact vengeance upon their neighbours.

Yet there is also an inverse, almost dialectical, alternative to this advanced cultural development. The rupture of conflict can re-emerge as external aggression in the enthusiasm of a passionate group identification. By idealising the leader, the once-internal aggression of conscience can be externalised. It is the tenacity of the mutually supportive identifications, in attachment to the great leader, that forces the conflictual aggression beyond the scope of the group. That is, internal aggression can be projected. In this state of communal overvaluation of the leader, 'conscience has no application to anything that is done for the sake of the object [i.e. the leader]; in the blindness of love remorselessness is carried to the pitch of crime' (Freud 1921, p113).

The projection of libidinal trends in the American reaction, mapped out in the aggression of their military response of warfare, is a rejection on the level of the ego alone. It is this that Lacan sought to categorise through his concept of the Imaginary. The ego is formed in a mirror stage, where the identification is the internalisation of an alterity, an otherness through which the ego finds identity. Whether a peaceful or a warlike ego, both would merely be inverses of the same specular relation. The whole American reaction of projection sustains itself on the level of the ego. And for Lacan, that is demonstrative of a psychotic mechanism.

Verwerfung and the refusal of dialogue

How is it that 11 September could result in a desire for war?

Most explanations of this have been mere tautologies. What occurred on 11 September was an act of war, it is said. And an act of war requires an act of war. Let us forget, for the moment, that its perpetrators are proponents of an Islamic jihad, whose very definition is a 'holy war'. At the uncertain moment of the first explosions, no one knew that this was committed on behalf of an Islamic terrorist group. Speaking at 9:30am, President Bush could only call the event an 'apparent terrorist attack'. Speaking from Barksdale Airforce Base in Louisiana at 13:04pm, the President was already declaring war on the perpetrators, even though they had not been identified. 'Make no mistake', he said, 'the United States will hunt down and punish those responsible for these cowardly acts'. It was as if the nature of the act itself – and not the identity of its organisers, or the message they had tried to convey – had invoked the sentiments of war. Why did this event not provoke a burning desire for dialogue and reconciliation?

War is a refusal of dialogue. It is a movement against reconciliation, order, and unity, towards strife, disunion, and conflict. The complexion of the American rhetoric after the attacks immediately refused to acknowledge any other discourse other than on its own terms. Analogous to a psychotic's narcissistic withdrawal, I would say that this is what determines the American megalomaniacal rhetoric. The war on the ground that would commence in Afghanistan precipitated from the self-enclosed speech of the Americans that was shut off from moderation or compromise from the first moment.

Despite the horror unleashed by these terrible acts, no one believes that they were sheer and meaningless acts of destruction. The terrorists chose their targets carefully. They selected the Twin Towers, symbols of American prosperity. They also targeted the Pentagon, centre of American military strength and intelligence. In other words, alongside their gruesome morbidity, these attacks were also a message. They were a form of speech, a sign of communication meant to speak out to the whole Western world. In Lacan's terms, the attacks were a signifier. The terrorists were attempting to speak out and communicate through their acts of brutality, to draw out a response and lure the Americans into a significatory exchange. Yet at no point has the American administration publicly sought to decipher that message. From the first, all that mattered was the impact of the events upon the United States and how they could eradicate this kind of activity form the face of the earth. If a message is supposed to initiate a dialogue, the United States simply did not hear it.

This American deafness, as an insensitivity to a call to dialogue, is manifest in the rhetoric of 'war against terror'. Instead of acknowledging the perpetrators as despicable but nonetheless human interlocutors, instead of accrediting any kind of communicative status upon them at all, it excludes them, by definition, from the right to dialogue. One would think that only the Americans (and those that have identified with them) are doing any of the talking. The terrorists, as speaking subjects, have been marginalised.

For Lacan, however, the entire domain of psychoanalysis is speech. Therefore, it is extremely significant when a speech act – no matter how brutal or violent – is completely missed because it has not even been heard. This is the result of the specific psychotic defence of foreclosure (*Verwerfung*). The psychotic cannot respond to the call of another person, cannot acknowledge the interpellation, because he is not embedded within the Symbolic structures of language. Foreclosure has denied the subject the structure of a fundamental signifier. Therefore, the psychotic remains trapped – frozen – at the level of the

Imaginary. That is, he remains trapped on the level of egological identification, where the only positions available for one's identity, and the ones that can be recognised, are those that have not acceded to the level of a social structure.

The 'fundamental signifier' is therefore the introduction of the social order through which the subject's ego is allocated a place in a grander scheme and thereby is able to recognise the appellation of a genuine Other person. In his famous formula in the Seminar on the psychoses, Lacan states that 'the Other is, therefore, the locus in which is constituted the I who is speaking with him who hears' (Lacan, 1993, p273). That is, the Other as Symbolic speech is the structural framework in which the speaking subject (the 'I') is positioned relative to the interlocutor (the 'you'). The relationship is not reciprocal but is imbedded and sustained by reference to a third party, who is not actual but structural, functioning as a support of the Imaginary dual relation. It is supported, Lacan says, by 'the supports of discourse, the presence of witnesses, indeed, of the tribunal before which the subject receives the warning or the opinion that he is called upon to reply to' (Lacan, 1993, p301).

That is why Lacan argues that the psychotic's discourse is characterised by 'mental automatism' (Lacan, 1993, p307). Because his/her speech lacks the fundamental signifier by which the Imaginary is framed by the Symbolic, his/her speech can only refer to the closed circle of its own egological circuit. The psychotic's reply is automatic because it speaks all by itself. It is not a genuine speech between Subjects within a Symbolic universe. Rather, it is a madman's rant to a subject who is simply the mirror image of an ego trapped in the Imaginary. When another person calls out to him/her and solicits a response within the field of speech, the psychotic is unable to reply because he/she is unable to recognise an appeal from the Other – a signifier from a subject who speaks from the Symbolic order, requesting an exchange on equal terms. 'Precisely because he is interpellated on a terrain where he is unable to respond', Lacan explains, 'the only way to react that can reattach him to the humanisation he is tending to lose is to make himself permanently present in this slender commentary on the stream of life that constitutes the text of mental automatism' (Lacan, 1993, p307).

Although one cannot go so far as to label the American reaction to 11 September as psychotic, this is the point at which it shares a similar structure. From the beginning the attacks were not understood to be an interpellation at all. Rather, the terrorists were demonised and defined in terms of their reciprocal relationship to the American position. In so far as a psychotic language expresses only the egological order, it can be said that America only sees itself in its enemies, precisely because they are merely the inverse, the 'other position' which is defined in mutual relation, exhibiting the full effulgence of their own aggression, turned inside out.

At least two aspects of the American political reaction to 11 September demonstrate how useful this psychotic structure of foreclosure is when trying to understand the event. First of all, the fact that the American political reaction manifested itself in rhetoric demonstrates the re-investment of language that Freud observed in the psychotic and that Lacan postulated as the essential symptom of psychosis. As an attempt at a cure, the re-alignment of the American position through Imaginary speech can be seen as a reconstitution of the American identity through the regression to narcissism. This phenomenon, however, was not limited to speech alone. Parallel to this, for example, was the sudden proliferation of American flags that were displayed across the country in the wake of the terrorist attacks. There can be no doubt that their purpose was to awaken a uniform sense of identity and pride, a revival of the ideal imago of a free and harmonious United States. A regeneration of the American identity was pursued by emphasising the common emblems of national unity. This can be nothing other than the retreat to identity formation on the level of the ideal ego. Secondly, certain tendencies present in the psychotic's experience of 'the end of the world' can also be seen in the American political reaction. While not going so far as an apocalyptic cataclysm, America's political position has redefined the very political reality of the globe. It has done so, furthermore, on its own terms: defined entirely in relation to the binary aggressive relationship that the United States has with its alter ego(s). The structure of a withdrawal of libidinal interest into the ego itself provides the framework by which we can understand the decomposition of the once-prevalent political reality.

This new political reality, where the world is defined relative to America's identity and interests, has its implications for a theory of the social body. At this stage, I can only sketch how this problem might be approached. As is latent in Freud, and made explicit in Lacan, it is the order of the signifier – the Law, the ego ideal of social obligation, the

Other – that sustains the essentially unstable ego identification. Without it, the bodily ego begins to fragment and the auto-erotic body re-emerges. When speaking about the body of the United States of America, however, one must not be led astray by the notion of a biological body. The body of a political State (at least in our modern times) is not an organism that breathes and feeds; its body is its territory, the delimited landmass by which it distinguishes itself from other political entities. As Freud argued in 'The Ego and the Id', 'the ego is first and foremost a bodily ego', not because it is the ego of a living biological entity, but because it 'is itself the projection of a surface' (Freud, 1923, p26). Without the structuring orientation of the fundamental signifier that distinguishes and sustains the 'I' and the 'you' within a greater social reality, however, this frontier begins to disintegrate. I would suggest that the structure of this fragmentation can be glimpsed in America's political policy of rhetorically identifying the victims of the attacks with humanity in general. America has responded, not only in defence of its own citizens, but first and foremost on behalf of all free and autonomous individuals everywhere. By doing so, this policy has extended America's interest far beyond its definable borders. 'It's a war against evil people who conduct crimes against innocent people' (Bush, Sept. 19). The American government is not only concerned about what happens to America, but what happens to all people who are identical to Americans. The identity of the nation is therefore dispersed and is not sustained by a position within the Symbolic universe of nation-states. This is not countered by the observation that the critical event took place on American soil. Because, complementary to the diffusion of American identification beyond its borders is the invasion of those borders by the Other. Suddenly, when the seeming impenetrability of the American identity was breached, the enemies of America multiplied, from the farthest regions of Asia, to deep within the borders of their own terrain. The famous 'Axis of Evil' that George W. Bush has proclaimed suddenly entangles America in numerous, irreducible conflicts all over the globe, with its enemies considered to be everywhere, and yet nowhere. They are potentially anywhere, planning their persecution, while simultaneously inside the United States as well, threatening devastation from within.

This is connected to the role that the leader, George W. Bush, has occupied during and since the crisis. Rather than sustain his Symbolic function as a State leader amongst the affiliation of other world leaders, occupying America's position within the international political order, his rhetoric suggests that he has occupied a more Imaginary function. He has spoken on behalf of the victims, identifying with them, and thereby idealising his political function, sliding from the ego ideal to the ideal ego of the populace. 'I wish I could comfort every single family whose lives have been affected', he proclaimed on 13 September. The tendency, therefore, of America to occupy a trans-national position in international affairs, in the infamous role of 'international policeman', would be coincident with the role of the President as an ideal imago and the proliferation of American aggressive relations that are progressively delivered from territorial considerations. Aside from these few hints, however, I cannot go further.

Conclusion

My position is not intended to be disapproval of the actions being taken against the enemies behind the New York attacks. The threat of further assaults demands a unified and steadfast reply. But there is a psychological factor at work, behind and within that reply, stretching to the hither side of reason, that the psychoanalytic concept of trauma can help to elucidate. Perhaps this reply is not entirely unconnected to the American tendency to reject psychoanalysis as a psychological method. If they reject this therapy at the level of the individual (preferring instead Ego Psychology, of course), then it should be no surprise that their international policies proceed in opposition to its warnings.

Notes

1. As was plainly evident on 11 September, this empathy was the most clearly marked immediate reaction to the bombings: a near universal outpouring of identificatory sympathy from both outside of America and within it. In this paper, I explicitly use the public statements of governmental officials as the privileged access to this psychological phenomenon. The next logical question is to ask what the basis is upon which this unitary psychical conglomeration is founded. As the main text indicates, this sympathy is based upon a recurrent structural relation. From this point of view, the events of 11 September are nothing but a concrete instance of the phenomenon of group formation in general. In any instance whereby a group is consolidated through political speech-making, we face the problems posed by Freud in his essay on 'Group Psychology' (Freud, 1921), which focuses upon the role of the leader and the projection of aggression beyond the group's boundaries. However, in so far as sympathetic identification

was not unanimous on 11 September and some pockets of dissent remained in opposition to the generally supported political reaction, a parallel (though tangential) problem can also be formulated: How does the American political and rhetorical reaction relate to internal dissension in its own ranks? That is, in order for individual statements of single politicians and Statesmen to become the dominant psychological attitude, there must be a complex process by which variant perspectives are either altered and incorporated or excised entirely from the political scene. In this way the current axiomatic function of the term 'America' would be rooted in a rhetorical and political transformation by which both externals and fellow nationals would be categorised (and perhaps even diabolised). Dissent both at home and abroad could then be repudiated in reference to this dominant regimatic discourse. However, though identification and not dissent, is an interesting question, it is one that strikes me as being tangential to the primary phenomenon of unity that we all observed so clearly. As well, being an issue of great complexity, it would require a full and separate investigation in its own right.

References

Fresneda, Carlos (2001) 'Richard Cheney y el FBI se comprometen a ayudar a España para luchar contra ETA', *El Mundo*, 16 October.

Freud, Sigmund (1966) *The Standard Edition of the Complete Psychological Works of Sigmund Freud*, James Strachey (ed), London: Hogarth Press, including:

(1895) *Project for a Scientific Psychology*, Volume I

(1905) *Fragment of an Analysis of a Case of Hysteria*, Volume VII

(1906) *My Views on the Part Played by Sexuality in the Aetiology of the Neuroses*, Volume VII

(1911) *Psycho-Analytic Notes on an Autobiographical Account of a Case of Paranoia (Dementia Paranoides)*, Volume XII

(1914) *On Narcissism: an Introduction*, Volume XIV

(1915) *The Unconscious*, Volume XIV

(1919) *Introduction to Psycho-Analysis and the War Neuroses*, Volume XVII

(1921) *Group Psychology and the Analysis of the Ego*, Volume XVIII

(1930) *Civilization and its Discontents*, Volume XXI

(1933) *Why War?*, Volume XXII

(1937) *Analysis Terminable and Interminable*, Volume XXIII

Lacan, Jacques (1977) 'The mirror stage as formative of the foundation of the I', in *Écrits: A Selection*, translated by Alan Sheridan, New York and London: W.W. Norton and Company, Inc.

Lacan, Jacques (1993) *The Psychoses: The Seminar of Jacques Lacan. Book III. 1955-1956*, translated by Russell Grigg, London: Routledge.

Zizek, Slavoj (10/07/2001) 'Reflections on WTC: Third Version'. Based on 'Welcome to the Desert of the Real' in Lacanian Ink 16. Taken from http://www.lacan.com/reflections.htm

Ethics and politics in psychology
Twilight dimensions

Maritza Montero

Abstract
A revision of the paradigmatic foundations of psychological theories is presented, arguing against the insufficiency of the predominant conceptions (Lincoln & Guba, 1985). As these conceptions limit the paradigmatic dimensions to three domains – ontology, epistemology, and methodology – two others are added: ethics and politics. These dimensions are defined, and discussed from a critical perspective. An ontological proposal based on a conception of the Other and the relation between the One and the Other (episteme of relatedness) is analysed, as is the distinction between ethics, morals and deontology. Politics, as the possibility for the person of expressing her/himself in the public space, is also discussed. The retrieval of ethics and politics from the secondary place given to both of them in social research is advocated.

It is well known how confusing and polysemous is the notion of paradigm used across the sciences (Masterman, 1975). Masterman's paper (1975) illustrates the point very well. I shall not discuss which, among the many meanings attributed to it, is the best or the worst. I shall go straight to the point: a paradigm is a mode of knowing used as a model, including both a conception of the cognisant subject and a conception of the world the person lives in, and of the relationship between them.

This supposes a systematic set of ideas and practices ruling interpretations about human activity, about its producers (Munné (1989) speaks of models of man, meaning human beings), about its origins, and about its effects on people and society. It also presents prevailing modes of doing in order to know those people and that society at a certain time (Montero, 1993). Its exemplar character consists, as Kuhn (1962: 13) has said, of providing a scientific community with models for explaining or describing problems and their solutions. It generates a stream of opinions and actions amongst those who produce science. Thus, in order to have a paradigm, now using Munné's words (1989), it is necessary 'to generate a scientific community, informal but well-differentiated. And that community is characterised by its own communication channels, by sharing the same epistemological approach, by its employment of common conceptual terms, by the use of one or several specific methods, and even by assuming a similar value scale' (Munné, 1989: 32).

The notion of paradigm, in a paradigmatic way, has been understood as a knowledge realm structured by three basic dimensions: ontology, epistemology and methodology. At least, that is the way it is currently presented in the social sciences, since Lincoln and Guba presented their model in 1985, further considered by Guba in 1990. The authors introduce these three aspects, implicitly assuming that they are the way to express scientific knowledge. And immediately, they begin examining, according to that 'troika', the paradigms that to their judgement have ruled the field of the social sciences during the twentieth century. Guba (1990) uses that trilogy of elements, after defining the concept of paradigm as a 'set of beliefs guiding action', be it in quotidian life, or in a systematic inquiry – a definition very similar, if not identical, to the way the notion of ideology has been defined in mainstream psychology.

Guba also states that both past paradigms and emergent ones can be characterised by the way in which those who propose them give answers to three basic questions, which can be characterised as ontological, epistemological and methodological (Guba, 1990: 17). Those questions should be the departure point to determine a research project, and how it is carried out.

—The first question (ontological) is, 'what is the nature of the "knowable"?' Or posed in a different way: 'What is the nature of reality?' (the nature of the object to be known).

—The second one (epistemological) is stated as: 'What is the nature of the relationship between the knower (the inquirer) and the known (or knowable)?'

—The third one (methodological) says: 'How should the inquirer go about finding out knowledge?' (Guba, 1990: 18)

I suppose no one in her wits (*paradigme oblige*) would argue against the pertinence of these three aspects so punctiliously presented by Lincoln and Guba; but I shall argue that this conception falls short. A paradigm does not end there. There is 'more fabric to be cut' in this task of defining and describing how knowledge is constructed in a research project (either naturalistic or experimentalist).

Lincoln and Guba (1985) and again Lincoln (1990:77-78) presented a comparative analysis of the paradigmatic structure of positivism, post-positivism, critical theory and 'social constructivism'. 'Social constructivism' was the denomination used by Lincoln (1990), as well as by Guba (1990), to refer to the monist perspective characterised by the constructed character of reality. I was charmed, as were many other researchers, by the elegant and apparently clear and simple way in which these two authors presented their analysis as a function of those three elements. At least that was so until I tried to use the Lincoln and Guba model to analyse which theories would preferentially correspond to each one of the paradigms they included.

So, several figures, tables and many paper balls later (after crossing and re-crossing my notes as well as feeling very cross), I ended up negotiating an accord with the model: things seemed to be more accessible, manageable and clear to me, when I used a prior classification: complexity versus simplicity. To that I had to add, when placing the paradigms, an extra cell to include theoretical productions in transit between paradigms. But I had to force the theories' admission and rejection criteria into those three main cells (ontology, epistemology and methodology). And also, some important and strongly determinant features of those theories had nothing to do with the table I was trying to produce. Finally, although the exercise was personally useful to me, since it elicited many a reflection, and showed the contradictions, I found that the model used was not as productive as it promised to be. In the end, what I had was a fixed table, which merely reflected a very particular view of the theoretical production examined. So I asked myself: were all the constituting and characteristic aspects typifying those practices and theories reflected in those three dimensions? Does that tri-dimensional interpretation of paradigms account for everything that is scientific work?

To answer that I had to go back to the beginning. Only this time I decided to start using as a point of departure everything that could not enter, or that would not have a place, in the previous table. Also I decided to start with an examination of my own practice, as well as that of other researchers. I examined not only theories that would not adjust to the table, but also those that perfectly fitted in. I then asked myself what had happened after I had answered the questions and looked at the paradigm that those theories belonged to.

The answer, of course, was that a lot was left out, although certainly one could determine who was knowing, what was being known, and how the knowing process was conceived, as well as the ways employed to produce that knowledge. What was being left out related to that aspect I mentioned at the outset, when I said what I understood a paradigm to be: the conception of the cognisant subject (though my definition is not so different from prior ones, for I am neither alone nor a pioneer in this search.)

Ethics and politics: out of the shadows

Two other dimensions had been omitted from the troika: ethics and politics. And this omission is the more evident when one reads the works of Guba and Lincoln (1989), Guba (1990), Lincoln (1990), Denzin and Lincoln (1998) and Lincoln (1999), as well as the works of many other researchers following their postulates. In their work, and in that of some others, one can find ethical as well as political concerns in connection with social research. But the omission is that ethics and politics are not seen as part of the model; they are presented as dignifying accessories, as aspects without which a work would be negatively considered. This happens in spite of the fact that in Guba and Lincoln's 1989 work a whole chapter is dedicated to 'Ethics and politics: the twin failures of positivist science'. There the political character of science is presented as residing in its being value-laden instead of value-free, as considered in positivist science. The same thing occurs when Barnes (1984, quoted by Smith, 1990) says that, 'the ethical and political commitment is intrinsic to the social research process'. Political factors and ethical issues are acknowledged, but after this has been done the way these factors are expressed in a paradigm is still ignored. Thus phrases like the one just quoted, though very impressive at first, come to sound like mere formal statements. Considering ethics and politics as part of a paradigm needs a more specific analysis.

In the following table can be seen the paradigm structure I am presenting, with the questions (to follow Guba's style) corresponding to each dimension.

PARADIGM STRUCTURE

DIMENSIONS	SCOPE	CHARACTERISING QUESTIONS
ONTOLOGY	"Being as being" (Aristotle). (Active) subject of knowledge. The being of knowledge. The being of the object known, or what things are. Reality.	What is the nature of the knowable? What is the nature of reality? (Guba, 1990) Who knows? Whom or what is known?
EPISTEMOLOGY	Relationship between knowing subject and known object. The construction of knowledge. The critical study of science, the study of knowledge.	What is the nature of the relationship between the knower (the inquirer) and the known (or knowable)? (Guba, 1990).
METHODOLOGY	Modes of production of knowledge.	What should someone do to produce knowledge? How should the inquirer go about finding out knowledge? (Guba, 1990)
ETHICS	Assessment judgement applied to the distinction between what is good and what is evil. Conception of the Other and of his/her place in the production of knowledge.	Who is the Other? What is the Other's place in the production of knowledge? What are the limits of good and evil?
POLITICS	What is related to collectively organised life in the public realm. What concerns civil rights and duties, as well as power relations and and their dynamics.	What type of relationship is had with the Other? For whom is knowledge produced? Who owns the knowledge produced?

Ethics and the production of scientific knowledge

In considering the two dimensions usually not explicitly acknowledged, let us begin with ethics. Firstly, I shall examine what is known as ethics when one speaks of science. Curiously, it is something that does not seem very different from what happens in common sense. What initially appears from that examination is that ethics and morals not only are mixed, but they are also used as synonyms. Secondly, and as a consequence of what has been said, sections about ethics usually are enumerations of norms that should be observed by researchers. Then, a new term should be added to that confusion: deontology. That is, the study of duties – duties to comply with during the practising of a profession or occupation.

Ethics has been defined within the field of philosophy (Lalande, 1953: 419) as the study that has as an object 'the assessment judgement concerning the distinction between what is good and what is evil'. According to this, ethics supposes a generic reflection of social relational character, from which derive specific commandments that each person should implement in her/his daily life. Its core is, as Aristotle (1952, V3: 1130) said: 'equity, based in justice'. Morals are that set of prescriptions, norms or rules, whose observance is exhorted in a particular time, society, or culture. As its etymology shows (morals comes from the Latin *mores*, that is, customs), morals are concerned with ways of doing and behaving.

Certainly, ethics and morals go together, the former influencing the latter, but they are not interchangeable. Nevertheless, as aforementioned, what usually is referred to, and found, in handbooks and scientific treatises is the set of rules to be followed in order to be considered morally respectable. At the same time, all this reflects an ethical standpoint, prior to those rules, that determines their sense and orientation. Then, what are called the 'codes of ethics' of different professions are sets of behavioural regulations pertaining to the moral order falling within the field, always applied, of deontology or theory of duties. And they reflect ethics because those norms suppose a conception of the world, of society, of the I (One) and the Other, as well as of the forms considered at a certain moment and in a certain space, as right and desirable for a society's common wellbeing.

Examples of this merge between ethics, morals and deontology can be found in the works of Smith (1990), House (1990), May (1980) and Barnes (1984; cited in Smith, 1990). Although some of the proposals

Smith presents for the regulation of the production of knowledge do include the Other, and transcend the moral level, they are enunciated in the same style, of behavioural rules to be observed. This author states that everything regarding the values intervening in a research is as important as the epistemological aspects, pointing out that researchers must be aware of the following issues:

- The necessity to be careful about any omission or carelessness in the treatment of anything regarding values.
- The necessity of including the perspective of the actors [other] present in the research context, so that the theory used by the researcher is co-ordinated with the actions carried out, according to that perspective.
- The necessity to account for the actions carried out by the researchers, in the same terms as it is done for those events executed by the subjects [other], in such a way that both worlds can relate.
- The need to be respectful of the 'human subjects" rights [other].
- The need to avoid bureaucratic management of the observance of 'ethical norms', which tends to postpone their fulfilment (Smith, 1990: 154-155).

The norms regulating scientific activity, the way theory is expressed, and their way of relating to the research object, fall into the realm of morals and translate into deontology. Likewise, deontological issues, which should be present in every scientific discipline, rule their practice and go along with their methods: the subject's worldview, their conceptions about the origins, application and property of the knowledge, and of the relationships that unite them to that world, belong to ethics.

Because of this, the questions posed by Hare in 1964 (Smith, 1990: 149), in relation to those activities, such as social research, which involve other people in their performance are ethical in nature. Those questions are:

- Why this bothers me? (referring to the specific research activity one is carrying out).
- Can I live with this?

And I would add another one:

- Would I like to have the same thing happening to me?

According to Hare (and I agree), when one faces questions such as these the decision one makes should be one of 'principles'. This means that Hare is placing the answer in the realm of values and of judgements relating to what is good or evil. Then, some fundamental ethical questions are:

- What are the interests motivating this research? (Asked by Fals Borda (1981), Smith (1990) and Rorty (1997))
- Who benefits from this research? (Fals Borda, 1981)
- Does this research harm anyone?

At the base of the act of knowing there is always a human being, as the One or as the Other. And the ethical realm thus configures a fundamental dimension in every paradigm, because in every conception of scientific activity there is, explicit or implicit, a conception of the Other. That Other is defined, by opposition or as complement, in the same way as is the cognisant subject. By 'cognisant subject' is understood the One who carries out the knowing activity (or the one that at least some times thinks of him/herself as the main actor in that activity). This is a point not to be treated lightly or to be considered as obvious: the conception of the Other (and of human beings in general) that supports a research project, theory or method frequently has to be deducted, as it is not clear, or is shadowed by contradictory information. Often a procedure or a principle is announced, while quite a different thing is done.

Ethics and otherness

What is the reason for making the conception of the Other the locus of Ethics? Why is it not enough to simply express it as part of the 'Ethics Code', or of a set of rules or commandments regulating the good citizen's (or researcher's) behaviour? After all, such rules seem to be necessary, useful, healthy and inevitable. But on closer analysis it can be revealed that a conception of the Other (for example, as someone close and alike to oneself, or as an alien) is always present in these rules, although usually covert. This means that the conception of the Other has been naturalised, accepted as something pertaining to what is considered as the natural order of things within the world. There is therefore no attempt to discuss or define it. And this can lead to the conceiving of that Other as another One, as someone not only close by proximity, but also by their similarity to the One from whose position those norms are being issued. Or it can mean condemning that Other to the realm of monsters, beasts, savages or the unclean.

That Other is also someone that even in her/his negative or opposing character is defined from the I, from the One – bad, where the One has defined what is good; dark where the light of clarity is defined as coming from the One's position. Good and evil are then constructed as a function of the relationship we have with the Other. We cause good and evil to the Other. Good and evil are inflicted upon us. This happens in the world we construct and inhabit, and all relationship with that world is essentially social.

This limitation of the Other reduces her/him to being the external part of the One, something like the adventuresome part of the I, the deviation we all secretly keep, defined as a function of prevailing norms. Enrique Dussel, an Argentinean philosopher living in Mexico, has reacted to this (1974) by presenting an epistemological and methodological modification or re-structuration: *analectics* (from the Greek *anas* meaning from beyond, from a higher plane – up there – what we could call *exteriority*). With analectics, Dussel wants to overcome the restricted character of dialectics by incorporating analogy as a mode of knowing – parallel and at the same time – opposed to the dialectics.

The restriction of dialectics resides in the internal ties between its elements. Thesis, anti-thesis and synthesis, all belong to the same realm. The three of them are enclosed in a totality, whose origin resides in the thesis. Thus, the thesis is such, because it precedes the confronting antithesis. Simultaneously, the thesis sets the horizon and the limits for the antithesis. Synthesis can only be in relation to the thesis and the antithesis, and the three combined constitute a totality generating (by the same sort of relationship, based in contradictions) a possible new totality.

There is a primary element in dialectics from which knowledge stems. And although it goes beyond the closed condition of syllogistic premises, the same three-part structure is still sustained through an element that stops being 'major' in dialectics, since it accepts the dialogue with its opposite, but nevertheless is part of a process of exchange coming from two elements that in some way complement each other.

Dussel (1974) defined analectics as an extension of dialectics (it is also called *ana-dia-lectics*), or as a 'moment of dialectics' incorporating a new possibility to the construction of knowledge: the excluded otherness or alterity. Otherness is constituted by those that not only are opposite or complementary, but also are different, unexpected, external. That otherness supposes accepting as a cognisant subject an unimagined Other. Someone who is not the same as the One (by opposition or by similarity).

Accepting a differing otherness, not constructed by the One, supposes admitting modes of knowing totally other; and it also supposes, necessarily, dialogue and relation with an Other in a plane of equality based in the acceptance of distinction, and not only in similarity or in complementarity.

Dussel's work, published extensively (from 1974 on) in Spanish, German, Portuguese and English, is one of the most outstanding contributions there has been to the philosophy of liberation; and its influence is also felt in the psychology of liberation. Ethics, issues concerning morals, exclusion, theology, politics, marxism, hermeneutics and discourse, have all been discussed in his writings (cf *Anthropos* journal, No 180, 1998).

Politics, science and knowledge

It is a common practice, when referring to politics outside of the partisan context, to immediately define it in a wide sense, making sure that those who hear us will not be confused, and think we are going to introduce some kind of defence or detraction of a political tendency. Usually the speaker tries to make sure that s/he will be cleared of any specific political affiliation. That happens because a single mention of the term politics scares, alarms or alerts even the drowsiest members of any audience. Things will be no different when one speaks of the political dimension of a paradigm. So, after a reminder about the ever-present origin of the word politics (that is, its Greek root *polis*, what belongs to the city, what concerns citizenry, what is public), I am going to point out why it constitutes a dimension in the structure of paradigms.

Punch (1998: 159), when dealing with ethics and politics in relation to qualitative research, says that, within this context, politics is understood as referring across the board, from the micropolitics of personal relationships to the culture and resources of research units and universities, to the power and policies of Government departments, and even the State's hand (heavy or not). And to all this is added 'the context of politics and its restrictions' [understood as the political arena], as well as the inevitable political condition inherent to science, as an activity crossed by values. Research, according to Punch, is influenced by this whole range of political manifestations.

Politics therefore refers, as announced, to public life and to how we relate with other people within it. But also, and this seems to be the core of politics, it refers to power and action lines. That is, to doing and saying within society. It is about having voice, about speaking out, and giving voice to those that have been spoken of, while left out in silence. The production of knowledge, therefore, has political consequences (and nowadays this is a commonplace), and can be the outcome of a specific policy or politics. Knowing or practising knowledge is political, as also is the holding of a particular place in the knowing relationship. As ethics resides in the recognition of the Other, and in accepting the active cognisant character of unlike others, the relationship arising from that recognition frees the One; for freedom does not reside in the isolation of others and from others, but in the intersubjectivity that, recognising the humanity of the Other, allows the One to also be human. That is why a paradigm has a political dimension; because it can be liberating, and it can be oppressive.

But, as we saw with ethics, in much research work the explicit or implicit allusions one finds about politics could easily drive the analyst along roads leading out of the very field s/he wanted to transit. Most of the time what one gets is information about the context of knowledge production and about its influence. And although this is important, it is only a fraction of what the field can yield. An example of this can be found in Smith (1990) and House (1990). Both authors use as an example the infamous Camelot Project carried out in Latin America by USA researchers and agencies during the mid and late 1960s. Both condemn – as happened at the time – the interventionist character of that Project, showing how it was designed to meddle with some Latin American countries' politics (understood as governmental action and orientation). But though there is an emphasis in their work on the moral (or should we say immoral?) aspects of this Project, concerning its sneaky ways, and the hiding of the real intentions, a concept of politics as part of the structure of the production of knowledge is absent. Actually, politics seems to be avoided. It is seen as a polluting notion, better kept apart from the research.

A paradigm is not the sum of its dimensions

The five dimensions I present here (ontology, epistemology, methodology, ethics, politics) are not separate components. Every epistemological expression is directly related to an ontological conception defining the object of knowledge. As a function of this a cognitive relation is produced. The method employed also reflects those two aspects. And, when dealing with ontology, epistemology and methodology, one necessarily enters the realm of ethics and politics. The basis of ethics, as aforementioned, resides in its conception of the Other, and in its understanding of the relationship of the Other with the cognisant subject, defined as the One; that is, in its definition of the Other as object or subject, as a cognisant being or as something to be known. Inequality is anti-ethical: it goes against freedom; and it is an effect of the power to discriminate, which falls into the political field. Moreover, the admission of the existence of values in the construction of knowledge also takes us into the political dimension, since those values determine who profits, who is excluded, who is included, who has access or not to that knowledge. Hence, the five dimensions continuously interact and cannot be taken apart.

As already mentioned, some of the authors that limit their conception of paradigm to three dimensions do include references to morals and deontology, sometimes to ethics, and, less frequently, to considerations of political order. But although some authors assert science's political character, it is not enough to admit that those aspects have to be considered; they also need to recognise the basic dimensional or constitutive character of such aspects in a paradigmatic structure.

The conception of Otherness which includes the possibility of a relationship with independent Others is derived from the critically examined works of Buber (1923/1956) and Levinas (1977). Their works can be considered as the foundation for what today has come to be called the 'episteme of relatedness' (Moreno, 1993), liberation philosophy (Dussel, 1988, 1998) and liberation psychology (Martín-Baró, 1986, 1990; Montero, 1990, 2000). The episteme of relatedness understands knowledge as the production of the relations constituted within social life. Dussel's philosophy of liberation can be used as an example of the integration of paradigm domains. With analectics, Dussel (1974; 1988; 1998) tries to extend the scope of dialectics by incorporating what is not linked to the One's (the I's) lifeworld, from where knowledge is mainly produced. Through analectics he introduces an epistemological conception (based in the relationship and in dialogue), creates a method, and constructs an ontology that has its ethical base in the conception of the unexpected Other. This also has political consequences: Liberation; being able to speak out; having access to public space; de-privatising what has been taken away from the citizens.

Dussel's contribution concerning liberation makes evident the oppression that a subjectivity imposes upon another subjectivity. Such domination gives way to an 'originary experience' (Dussel, 1998) lived by a variety of social categories: the colonised; the poor; the dark-skinned; Jews; women; children; Third World countries. The assertion of the other as Other originates the possibility of negating the dialectic negation (analectics), and that possibility can be achieved through a praxis both ethical and political: the praxis of liberation (Dussel, 1998; Montero, 2000).

From an ontology (ontology of relatedness) based not in the individual Being, not in the One, but in the relationship between the One and the Other (Montero, 1999b), arises that episteme of relatedness: that is, a systematic conception of the relation between subject and object of knowledge, providing a referential place for the theoretical and methodological construction of a particular time. The epistemological dimension is then integrated by knowing through relationships. The One recognises him/herself as such because of the admitted presence of the Other and because of the relationship they keep. One is in the relation, and One cannot be outside the relationship. Individuality is then an element of the relation, constructed within the relation, and by the relation.

This episteme of relatedness is a critical challenge to the truth-value of an affirmation that has sustained the psychological and philosophical building housing modern science: the empire of the individual as sovereign of consciousness, as sole and unique entity among millions of equals. A social being *par excellence*, and yet defending an individuality, that, paradoxically, can only exist if there is a group and a society within which to be individualised. And the paradox becomes yet more evident through the fact that the individual is defined by what denies her/his individuality, and every now and then condemns individuality.

Nevertheless, the episteme of the relation does not expel the individual. It does not mean either the de-personalising, or the disappearance, of each individual's distinctiveness. It refers to a phenomenon in which One is with the Others, without stopping being singular. But One is in the relation, One is not in isolation. No one can exist without the other, unless, as Aristotle (1952) posed it, we are either wild animals or gods. And it is from that singularity that arises the necessity to recognise the Other in its distinctiveness, and not just as the extension of the One, either as its complement or as its opposite.

Camps (1993) illustrates this contradiction by saying that:

> the individual stops being such when s/he abdicates his/her autonomy. To be individualistic in the sense usually given to the term, to think only about one's own survival and that of the group one belongs to, to be selfish, that is not to be autonomous ... because it is to blindly adapt to the established norms.

And to do that ... 'one has to avoid by all means the permeability of other behaviours and lifestyles'. And yet she adds, not without a certain shyness: 'autonomy ... is not incompatible with dialogue and with the necessity of the other' (Camps, 1993:23,24). In Camps's perspective, the individualism that transforms people into numbers is rejected. She points out the necessity of accepting a diversity-Other, the otherness which makes an autonomous self; or (as Levinas would say (1977/1995)) that frees ourselves.At the same time, both still keep the I, the individual as ontological unity.

Community social psychology, as produced in Latin America during the last thirty years, has provided fertile ground in the development of this perspective. Its liberating orientation, especially its consideration of community members as co-producers of knowledge and internal agents of change, sustaining a dialogical relation with psychologists (external agents of change), has provided a nourishing praxis (cf Serrano-García and Rosario-Collazo, 1992; Montero, 1994, 1999a). With the same orientation, Prilleltensky and Gonick (1996) presented what they called a 'psychology of oppression', which more recently has led the first author (Prilleltensky, 1999) to propose a critical psychology praxis oriented towards goals similar to those posed by the psychology of liberation: to produce social change intended to fight social and psychological conditions of inequality. In general, the critical psychology movement promotes what can be defined as a politically oriented practice, in the sense of searching for a better society (Prilleltensky and Fox, 1997). And in 1999, Lincoln told how her epistemological conception had changed: she had discarded the 'voyeur' approach, to focus on the relationship between subject and object of research; and considered that s/he who wants to know and those holding the sought-after knowledge co-create new knowledge (Lincoln, 1999: 53). Lincoln interprets this as a collapse of the distinction between ontology and epistemology, since the known object is also a knower-subject. As said before, the ontology of relatedness considers that beings are constituted in and by relations, and therefore knowledge is constructed within the relation, due to its dynamics. Ethics, with the consideration of the Other in its diversity, expands the totality by inclusion.

Conclusion

If the presence of ethics and politics in the production of knowledge has been recognised by some analysts, they have been assigned a fuzzy or dim place, and are not assumed to be dimensions of paradigmatic structure. Gnosiologists, and those in general concerned with the study of science, do attempt to discover or uncover the theoretical foundation underlying the work of an author, the methods they employ, and (though in a lesser degree) the model of human being inhabiting the explanation, study or interpretation. But they miss out on key aspects of analysis. Denzin and Lincoln (1998: 22) say, with reference to the current state of qualitative research, that 'new epistemologies from previously silenced groups' are emerging to offer solutions to the problem of the representation of the 'other'. This is to be welcomed, since it is likely to make social sciences and psychology more sensitive to the fact that caring about the other can lead to the analysis of ethical and political aspects in a paradigm. Such a process could also help to bring ethics and politics out of the shadows, so that they stop being paradigmatic twilight dimensions.

Nevertheless, the current imprecise and blurred condition is unacceptable, because as is nowadays widely recognised, every form of knowledge construction at least nominally includes the ethical and political. Usually this is done in a naturalised way, whereby they are presented as elements belonging to the object to be known, intrinsic to it; or they are referred to as if they were part of the research rituals, part of the multiple gestures of quotidian scientific doing, as if they were part of the essence of being and living. Thus a vanishing act takes place, that limits to three the recognised aspects of paradigms, hiding the conception of the Other, and reducing the cognisant being, by not considering the nature of the relationship that, as knowledge producers, the One has with the Other. That conception limits the very relationship. That is why in the research agenda of those who would like to produce knowledge, a critical approach to the study of the construction of knowledge should be included.

References

Anthropos (1998) 180, Enrique Dussel, *Un proyecto ético político para América Latina*, Barcelona, Spain. Whole issue.

Aristotle (1952) *Nichomachean Ethics*, Chicago, USA: *Encyclopedia Britannica*, The University of Chicago, Vol 9: 334-436.

Buber, M. (1923/1956) *Yo y Tu* [I and thou] Buenos Aires, Argentina: Galatea/Nueva Visión.

Camps, V. (1993) *Paradojas del individualismo* [Paradoxes of individualism], Barcelona, Spain: Drakontos.

Denzin, N. & Lincoln, Y. (1998) 'Introduction. Entering the field of qualitative research', in N.K. Denzin & Y.S. Lincoln (eds), *The Landscape of Qualitative Research. Theories and Issues*: 1-34. London: Sage.

Dussel, E. (1974) *Método para una filosofía de la liberación* [Method for a liberation philosophy], Salamanca, Spain: Sígueme.

Dussel, E. (1988) *Introducción a la filosofía de la liberación* [Introduction to liberation philosophy], Bogotá, Colombia: Nueva América.

Dussel, E. (1998) *Un proyecto ético político para América Latina* An ethical-political project for Latin America, *Revista Anthropos* 180, whole issue.

Fals Borda, O. (1981) *Ciencia propia y colonialismo intelectual* [Indigenous science and intellectual colonialism], Bogota, Colombia: Carlos Valencia Editores.

Guba, E. G. & Lincoln, Y. (1989) *Fourth generation evaluation*, London: Sage.

Guba, E. G. (1990) 'The alternative paradigm dialog', in E. Guba (ed), *The paradigm dialog*: 17-27, Newbury Park, USA: Sage.

House, E. R. (1990) 'An ethics of qualitative field studies', in E. Guba (ed), *op. cit.* Kuhn, T.S. (1962) *The structure of scientific revolutions*, Chicago, USA: University of Chicago Press.

Lalande, A (1953) *Vocabulario técnico y crítico de la filosofía* [Technical and critical vocabulary of Philosophy], Buenos Aires, Argentina: El Ateneo.

Levinas, E. (1977) *Totalidad e infinito. Ensayos sobre la exterioridad* [Totality and Infinite], Salamanca, Spain: Sígueme.

Levinas, E. (1989) 'Time and the Other', in S. Hand (ed), *The Levinas Reader*: 37-58. Oxford, UK: Blackwell.

Lincoln, Y. and Guba, E.G. (1985) *Naturalistic Inquiry*, Beverly Hills, USA: Sage

Lincoln, Y. (1990) 'The making of a constructivist: A remembrance of transformations past', in E.G. Guba (ed), *op. cit.* 67-87.

Lincoln, Y (1999) 'Imperativos éticos en la enseñanza de la investigación cualitativa en psicología' [Ethical imperatives in the teaching of qualitative research in psychology] *Revista AVEPSO*, XXII (2): 51-66.

Martín-Baró, I. (1986) 'Hacia una psicología de la liberación' [Towards a psychology of liberation], *Boletín de Psicología*, UCA El Salvador, 22: 219-231.

Martín-Baró, I. (1990) 'Retos y perspectivas de la psicología en América Latina' [Challenges and perspectives for psychology in Latin America], in G. Pacheco and B. Jiménez (eds), *Psicología de la liberación para América Latina* [Liberation psychology for Latin America]: 51-80, Guadalajara, México: Universidad de Guadalajara – ITESO.

Masterman, M. (1975) 'La naturaleza de los paradigmas' [The nature of paradigms], in Lakatos, I. and A. Musgrave (eds), *La crítica y el desarrollo del conocimiento* [Development and critique of knowledge]: 159-202, México: Grijalbo.

May, W. (1980) 'Doing ethics: the bearing of ethical theories in fieldwork', *Social Problems*, 27: 358-370.

Montero, M. (1990) 'Psicología de la liberación: Propuesta para una teoría psicosociológica' [Liberation psychology. Proposal for a psychosocial theory], in H. Riquelme (ed), *Otras realidades, otras vías de acceso*: 133-149. Caracas, Venezuela: Nueva Sociedad.

Montero, M. (1993) 'Permanencia y cambio de paradigmas en la construcción del conocimiento científico' [Permanence and change of paradigms in scientific knowledge construction] *Interacción social* [Social interaction] Spain, 3: 11-24.

Montero, M. (ed) (1994) *Psicología Social Comunitaria. Teoría, método y experiencias* Community Social Psychology. Theory, method, experience, Guadalajara, Mexico: University of Guadalajara Press.

Montero, M. (1999a) 'Retos y perspectivas de la psicología de la liberación' [Challenges and perspectives of liberation psychology], *Estudios centroamericanos* [Central American studies] UCA, El Salvador, 601-602: 1123-1135.

Montero, M. (1999b) 'Los Unos y los Otros: de la individualidad a la episteme de la relación' The One and the Other: From individuality to the episteme of relatedness *Revista AVEPSO*, XXII (2): 67-84.

Montero, M. (2000) 'Constructing the Other, liberating the Self', Stockholm, Sweden: Paper presented at the XXVII International Congress of Psychology.

Moreno, A. (1993) *El aro y la trama. Episteme, modernidad y pueblo* The hoop and the weave. Episteme, modernity and the people, Caracas, Venezuela: Centro de Investigaciones populares.

Munné, F. (1989) *El individuo y la sociedad* [Individual and Society], Barcelona, Spain: PPU.

Prilleltensky, I. (1999) 'Critical Psychology Praxis', in *La Psicología al fin del siglo* [Psychology at the end of the century], (Keynote address at the XXVII Interamerican Congress of Psychology): 279-305, Caracas, Venezuela: Interamerican Society of Psychology.

Prilleltensky, I. & Fox, D. (1997) 'Introducing Critical Psychology: Values, assumptions, and the status Quo', in Fox, D. & Prilleltensky, I. (eds), *Critical Psychology. An Introduction*: 3-20. London: Sage.

Prilleltensky, I. & Gonick, L. (1996) 'Polities change, oppression remains: On the Psychology and Politics of Oppression', *Journal of Political Psychology*, 17: 127-148.

Punch, M. (1998) 'Politics and ethics in qualitative research', in N.K. Denzin & Y. Lincoln (eds), *The landscape of qualitative research*, Theories and issues: 156-184, Thousand Oaks, USA Sage.

Rorty, R. (1997) *Esperanza o conocimiento? Una introducción al pragmatismo* [Hope or knowledge? An introduction to pragmatism], Buenos Aires, Argentina: FCE.

Serrano-García, I. & Rosario-Collazo, W. (eds), (1992) *Contribuciones puertorriqueñas a la psicología social comunitaria* Puerto-rican contributions to Community Social Psychology, San Juan, Puerto Rico: Puerto Rico University Press.

Smith, L.M. (1990) 'Ethics, field studies, and the paradigm crisis', in E. Guba (ed) *op. cit*: 139-57.

Dialectics of subjectivity: North-Atlantic certainties, neo-liberal rationality and liberation promises

Dimitris Papadopoulos

Abstract
Although the notion of subjectivity has been the target of acute criticism, it seems that it has withstood this repudiation and achieved a new efficacy in post-structuralist, feminist and discursive trends, and in the Marxian or post-Marxist accounts. In this paper I want to skip an intrinsic examination of the theoretical-philosophical development of subjectivity and focus instead on the interpersonal and mental realities that are produced through the use of this concept. I want to assert that by applying it we are effectively engaged in constituting new domains of the social. These domains correspond to dominant neo-liberal reason, characterised by transnational capitalism, the disintegration of the welfare state, individualisation processes, and the domination of high technology. If we accept that the critical accounts mentioned at the beginning represent specific forms of involvement in power relations established in particular sites, as well as in their interconnections throughout the neo-liberal world system, then we have to raise the question of how it is possible, if at all, to identify the 'critical' or 'emancipatory' moment in these approaches.

thou shalt be a diaspora in all kingdoms of the earth[1]

1.
One of the common points of departure for the various alternative psychologies which have emerged in the last three decades has been to

question the conditions of theory production in mainstream psychology.[2] Most critical trends begin with the assumption that traditional psychology commits the so called objectivistic fallacy (cf Haraway, 1997; Canguilhem, 1979; Bourdieu, 1980): that is, the ontologising of knowledge and, consequently, the naturalisation of the relationships through which such knowledge is fabricated. A major consequence of this gnostic strategy is the insertion of an empiricist stance throughout the experimental and research methodology (cf Toulmin & Leary, 1985; Holzkamp, 1996).

While the critical investigation of the psy-complex – i.e. the scientific and professional 'complex of discourses, practices, agents and techniques, deployed within schools, clinics, the juridical and penal processes, the factories and the army' (Rose, 1985: 9; and cf Danzinger, 1990; Jaeger & Staeuble, 1978; Sonntag, 1990) – plays a central role in the assembly of critical psychological agendas, the construction of the subject of critical psychologies eludes a close scrutiny of its own production conditions. My quest in this paper is to trace the social and institutional spaces which have allowed critical theories and practices, especially the notion of subjectivity and subjectification, to come into being.

The ideas presented here are an attempt to interrogate the tacit presuppositions of my own work within critical psychology. In particular, to unravel some of the reasons why terms such as subjectivity, subjectification, sense, etc, enjoy a privileged and self-sufficient methodological position in my recent work projects (Papadopoulos, 1999). While reading a small piece by bell hooks (1992) and fumbling about in my memory for the foundations of my convictions and practices, I realised how difficult it is to escape the unbreakable complicity between subjectivity, difference, and exclusion. I mean that the routinisation of difference, and the unrestrained enunciation of subjectivity, often fabricate exclusion in other remote sites. Subjectivity and difference tend towards structuring the world in terms of the binary code belonging/not belonging, or fitting/not fitting; and this code appears to have a self-evident, quasi-natural validity in the day-to-day transactions of life. This is something bell hooks describes when she asks if the white men, mostly street vendors, were conscious of the terrifying appearance of whiteness in the living rooms of black neighbourhoods (hooks, 1992: 341).[3] What I am trying to address here is not only the politics of subjectivity but also its ordinary phenomenology on an intersubjective level. This paper casts doubt upon the assertion that the ethical or political commitment of critical psychology is axiomatically given in the categories and conceptions employed in critical intervention.

Proceeding from the assumption that we reject an essentialist or teleological definition of subjectivity, we have to examine all the paths – be they techniques, discourses, social practices or societal landscapes – which let the critical narratives and policies emerge as true. I mean that since we cannot ground the key concepts of the various critical psychologies metaphysically, we have to view the critical discourse itself as a construction, indeed a very specific construction, which *springs from* as well as *participates in* the formation of our social realities. Critical accounts establish, in exactly the same manner as other mainstream psychological trends, regimes of truth (Foucault, 1969; Rose, 1996), in the middle of concrete social and institutional spaces. Moreover, critical psychologies, similar to mainstream psychological theories and practices, promote closures or attachments, mark differences and coalitions, and finally alter the conditions under which certain suppressed aspects of social phenomena become intelligible and amenable to change.

By challenging mainstream psychology, the critical accounts claim recognition for their ability to organise relationships between human beings in particular ways. In other words, they claim to empower specific subjects as speaking subjects who should be included in community, state, and global decision-making. But a crucial problem arises here: Who is this subject in whose name the critical psychologist is speaking? Who is this subject finding its voice through the liberation practices of critical psychology? Do the critical approaches constitute an emancipatory discourse or do they merely represent a particular facet of a historically determined mode of social regulation?

As Nikolas Rose says, 'the social reality of psychology is not a kind of disembodied yet coherent "paradigm", but a complex and heterogeneous network of agents, sites, practices, and techniques for the production, dissemination, legitimation, and utilisation of psychological truths' (Rose, 1996: 60). In this paper, I want to suggest that we should *also* understand critical psychologies as a partial force in the construction of these social networks. That means that we should – exactly as when we are deconstructing mainstream psychology – dismiss the idea that critical psychologies represent either a pre-discursive subject outside the domination of power relations, or the post-discursive subject of our desires.

2.

Yet, the rejection of the idea that the constitutive element of critical psychological accounts could be a universal liberation project obliges us to look for the rootedness of the critical psychologies in concrete geopolitical constellations. Specifically, we have to follow the vestiges of the implicit images of the person, of the entailed vocabularies about the self and the other, of the invisible techniques used to sustain intersubjective communication, and finally of the practices employed to manage and to rationalise social relationships.

The disciplining and standardisation of human individuality (Foucault, 1975) could be understood as the pivotal project of (traditional) psychology. This enterprise takes place against the background of the genesis of the modern understanding of the self and of 'the growth of forms of inwardness' (Taylor, 1989: 186; see also Hobsbawm, 1995: 420ff).[4] The broad validity and the social technological attitude of mainstream psychology depend precisely on a unification of a doubled-sided process, that is, the interaction between the 'context of application' and the 'context of investigation' (Danziger, 1990: 191; see also 1979). In the course of professionalisation, psychology concentrated on the triaxial task: education/adaption, suffering/repair, delinquency/correction (Staeuble, 1985) (this triangular scheme was later extended by the AI and neurosciences with the addition of a fourth prime task: the simulation of human brain processes in automated cyber-devices); psychology transcribes the abstract knowledge about the individual into local technologies of the self and the other. The crucial target in this ongoing endeavour could be understood as the struggle to visualise individuality, self and difference, and to render them amenable to management, codification and simulation.

In this paper, I want to assert that critical psychologies, instead of establishing a counter discourse, are linked to and indeed closely follow this project (cf Foucault, 1976). Since individuality is more than a mere theoretical construction, the disapproval of the individualistic perspective on the self cannot be simply a matter of an intellectual decision; it is rather a particular historic-cultural way of organising and sustaining social relations, and of positioning actors in dialogical, intersubjective contexts.[5] The reign of different languages of individuality is much more than a mere game with signs and symbols; it is rooted in our contradictory social realities, it is a matter of our historically situated and semiotically organised materiality, where bodies and lives are at stake.

Thus, the construction of the psychological subject is always a material, practical question. In this sense the common, fashionable oppositions between construction and deconstruction, or between the logic of discovery and the logic of critique (e.g. Burman, 1994; Sampson, 1989), are essentially both aspects of one and the same trajectory: the struggle to determine the conditions and the terms of visibility in the historical-cultural space. The quest for visibility is nothing more than a campaign to order the social (see Waldenfels, 1989: 337), and, in this sense, critical psychologies are also keen on proposing and realising their own visions of how social relations should be arranged. Different regimes of truth in psychology – be it mainstream or alternative – are consistent and linked to different attempts to fabricate valuable, applicable knowledge as a way of insinuating transformational modes of social and institutional relations into practical technologies.

3.

What has happened in the last three decades is that by using the concept of subjectivity some critical accounts tried to formulate an alternative theory and praxis of individuality. We can delineate two principal interpretations of subjectivity.

In the marxian and post-marxian tradition of argumentation, subjectivity represents the ability of the individual to transform the material world according to its own first-person-standpoint in social practice (Holzkamp, 1983; Tolman & Maiers, 1991).[6] Three categories are employed to underpin this notion: action, agency and societal conditions. Derived from soviet activity theory (Leontjew, 1977), the concept of action grasps the relational nature of subjectivity. We are not dealing here with a linear determination of the subject by his or her circumstances, nor are we supposing a solipsistic constitution of the psychic processes and a free-flow of the subject beyond social contingencies. The concept of action stresses a relation of possibility towards the surrounding environment, which implies the idea of subjective agency, i.e. the perception of the alternative possibilities inherent in a particular context and the potency to act from a subjective perspective

(Maiers & Tolman, 1996). Acting from this first-person-standpoint and having subjective grounds for action (Maiers, 1996) presupposes the anchorage of the individual in space and time and introduces the concept of location in specific societal conditions (Dreier, 1997). These conditions represent structures of meaning, of material constraints and possibilities, and of institutional impediments and opportunities, which together form the subjective context of action. And it is precisely this positionality of the subject and the embeddedness of subjectivity in contradictory social contexts which characterises the critical psychological project: The empowerment of the individual 'toward extended control over one's own life conditions through participation in societal provisioning' (Holzkamp, 1984, 60f.; further 1983).

The second strand in current interpretations of subjectivity has a post-structuralist origin. It neglects the existence of inner states and psychic processes and asserts that subjectivity comes into being through people's discursive transactions in concrete sociocultural contexts (this notion exists in many variations, catering to all purposes and tastes: Gergen, 1996; Harré & Gillett, 1994; Hollway, 1984; Parker, 1992; Walkerdine, 1987; there is also a certain affinity of these approaches to discursive or dialogical accounts: Potter & Wetherell, 1987; Shotter, 1992). Three ideas are used to support this notion: discourse, positionality, and difference. Subjectivity emerges via the positionality (cf Davies & Harré, 1990) of human beings in discourses (cf Parker, 1992). In other words, subjectivity is difference, and difference is a metonymy which is used to provide a topography of various locations within apparatuses and technologies of power and control. Such an understanding of subjectivity as difference defines the critical project in the post-structuralist tradition of argumentation: it is the 'production of new positions and subjectivities', it is the attempt to render the psy-complex 'open for new possibilities' (Burman, 1996: 7), to invent means of 'elaborating resistance' (Burman, 1996: 9), and finally nothing less than an opportunity of discussing 'ways of changing the world' (CPAR, 1999: 1) and creating a 'better society' (Prilleltensky & Fox, 1997: 13).

4.
Despite the different origins and heritages of these critical traditions, we can trace a common view of individuality as a relational self that aims to achieve a possible maximisation of its influence on the forma-

tion of the surrounding power-pervaded circumstances. What is usually presented under the guise of subjectivity as an alternative conceptualisation of individuality or the self is in fact an articulation of a new governmental rationality which can be situated in the long tradition of social technologies in psychology.[7] In this sense, government refers to the interdependence between the practices of individual agents and the way political and social power is exercised in a specific society (for a detailed discussion see Gordon, 1991; Foucault, 1978).

This reconstruction of the idea of individuality, which avoids the pitfalls of methodological individualism, atomism and 'asociality of the self', corresponds with a new understanding of the issue of power (an issue which mainstream psychology traditionally leaves out of consideration or conceives of only as a special research field within social psychology). The former notion of power as a monistic entity – penetrating, contaminating, prescribing and, finally, regulating the individual's existence through the inescapable force of disciplinary mechanisms – is gradually replaced by a view of power which functions through the open control and self-control of each individual. Power is much more disseminated in various individualising modalities which could be described as government techniques of self-enterprising individuals.[8]

The concept of government rests on the idea that power can be grasped only as a communicative, intersubjective practice based on existing societal constraints and conditions, and thus implies acting upon present or coming circumstances in order to facilitate or to nullify possible relationships between people (Foucault, 1982b). This governmental theme demythologises traditional objectivist knowledge in mainstream psychology, which hitherto attempted to reveal in the politically hermetic and aseptic brain of the abstract and acontextual human being what the essentials of subjectivity are. The notion of government seeks a comprehension of subjectivity in the factual interrelations of people in existing sociocultural conditions. This understanding of subjectivity is not an undertaking evolving outside of the lifeworld in which people dwell, but is a real time venture which monitors, modifies, builds, and rebuilds the life conditions of the participating subjects. In this sense, the research on subjectivity is not a neutral enterprise, but an active force for organising and reorganising the socio-political conditions of existence, and necessarily implies a notion of 'better' government. This entails a vision of how interpersonal relationships should be exercised, how social and political inclusion could be achieved, and finally how exclusion of individuals or communities could be undermined. Subjectivity is not just an intellectual instrument; it is a historically value-laden form for relating to ourselves and to others and for regulating our social practice.

Thus, when critical psychologies claim to offer a new slant on subjectivity they are actually referring to a new type of government in which the subjects assemble themselves, arrange their relationships and perform their existence through various subjectification processes (instead of adopting predefined developmental tasks). And if subjectification is not to become a catachresis, and is still concerned with the idea of how individuals transform their selves to subjects, then we have to identify the concrete contexts in which the notions of subjectivity, power and difference emerge.

In the first place, this means that we have to recontextualise and repoliticise the transhistorical assumptions inherent in Marxist or poststructuralist ideas: primarily the notion of interest in the marxian accounts, and the will to power in the poststructuralist theories. These transhistorical categories seem so untouchable because they feed our illusions and superstitions of secular salvation: the illusion, for example, of marxian critical psychology that the individual or a community of individuals has the ability to extend its action capacity till it achieves a generalised, omnipotent insight into the complexity of historical development; or, in the post-structuralist accounts, the illusion of light-hearted, self-liberating cyber-performances unfolding 'above' the discursive practices.

Disregarding these day-dreams – or better still comprehending them as political instruments of mobilisation and justification for specific mass-democratic purposes – I would like, first of all, to suggest that the discursive, relational or subjective self, rather than constituting a radical theoretical shift, is in fact a way of grasping subjectification processes unfolding in North-Atlantic countries in the last three decades, where neo-liberal rationality has come to dominate social and political reason. In a second move, I will try to show that the symbiotic development of critical psychologies and neo-liberal rationality implicates a closure which is only apparent if we introduce a world-system analysis.

5.
Neo-liberalism can be understood as a government doctrine that opposes protectionism, interventionism, and central economic plan-

ning in the modern state, and rehabilitates the individual as the historic subject of the modern era, combating conservatives' preference for traditional collectives or socialists' all-humanity-visions (Wallerstein, 1995). Milton Friedman summarised it as early as 1962, saying that 'a liberal is fundamentally fearful of concentrated power' (Friedman, 1962).

I will depict two major social changes which have allowed the neo-liberal ideology to attain the complete command of North-Atlantic societies. The first concerns the function and development of state power. According to Marx (1857), distribution determines individuals' share of produced wealth. The political and constitutional authorities of the modern state constitute the power instances which constantly target the definition and redefinition of the forms and outcomes of distribution. Power is, in that sense, the by-product of antagonistic interests concentrated in the political institutions of the modern state. The ongoing dissolution of the welfare state, the ascent of deregulation and market ideologies in the 1970s and 1980s (carried out via parliament through the success of the New Right; Barry, 1987), and the increasing role of transnational institutions and multinational companies, undermine the primary role of the state in the organisation of distribution policies. We observe a growing contrast between democracy and capitalism (Offe, 1972), which consists in an extensive legitimation crisis of state politics and state economics (Wolfe, 1977; O'Connor, 1973). The neo-liberal answer to this crisis is primarily a reconsideration of the way power is exercised: it is no longer the privilege of state authorities mediated through a complex centripetal arrangement of various social forces. Power is gradually allocated to the action radius of each individual or separated groups of individuals with common interests. The state should occupy the least possible space in social, transactional life – at least this seems to be the postulate of the neo-liberal project.

The second social change takes place on the level of the machine. A machine is a means for ordering space, time, motion, desires; and in this sense machines are operative in constructing forms of life (Marx & Engels, 1845; Gramsci, 1992: 529ff.; Winner, 1989). We can delineate two phases in the history of machines: a concentric and an excentric one. In the first, machines reflect human thought and action, that is knowledge and anticipation, desire and instrumental rationality. This phase, in which a machine is a tool, is typical for the fordist mode of production (Aglietta, 1976; Edwards, 1979; Hirsch, 1985). In the second phase, machines are not only tools or predictable instruments but now they also produce sense in exactly the same manner as human beings produce it, and as such they give birth to new machines. The image of the all-powerful subject as a (male) human being can no longer be taken for granted. The algorithms of the new post-fordist machines not only model and simulate reality, but they also build reality by means of non-linear links and connections, dismantlings and recombinations across human-machine systems (Haraway, 1985). Neo-liberalism is a form of life that is based on this new technological form of production.

Surely the aim of neo-liberalism is to reduce the social and the political to the market, not only because the possibility of recognising the reality to be governed is fundamentally rejected (replaced by the idea of 'spontaneous order', Hayek, 1973: Vol. 1, 35ff., and of 'unknown ends', Hayek, 1973: Vol. 2, 15ff.), but also because effective politics depends on economics, economics (and above all drastic economics) on finance, and, finally, finance on the market. But these are perhaps not the definitive reasons for the overall domination of neo-liberalism. As Fredric Jameson says, 'the reasons for the success of market ideology can not be sought in the market itself' (Jameson, 1991: 266f.). The pervasive strength of neo-liberalism should perhaps be sought in the combination of more effective strategies for the accumulation of capital *with* a transformation of government chiefly supported by a new understanding of the relations between individuals which stresses the aspect of *exchange* between them. Neo-liberalism thus raises the moment that Marx called 'Austausch' – i.e. the redistribution of the already distributed wealth through the acquisition of *particular* products according to the subjective needs and position of each individual (Marx, 1857) – to a basic normative and substantive anthropological principle. The neo-liberal governmentality of exchange forces the *use* of state politics – against which neo-liberalism is hypocritically 'allergic' – to achieve an 'artefactual' (Hindess, 1996) social regime where the biggest possible autonomy of every independent individual is secured.[9]

To change the point of view: the 1986 Nobel Prize winner in economic sciences and decided opponent of the 'Keynesian episode in economics' (Buchanan, 1998: 24), James Buchanan, classifies not only economy as a form of exchange, but also politics. In doing so he introduces a fundamental new optic on the idea of government: the politicisation of the market (Buchanan & Tullock, 1962). Such an understanding has far-reaching consequences for the governmental techniques employed by neo-liberalism. These are primarily based on the assumption that government has to construct a space where enterprising and competitive individuals participate and interact at their own expense and where the decisions obtained in this way produce the best possible effects (Ramonet called it the 'state-individual' or the individual as state; Ramonet, 1999: 4). Individuals as social agents have a stake, interest and a possible return from their participatory actions (Buchanan, 1986; cf. Burchell, 1996).

In such an account we observe some prerequisites which reveal striking resemblances to the notion of subjectivity and positionality discussed at the beginning of this paper,[10] especially the idea that liberal government is only possible if it arises as a relationship between individuals who are constituted solely as subjects of power. This idea brings in its wake the conviction that the relative autonomy of the individual is based, not only on an abstract liberation from coercions of the social, but also on accountability for the self and for (some) others. The self-enterprising individual of neo-liberal rationality is a relational self, emerging through its positionality in interactive practices.

The elevation of the concept of exchange to the ruling doctrine of neo-liberal governmentality signifies that subjectivity is becoming the primary source of social organisation and of economic prosperity. When Friedman expresses his fear of 'concentrated power', or Buchanan declares the 'failure of government', both of them, instead of dismissing power and government, are in fact flirting with a modified idea of governmentality which consists in the assertion that it can only be effective and profitable if it is 'acting at a distance' on the individual or the community (Latour, 1987: 222; cf Miller & Rose, 1994). The prevalence of this exchange governmentality, that is the commodification and capitalisation of North-Atlantic neo-liberal societies, means more than a pure economic reorganisation or mere financialisation of them: it means that subjectivity (and the social dispositions of the individual; see Bourdieu, 1986; 1994) is also capitalised. Is this commodification of subjectivity also being carried out by critical psychology? Does the commodification of alterity, otherness and difference represent an aspect of the neo-liberal governmentality in progress?

6.

Do the critical psychologies write their stories within a *'historical* closure' (Derrida, 1967: 93, emphasis J.D.)? And because we can only answer this question in the affirmative, we have to look for the different refractions which take place when critical psychologies actively apply their conceptions. The first refraction is a humanistic attitude, that is the narration of difference and subjectivity and the politics of inclusion.[11] But as soon as we investigate the other side of humanism, its 'target group', we can see another direction of the refraction. In this scenario humanism constitutes itself as a coherent discourse only in so far as it designates some others as the 'marginal Other' (Mohanty, 1991); and this refraction is only possible because the ideas of critical psychology necessarily fall on the surface of a hierarchically structured world-system. The historical closure within which we tell our stories is not primarily the appropriation of critical psychologies by the neo-liberal project (at this level critical psychologies remain *somehow* still 'critical' and can enjoy their status as counter or corrective forces), but instead consists in the fact that North-Atlantic neo-liberal rationality – among its reformist-healing or radical-antisystemic discourse-satellites – is the hegemonic project in our transnational world-system – that is the tendency for structural unification of the planet as a capitalist world economy and geoculture (Wallerstein, 1989; 1991; Altvater & Mahnkopf, 1996; Braudel, 1976).

In such a constellation critical work is put in jeopardy under the pressure of a seemingly unresolvable contradiction between two poles. Firstly, the need to reveal global power networks which, using primarily racist, sexist and underdevelopment discourses, maintain the reproduction of North-Atlantic neo-liberal dominance. This entails the accelerated destruction of the social and economic basis of entire regions and increases inequality and poverty (Gabriel, 1997; Wallerstein, 1990; Wolf; 1982; Zapatista encuentro, 1996). In the light of the 'structural adjustment policies' imposed by transnational organisations,[12] especially the Organisation for Economic Co-operation and Development, the International Monetary Fund, and the World Trade Organisation, a *macrological* perspective seems to be indispensable for any critical project. Secondly, it is difficult to overlook the fact that such a perspective eliminates the possibility of 'the narration of the periphery', neglects the irreducible significance of local and territorial differentiation, and assumes that power and politics are exclusively determined by the coloniser and the transnational companies and organisations (Bhabha, 1990; Sahlins, 1994; the claim for a multivocal psychology divided into different indigenous psychologies reflects this second perspective, cf. Kim, 1997).

The mere juxtaposition or exclusion of these two perspectives is what characterises the critical psychological project: the structuring of the world in binary terms. How to represent subjectivity and at the same time reflect thoroughly the conditions of its fabrication? How to write the project of critical psychologies using the concept of subjectivity when we already know that its implicit ethical desideratum, namely the inclusion and enunciation of the oppressed, is a highly controversial and ambiguous path?

7.

Subjectification and subjectivity are thus not thinkable outside power contested hierarchies. Hierarchy implies the enunciation of hegemony, and hegemony tends towards homogenisation (cf Holz, 1992). While establishing a claim for inclusion, critical psychologies enter the political and articulate hegemonial projects. The idea of subjectivity and subjectification serves as a necessary step for the elaboration of the homogenisation processes underlying these projects. What really determines these processes? Which are the invisible prerequisites of hegemony and where is the force for homogenisation coming from?

In the post-structuralist tradition of argumentation the basic components of the category of subjectification – the ideas of positionality, textuality, and difference – are presented as if they had an overriding epistemic validity lacking any geopolitical determinations (Smith, 1988: 206ff.; Spivak, 1999). This 'view from nowhere' (Bordo, 1990: 136) renders the 'subject of the subjectification processes' inscrutable: that is, the exhaustive driving force of neo-liberal rationality which serves to conserve the North-Atlantic as a generic intact subject (cf Hildebrand-Nilshon, Motzkau & Papadopoulos, 2001). In such a scheme the representation of Otherness and of subordination, in so far as it is located outside or in the periphery of the 'North-Atlantic "dispositif"', is an arbitrary and idealised one, which takes shape according to the projections and inclinations of each particular intellectual. In any case the Other and the oppressed, in whose name critical work is done, 'never rise above the debilitating generality of their "object" status' (Mohanty, 1991: 71).

The seemingly opposite but in fact complementary stream in critical psychology, the marxian inspired accounts, preserve the North-Atlantic as a generic intact subject by employing an opposite logic: these marxian accounts represent Otherness, suppression, and local rebellion as a mere function or as a spontaneous remote effect of a central power. The Other and the oppressed overcome their 'object status' (which they posses by definition) as far as they question the all-embracing North-Atlantic subject. When such oppressed groups organise peripheral revolts or acts of subversion which do not take account of the centre or the 'wholeness', they are deprived – regardless of the revolutionary platitudes and the feelings of paternalistic solidarity – of their possibility of responsible self-articulation and so retain their object status (see Guha, 1994): how do critical intellectuals perceive these contemporary forms of 'peasant insurgency' which regularly break out in the suburbs of many western cities?).

The metropolitan rhetorics of critical psychologies can only unfold against the background of an obliterated hinterland. The literal meaning of the word 'hinterland' consists in the material and symbolic construction of the world in binary terms. The allegory consists in the unexamined representation of Otherness (this imagined community of the inhabitants of hinterland ...) as a coherent abstraction and unified object of subordination beyond history and social conditions.

What displacements of meaning arise through the use of the concept of subjectivity? At the level of theory, subjectivity supports the symbolic presence of specific subjects which implies *at the same time* the symbolic anonymity of other subjects. At the level of practice, subjectivity unavoidably demands enunciation, coalition and inclusion politics and *simultaneously* initiates the effacement of bodies in pain and violence. Subjectivity is a conflicting and liminal enterprise: for in it coexist in parallel a gesture of obliteration and a gesture of expressibility.

8.

If the occurrence of the concepts of subjectivity and subjectification (as a particular conceptualisation of individuality) is symptomatic for the integrative ambivalence of North-Atlantic neo-liberal rationality, the liminality of subjectivity signifies the vulnerable, transitional and polarised character of the contemporary situation.

The end of the 1990s seemed to bring with it a crisis of neo-liberalism (see the contributions in Bischoff, Deppe & Kisker, 1998; Hobsbawm, 1999; Wallerstein, 1998). Such a crisis means anything but a radical revision or overhaul of the political and economic programme which neo-liberalism has been applying for at least thirty years. On the contrary, it means that neo-liberal economic policy becomes a planetary norm and that neo-liberal governmentality increasingly penetrates social consciousness.

The crisis of the neo-liberal doctrine lies in the disintegration of social, political and economic structures which are in reality indispensable for the sustaining of liberal societies and the world-economy (at least in the form we have been acquainted with up to now). In the long run, neo-liberalism could not serve the purpose for which it was conceived (except of course the temporary acceleration of capital accumulation), and unwittingly promotes a widespread delegitimisation of its own governmentality. The changes which the state has undergone clearly illustrate this failure: transnational organisations and corporations need the nation-state as much as ever; but the state has had to undergo a process of transformation (Hirsch, 1998) which, due to the consequences of the initial neo-liberal policies, has far exceeded the expectations being placed upon it.

In neo-liberal conditions of deepening polarisation and growing vulnerability, becoming an *enunciative subject of power* – be it an individual, a community, an institution, or a group for collective action – will be perhaps one of the most vivid and influential resources for political and social intervention.[13] Subjectivity seems to undertake such a task, namely to be one of the social technologies appropriate for the positioning of individuals and communities in the neo-liberal arrangement of power. Under this guise its ethical and political commitment can not be necessarily linked to a certain liberation project – however this project may be defined; and more than that, its ethical and political commitment seem to be biased by the socialisation practices immanent in the movement of neo-liberal power. Surely the past of the idea of subjectivity is combined with a particular historic emancipatory movement (both in its Marxian or poststructuralist understanding) which challenged the ruling universalism of the fetishised male, North-Atlantic subject. Nevertheless, the present and future of subjectivity seem to reveal an irresolute and liminal enterprise: they seem to be linked to specific forms of the regeneration of neo-liberal domination. As Wallerstein says: 'The revolutions never worked the way their proponents hoped or the way their opponents feared' (Wallerstein, 1998: 13).

I am grateful to Douglas Henderson for his constructive comments and editing assistance.

Notes

1. Deuteronomium 28, 25, in *Septuaginta*, Alfred Rahlfs (ed), Stuttgart: Deutsche Bibelgesellschaft, 1979, p337.
2. The handling of mainstream psychology as a solid and coherent 'dispositif' has only a heuristic relevance for my argumentation in this paper since mainstream psychology seems to be a highly fragmented, inconsistent and eclectic discourse (cf Graumann, 1973; Koch, 1985).
3. bell hooks: 'As child I did not know any white people. They were strangers, rarely seen in our neighbourhoods. The 'official' white men who came across the tracks were there to sell products, Bibles, insurance. They terrorised by economic exploitation. What did I see in the gazes of those white men who crossed our thresholds that made me afraid, that made black children unable to speak? Did they understand at all how strange their whiteness appeared in our living rooms, how threatening? Did they journey across the tracks with the same 'adventurous' spirit that other white men carried to Africa, Asia, to those mysterious places they would one day call the third world? Did they come to our houses to meet the Other face to face and enact the coloniser role, dominating us on our own turf?' (hooks, 1992: 341)
4. The modern treatment of individuality should not be confused with the concept of methodological individualism (cf Bhaskar, 1989), which represents only one – even if widespread – definition of individuality.
5. For one of the major reasons for repudiating social constructionism is that it believes that our knowledge about the being or social affairs 'can always be analysed in terms of statements about our knowledge' (Bhaskar, 1989: 13; Bhaskar marks this problem as 'epistemic fallacy'). Furthermore, such a gnosiological view introduces a peculiar form of essentialism: the 'notion of the social as an essence', as Spivak describes it (Spivak, 1993: 294). It is obvious that such an approach inevitably implies an affirmative attitude towards existing social relations.
6. In this treatment of 'Berlin Critical Psychology' I can not touch on the radical and far-reaching consequences of the theory for psychological methodology (e.g. Holzkamp, 1988; 1993) and the recent turn to new agendas (Holzkamp, 1996; Osterkamp, 1999).
7. The prerequisite of the self as the place where a kind of 'unification' of action and subjective emotions in time and space takes place, whatever this unification might be, seems to be a common starting point – even if it is not always explicitly mentioned – for most alternative accounts (cf Bruner, 1995; Harré, 1983; 1995; Holzkamp, 1996).
8. Cf Hildebrand-Nilshon & Papadopoulos, 1998, and originally Foucault, 1982b; 1983; 1984. As is well known, Foucault describes this form of power as 'bio-power' (Foucault, 1976; 1982a).
9. The proclaimed antistatism of neo-liberalism seems to be an ideological flop. As Wallerstein says: 'Well, at least the liberals – champions of individual freedom and of the free market – remained hostile to the state? Not at all! From the outset, liberals were caught in a fundamental contradic-

tion. As defenders of the individual and his rights vis-à-vis the state, they were pushed in the direction of universal suffrage, the only guarantee of a democratic state. But thereupon, the state became the principal agent of all reforms intended to liberate the individual from the social constraints inherited from the past. This in turn led the liberals to the idea of putting positive law at the service of utilitarian objectives' (Wallerstein, 1995: 83). In addition, a typical tactic of neo-liberalist economic management consists, on the one hand, in the externalisation of the costs and the socialisation of loss through the use of state mechanisms and, on the other hand, in the privatisation of the profits (cf Haug, 1999).

10. This is certainly the case if we attempt to temporarily purify neo-liberalism from its social-darwinistic, pan-selectionistic (Gould, 1997) ideological assumptions which rigorously emphasise the concepts of selection, adaptation and self-preservation at the level of the *single* individual. It must be stressed here that the appeal of such biologistic-evolutionist ideologies is by no means limited to liberalism (especially to the liberalism influenced by Hayek; cf. Hayek, 1973, Vol. 1), but has actually appealed to a wide range of political ideologies in the 19th and 20th century, from fascism (e.g. the apotheosis of warfare and of the banal theme of the 'survival of the fittest') and conservatism (e.g. Schmitt, 1932) to pragmatical (e.g. Kondylis, 1984) or socialist (cf. Bayertz, 1982) theories.

11. The humanist attitude feeding the liberation project is entailed *mutatis mutandis* in all critical psychologies, even if in the post-structuralist, scepticist accounts it is conceived as a kind of 'short' or 'weak' humanism which divides the unquestioned neutrality and univocality of the humanist ideal in several sub-conceptions springing from different social and cultural locations and perspectives.

12. Such policies enforce the removal of protection regulations and facilitate the unconditional access of the market to all sectors (e.g. the 'Multilateral Agreement on Investment', cf. Glunk, 1998; or the 'Enhanced Structural Adjustment Facility' of the IMF, cf. Falk, 1998).

13. How subjectification processes unfold and how the subject transforms itself to become a subject of power is an issue which can be grasped in various ways. For example, the traditional understanding is based on the assumption that individual or collective political action is predetermined by certain essentialist characteristics of the subject (race or gender stereotypes, belonging to a class, identification with a culture or lineage, etc, are ways to conceptualise subjectivity as predefined). More recent critical accounts question this essentialist notion of political action by introducing a situated perspective of socio-political action (cf for example the accounts for 'coalition', 'transversal' or 'standpoint' politics in Spivak, 1990, 59ff.; Yuval-Davis, 1994; Harding, 1994 respectively). But even in these accounts we are dealing with the idea of an enunciative subject of power which is compatible with the regulation practices disseminated in the neo-liberal and transnational world system.

References

Aglietta, M. (1976) *A theory of capitalist regulation. The US experience*, London: NLB, 1979.

Altvater, E., & Mahnkopf, B. (1996) *Grenzen der Globalisierung: Ökonomie, Ökologie und Politik in der Weltgesellschaft*, Münster: Westfälisches Dampfboot.

Barry, N. P. (1987) *The new right*, London: Croon Helm.

Bayertz, K. (1982) 'Darwinismus als Ideologie. Die Theorie Darwins und ihr Verhältnis zum Sozialdarwinismus', *Dialektik* 5: 105-120.

Bhabha, H. K. (1990) 'DissemiNation: time, narrative, and the margins of the modern nation', in H. K. Bhabha (ed), *Nation and Narration* 291-322, London: Routledge.

Bhaskar, R. (1989) *Reclaiming reality: A critical introduction in contemporary philosophy*, London: Verso.

Bischoff, J., Deppe, F., & Kisker, K. P. (1998) 'Neoliberalismus – ein Schimpfwort?', in J. Bischoff, F. Deppe, & K. P. Kisker (eds), *Das Ende des Neoliberalismus? Wie die Republik verändert wurde* 7-14. Hamburg: VSA.

Bourdieu, P. (1980) *Sozialer Sinn. Kritik der theoretischen Vernunft*, Frankfurt/M.: Suhrkamp, 1987.

Bourdieu, P. (1986) 'The forms of capital', in J. G. Richardson (ed), *Handbook of theory and research for the sociology of education* 241-258. New York: Greenwood.

Bourdieu, P. (1994) 'Structures, habitus, power: Basis for a theory of symbolic power', in N. B. Dirks, G. Eley, & S. B. Ortner (eds), *Culture/power/history. A reader in contemporary social theory* 155-199, Princeton, NJ: Princeton University Press.

Bordo, S. (1990) 'Feminism, postmodernism, and gender-scepticism', in L.J. Nicholson (ed), *Feminism/postmodernism* 133-153. London: Routledge.

Braudel, F. (1976) *Die Dynamik des Kapitalismus*, Stuttgart: Klett-Cotta, 1991.

Bruner, J. (1995) 'Meaning and self in cultural practice', in D. Bakhurst & C. Sypnowich (eds), *The social self* 18-29. London: Sage.

Buchanan, J. M. (1986) *Liberty, market, and state. Political economy in the 1980s*, Brighton: Harvester Wheatsheaf.

Buchanan, J. M. (1998) 'Has economics lost its way? Reflections on the economists' enterprise at century's end', in J. M. Buchanan, & B. Monissen (eds), *The economists' vision. Essays in modern economic perspectives* 17-29. Frankfurt/M.: Campus.

Buchanan, J. M., & Tullock, G. (1962) *The calculus of consent. Logical foundations of constitutional democracy* Ann Arbor: The University of Michigan Press (Ann Arbor Paperbacks, 1965).

Burchell, G. (1996) 'Liberal government and techniques of the self', in A. Barry, T. Osborne, & N. Rose (eds), *Foucault and political reason. Liberalism, neo-liberalism and rationalities of government* 19-36. London: University College London Press.

Burman, E. (1994) *Deconstructing developmental psychology* London: Routledge.

Burman, E. (1996) 'Psychology discourse practice: From regulation to resistance', in E. Burman, G. Aitken, P. Allred, R. Allwood, T. Billington, B. Goldberg, A. J. Gordo López, C. Heenan, D. Marks, & S. Warner (eds), *Psychology discourse practice: From regulation to resistance* 1-14. London: Taylor & Francis.

Canguilhem, G. (1979) *Wissenschaftsgeschichte und Epistemologie. Gesammelte Aufsätze*, Frankfurt/M.: Suhrkamp.

CPAR (1999), Critical Psychology & Action Research – International Conference 13-16 July 1999, First call for papers, Bolton: Discourse Unit.

Danziger, K. (1990) *Constructing the subject. Historical origins of psychological research*, New York: Cambridge University Press.

Davies, B., & Harré, R. (1990) Positioning: Conversation and the production of the selves. *Journal for the Theory of Social Behavior* 20: 43-63.

Derrida, J. (1967) *Of Grammatology*, Baltimore: The John Hopkins University Press, 1998.

Dreier, O. (1997) *Subjectivity and social practice*, Aarhus: Center for Health, Humanity, and Culture, University of Aarhus.

Edwards, R. (1979) *Herrschaft im modernen Produktionsprozess*, Frankfurt/M.: Campus, 1981.

Falk, R. (1998), *Der IWF und die Armen. Zur Kritik der Strukturanpassungspolitik des IWF am Beispiel der ESAF*, Bonn: WEED.

Foucault, M. (1969) *Archäologie des Wissens*, Frankfurt/M.: Suhrkamp, 1981.

Foucault, M. (1975) *Überwachen und Strafen. Die Geburt des Gefängnisses*, Frankfurt/M.: Suhrkamp, 1994.

Foucault, M. (1976) *Sexualität und Wahrheit, Bd. I: Der Wille zum Wissen*, Frankfurt/M.: Suhrkamp, 1983.

Foucault, M. (1978) 'Governmentality', in G. Burchell, C. Gordon, & P. Miller (eds), *The Foucault effect: Studies in governmentality* 87-104. Chicago: University of Chicago Press, 1991.

Foucault, Michel (1982a) 'Warum ich Macht untersuche: Die Frage des Subjekts', in H.L. Dreyfus, & P. Rabinow, *Michel Foucault. Jenseits von Strukturalismus und Hermeneutik* 243-250. Weinheim: Beltz Athenäum, 1994.

Foucault, Michel (1982b) 'Wie wird Macht ausgeübt?', in H.L. Dreyfus, & P. Rabinow, *Michel Foucault. Jenseits von Strukturalismus und Hermeneutik* 251-261. Weinheim: Beltz Athenäum, 1994.

Foucault, Michel (1983) 'Zur Genealogie der Ethik: Ein Überblick über laufende Arbeiten', in H.L. Dreyfus, & P. Rabinow, *Michel Foucault. Jenseits von Strukturalismus und Hermeneutik* 265-292. Weinheim: Beltz Athenäum, 1994.

Foucault, Michel (1984) 'The ethic of care for the self as a practice of freedom', in James Bernauer, & David Rasmussen (eds), *The final Foucault* 1-20. Cambridge: MIT Press, 1988.

Friedman, M. (1962) *Kapitalismus und Freiheit*, München: DTV, 1976.

Gabriel, L. (ed) (1997) *Die globale Vereinnahmung und der Widerstand Lateinamerikas gegen den Neoliberalimsus*, Frankfurt/M.: Brandes und Apsel/Südwind.

Gergen, K. J. (1996) *Das übersättigte Selbst. Identitätsprobleme im heutigen Leben*, Heidelberg: Karl-Auer.

Glunk, F. R. (1998) *Das MAI und die Herrschaft der Konzerne. Die Veränderung der Welt durch das Multilaterale Abkommen über Investionen*, München: DTV.
Gould, S. J. (1997) 'Ultra-Darwinismus. Die Evolutionstheorie zwischen Dogmatismus und Offenheit', *Lettre* 38: 82-90.
Gordon, C. (1991) 'Governmental rationality: An introduction', in G. Burchell, C. Gordon, & P. Miller (eds), *The Foucault effect: Studies in governmentality* 1-51. Chicago: University of Chicago Press.
Gramsci, A. (1992) *Gefängnishefte* Bd. 3: Hefte 4-5, K. Bochman, & W. F. Haug (wd). Hamburg: Argument.
Graumann, C. F. (1973) 'Zur Lage der Psychologie', in G. Reinert (ed), *Bericht über den 27, Kongress der Deutschen Gesellschaft für Psychologie in Kiel 1970* 19-37. Göttingen: Hogrefe.
Guha, R. (1994) 'The prose of counter-insurgency', in N. B. Dirks, G. Eley, & S. B. Ortner (eds), *Culture/power/history. A reader in contemporary social theory* 336-371. Princeton, NJ: Princeton University Press.
Haraway, D. (1985) 'Ein Manifest für Cyborgs. Feminismus im Streit mit den Technowissenschaften', in D. Haraway, *Die Neuerfindung der Natur. Primaten, Cyborgs und Frauen* 33-72. Frankfurt/M.: Campus, 1995.
Haraway, D. (1997) *Modest_Witness@Second_Millenium. FemaleMan©_Meets_OncoMouse™*, London: Routledge.
Harding, S. (1994) *Das Geschlecht des Wissens. Frauen denken die Wissenschaft neu*, Frankfurt/M.: Campus.
Harré, R. (1983) 'Identity projects', in G. M. Breakwell (ed), *Threatened identities* 31-51. New York: Wiley.
Harré, R. (1995) 'Discursive psychology', in J.A. Smith, R. Harré, & L. van Langenhove (eds), *Rethinking psychology* 143-159. London: Sage.
Harré, R., & Gillett, G. (1994) *The discursive mind*, London: Sage.
Haug, W. F. (1999) *Politisch richtig oder richtig politisch. Linke Politik im tranationalen High-Tech-Kapitalismus*, Hamburg: Argument.
Hayek, F. A. (1973) *Law, legislation and liberty. A new statement of the liberal principles of justice and political economy*, Vol. 1: Rules and Order. Vol. 2: The mirage of social justice. Vol 3: The political order of a free people, London: Routledge and Kegan Paul, Vol. 1: 1973; Vol. 2: 1976, Vol. 3: 1979.
Hildebrand-Nilshon, Martin, Motzkau, Johanna, & Papadopoulos, Dimitris (2001) 'Reintegrating sense into subjectification', in J. R. Morss, N. Stephenson, H. van Rappard (eds), *Theoretical issues in psychology* 289-300. Boston: Kluwer Academic Publishers.
Hildebrand-Nilshon, M., & Papadopoulos, D. (1998) 'Short stories about identity. The tension between self-articulation and the regulation of the self', Paper presented at the 4th congress of the International Society for Cultural Research and Activity Theory (ISCRAT), Aarhus, Denmark, June 7-11, 1998.
Hindess, B. (1996) 'Liberalism, socialism and democracy: Variations on a governmental theme', in A. Barry, T. Osborne, & N. Rose (eds), *Foucault and political reason. Liberalism, neo-liberalism and rationalities of government* 65-80. London: University College London Press.

Hirsch, J. (1985) 'Fordimsus und Postfordismus. Die gegenwärtige gesellschaftliche Krise und ihre Folgen', *Politische Vierteljahresschrift* 26: 160-182.

Hirsch, J. (1998) *Vom Sicherheitsstaat zum nationalen Wettbewerbsstaat*, Berlin: ID Verlag.

Hobsbawm, E. J. (1995) *Das Zeitalter der Extreme. Weltgeschichte des 20. Jahrhunderts*, München: Carl Hanser.

Hobsbawm, E. J. (1999) 'Der Tod des Neoliberalismus', in S. Hall, E. J. Hobsbawm, M. Jaques, S. Moore, & G. Mulgan, *Tod des Neoliberalismus – Es lebe die Sozialdemokratie? Marxism Today: Eine Debatte* 7-21. Hamburg: VSA.

Hollway, W. (1984) 'Gender difference and the production of subjectivity', in J. Henriques, W. Hollway, C. Urwin, C. Venn, & V. Walkerdine (eds), *Changing the subject. Psychology, social regulation and subjectivity* 227-260 London: Methuen.

Holz, H. H. (1992) 'Philosophische Reflexion und politische Strategie bei Antonio Gramsci', in H.H. Holz, & G. Prestipino (eds), *Antonio Gramsci heute. Aktuelle Perspektiven seiner Philosophie* 9-28. Bonn: Pahl-Rugenstein.

Holzkamp, K. (1983) *Grundlegung der Psychologie* Frankfurt/M.: Campus.

Holzkamp, K. (1984) 'Societal and individual life processes', in C. W. Tolman & W. Maiers (eds), *Critical psychology. Contributions to an historical science of the subject* 50-64. New York: Cambridge University Press, 1991.

Holzkamp, K. (1988) 'Die Entwicklung der Kritischen Psychologie zur Subjektwissenschaft', in G. Rexilius (ed), *Psychologie als Gesellschaftswissenschaft* 298-317. Opladen: Westdeutscher Verlag.

Holzkamp, K. (1993) 'Was heisst 'Psychologie vom Subjektstandpunkt'? Überlegungen zu subjektwissenschaftlicher Theoriebildung', *Journal für Psychologie* 1: 66-75.

Holzkamp, K. (1996) 'Psychologie: Selbstverständigung über Handlungsbegründungen alltäglicher Lebensführung', *Forum Kritische Psychologie* 36: 7-112.

hooks, bell (1992) 'Representing whiteness in the black imagination', in L. Grossberg, C. Nelson, & P. A. Treichler (eds), *Cultural studies* 338-346. London: Routledge.

Jaeger, S., & Staeuble, I. (1978). Die gesellschaftliche Genese der Psychologie. Frankfurt/M.: Campus.

Jameson, F. (1991) *Postmodernism, or, the cultural logic of late capitalism*, Durham: Duke University Press.

Kim, C. W. (1997) Baustein für einen kulturpsychologischen Diskurs: Dekonstruktion des unilinearen Entwicklungsgedankens, Berlin: Dissertation (Fachbereich Erziehungswissenschaft und Psychologie der Freien Universität Berlin).

Koch, S. (1985) 'The nature and limits of psychological knowledge: Lessons of a century qua 'science'', in S. Koch, & D. E. Leary (eds), *A century of psychology as science* 75-97. New York: McGraw Hill.

Kondylis, P. (1984) *Macht und Entscheidung. Die Herausbildung der Weltbilder und die Wertfrage*, Stuttgart: Klett-Cotta.

Latour, B. (1987) *Science in action: How to follow scientists and engineers through society*, Cambridge, MA: Harvard University Press.
Leontjew, A. N. (1977) *Probleme der Entwicklung des Psychischen*, Frankfurt/M.: Athenäum.
Maiers, W. (1996) 'Der Subjektbegriff der Kritischen Psychologie', in M. Heinze, & S. Priebe (eds), *Störenfried Subjektivität. Subjektivität und Objektivität als Begriffe psychiatrischen Denkens* 167-221. Würzburg: Königshausen und Neumann.
Maiers, W., & Tolman, C. W. (1996) 'Critical psychology as subject-science', in I. Parker, & R. Spears (eds), *Psychology and society. Radical theory and practice* 105-115. London: Pluto.
Marx, K. (1857) 'Einleitung', in K. Marx, Grundrisse der Kritik der politischen Ökonomie 3-31, Berlin, DDR: Dietz, 1974.
Marx, K., & Engels, F. (1845), Die deutsche Ideologie, in Marx, K., & Engels, F., MEW. Bd. 3. Berlin, DDR: Dietz, 1987.
Miller, P., & Rose, N. (1994) 'Das ökonomische Leben regieren', in J. Donzelot, D. Meuret, P. Miller, & N. Rose, *Zur Genealogie der Regulation. Anschlüsse an Michel Foucault* 54-108. Mainz: Decaton.
Mohanty, C. T. (1991) 'Under western eyes. Feminist scholarship and colonial discourses', in C. T. Mohanty, A. Russo, & L. Torres (eds), *Third world women and the politics of feminism* 51-80. Bloomington, Ind.: Indiana University Press.
O'Connor, J. (1973) *Die Finanzkrise des Staates*, Frankfurt/M.: Suhrkamp, 1974.
Offe, C. (1972) *Strukturprobleme des kapitalistischen Staates. Aufsätze zur politischen Soziologie*, Frankfurt/M.: Suhrkamp.
Osterkamp, U. (1999) 'On psychology, ideology and individuals' societal nature', Theory & Psychology 9: 379-392.
Papadopoulos, D. (1999) *Lew S. Wygotski – Werk und Wirkung*, Frankfurt/M.: Campus.
Parker, I. (1992) *Discourse dynamics. Critical analysis for social and individual psychology*, London: Routlege.
Potter, J., & Wetherell, M. (1987) *Discourse and social psychology. Beyond attitudes and behaviour*, London: Sage.
Prilleltensky, I., & Fox, D. (1997) 'Introducing critical psychology: Values, assumptions, and the status quo', in D. Fox, & I. Prilleltensky (eds), *Critical psychology. An introduction* 1-20. London: Sage.
Ramonet, I. (1999) 'Nouvel ordre global', *Le Monde Diplomatique*, June 1999, 1; 4-5.
Rose, N. (1985), *The psychological complex: Psychology, politics, and society in England, 1869-1939*, London: Routledge & Kegan Paul.
Rose, N. (1996) *Inventing our selves. Psychology, power, and personhood*, New York: Cambridge University Press.
Sahlins, M. (1994) 'Cosmologies of capitalism: The trans-pacific sector of 'the world system', in N. B. Dirks, G. Eley, & S. B. Ortner (eds), *Culture/power/history. A reader in contemporary social theory* 412-455. Princeton, NJ: Princeton University Press.

Sampson, E. E. (1989) 'The deconstruction of the self', in J. Shotter & K.J. Gergen (eds), *Texts of identity* 1-19, London: Sage.
Schmitt, C. (1932) *Der Begriff des Politischen. Text von 1932 mit einem Vorwort und drei Corollarien*, Berlin: Duncker und Humblot, 1963.
Shotter, J. (1993) *Cultural politics of everyday life*, Toronto: University of Toronto Press.
Smith, D. (1998) *Der aktive Text. Eine Soziologie für Frauen*, Hamburg: Argument.
Sonntag, M. (1990) 'Einleitung: Theorieprobleme "historischer Psychologie"', in M. Sonntag (ed), *Von der Machbarkeit des Psychischen* 1-18. Pfaffenweiler: Centaurus.
Spivak, G. C. (1990) *The post-colonial critic. Interviews, strategies, dialogues*, S. Harasym (ed), London: Routledge.
Spivak, G. C. (1993) 'Subaltern Talk', in G.C. Spivak, *The Spivak Reader* 287-308, D. Landry, & G. MacLean (eds). London: Routledge.
Spivak, G. C. (1999) *A critique of postcolonial reason: Toward a history of the vanishing present*, Cambridge, MA: Harvard University Press.
Staeuble, I. (1985) '"Subjektpsychologie" oder "subjektlose Psychologie" _ Gesellschaftliche und institutionelle Bedingungen der Herausbildung der modernen Psychologie', in M.G. Ash, & U. Geuter (eds), *Geschichte der deutschen Psychologie im 20. Jahrhundert. Ein Überblick* 19-44. Opladen: Westdeutscher Verlag.
Taylor, C. (1989) *Sources of the self: The making of modern identity*, Cambridge, MA: Harvard University Press.
Tolman, C. W., & Maiers, W. (eds) (1991) *Critical psychology. Contributions to an historical science of the subject*, New York: Cambridge University Press.
Toulmin, S., & Leary, D. E. (1985) 'The cult of empiricism in psychology, and beyond', in S. Koch, & D.E. Leary (eds), *A century of psychology as science* 584-617. New York: McGraw-Hill.
Waldenfels, B. (1989) 'Das Rätsel der Sichtbarkeit. Kunstphänomenologische Betrachtungen im Hinblick auf den Status der modernen Malerei', *Kunstforum* 100: 331-341.
Walkerdine, V. (1987) *The mastery of reason: Cognitive development and the production of rationality* London: Routledge.
Wallerstein, I. (1989) *Der historische Kapitalismus*, Hamburg: Argument.
Wallerstein, I. (1990) 'Die Konstruktion von Völkern: Rassismus, Nationalismus, Ethnizität', in E. Balibar, & I. Wallerstein (eds), *Rasse, Klasse, Nation. Ambivalente Identitäten* 87-106. Hamburg: Argument.
Wallerstein, I. (1991) *Unthinking social science. The limits of nineteenth-century paradigms*, Cambridge: Polity Press.
Wallerstein, I. (1995) *After liberalism*, New York: The New Press.
Wallerstein, I. (1998) *Utopistics, or, historical choices of the twenty-first century*, New York: The New Press.
Winner, L. (1989) *The whale and the reactor. A search for limits in an age of high technology*, Chicago: The University of Chicago Press.
Wolf, E. J. (1982) *Europe and the people without history*, Berkeley: University of California Press.

Wolfe, A. (1977) *The limits of legitimacy. Political contradictions of contemporary capitalism*, New York: The Free Press.

Yuval-Davis, N. (1994) 'Women, ethnicity and empowerment', in K.K. Bhavani & A. Phoenix (eds), *Shifting identities – shifting racisms. A Feminism & Psychology Reader* 179-197, London: Sage.

Zapatista encuentro (1996), *Documents from the 1996 Encounter for Humanity against Neoliberalism*, New York: Seven Stories Press, 1998.

A plurality of selves?
An illustration of polypsychism in a recovered addict

Peter Raggatt

Abstract
To meet the challenges of rapid social change and growing cultural hybridisation, psychologists must find new ways to study personality processes unconstrained by older Enlightenment models that promote self-contained individualism. This research aims to contribute to that challenge. In trying to come to terms with issues surrounding the meaning of 'self' and 'identity' in a postmodern landscape, I have developed and refined a method for mapping the multiplicity of the self. The Personality Web protocol combines structured interviewing and qualitative analyses with multidimensional scaling statistical methods. The goal is to map the history and development of an individual's life-world from the viewpoint of alternative narrative voices which constitute a polypsychic self. The method of analysis is described here with reference to the case study of Sean, a former addict. Sean's story provides a powerful illustration of opposing narrative voices in the self. It is argued that dialogical oppositions in the self are defined by moral concerns, and by a matrix of social, political and cultural positioning.

In this paper I present a case for the plurality or multiplicity of the self, describe a method for empirically examining the plural self, and detail a case study to illustrate the arguments proposed. To begin any discussion of the self, however, requires cultural and historical grounding. In the western world, the past three hundred years have witnessed the flowering of 'self-contained individualism', an ideology borne along by Enlightenment ideals of rationalism, progress, personal agency and individual liberty (Sampson, 1985, 1989). In this world the ego was constructed as an idealised, coherent, integrated entity. Within the discipline of psychology, the person was defined by the 'consistency' and 'predictability' of their behaviour. 'Personality' was assumed to have a fixed centre or stable core, and individuals were assumed to carry around certain fundamental, distinctive and predictive attributes (such as traits, motives, and schemas).

Now there is an emerging view in the social sciences that this model no longer engages with our experience of the world, or with social conditions prevailing at the turn of the millennium (e.g. conditions imposed in the processes of 'globalisation' and social 'saturation') (Gergen, 1991). In particular, emerging perspectives in social constructionism and critical psychology have sought to 'deconstruct' the self as a locus of agency (for example, see Kvale, 1992). Influenced by European scholars including Bakhtin (1929/1984), Barthes (1966/1988) and Foucault (1969/1988), the social constructionists have argued for a deconstruction of the *psyche*, akin to the literary theorists 'death of the author' (Bradley, 1993; Gergen, 1991; Shotter, 1993). What remains, in this view, is a socially constituted narrative of relationship, the locus of which is not centred in individuals, but rather is constituted by language, and lies 'out there', at the boundaries or linkages between individuals and the enveloping culture (Shotter, 1999). From this perspective, 'personality' is in danger (once more) of being critically theorised out of existence.

Everyday polypsychism

I do not intend here to follow the social constructionists (or the radical behaviourists for that matter!), in taking a strong anti-foundationalist stance towards 'the problem of reifying the individual'. Rather, I shall begin from a middle position and from an everyday observation that helped spark the present work – that to varying degrees we lead a Jekyll and Hyde existence. In this approach, there is no singular, monologic account of a life, no completely integrated narrative identity; rather, there is a *plurality* of frequently conflicting subjectivities, alternative stories about our lives. Our mental life, I suggest, is characterised by a multiplicity of subjectivities or dominant voices (Raggatt, 2000).

This is not a new idea. In the Netherlands, Hermans and his associates (Hermans, Kempen & Van Loon, 1992; Hermans & Kempen, 1993), inspired by the writings of James (1890) and Bakhtin (1929/1984), have been using the concept of a multi-voiced 'dialogical self' in their clinical research and practice. In Britain, for some years now, critical psychologists influenced by the writings of the French post-structuralists have been arguing for a radical change in the way psychology constructs its subject (e.g. Davies & Harre, 1990; Henriques, Hollway, Urwin, Venn, & Walkerdine, 1984). In America, a new generation of psychologists have explored conceptions of a 'multistable' or decentred self, from a range of perspectives including psychoanalytic, cognitive, cross-cultural and critical theory (e.g. Gergen, 1991; Gregg, 1991; Markus & Nurius, 1986; Sampson, 1989). Most recently, many of the contributors to Rowan and Cooper's recent text on the plural self (1999) make the assumption that we are 'polypsychic' beings.

The self, in this new framework, has no unidimensional core or centre of 'ego-integration' in the Eriksonian sense (e.g. Erikson, 1959). Instead, competing versions of 'the self' are theorised to emerge as voices in narrative form. Moreover, recognition of dialogue and/or conflict among these 'voices' is just as important for understanding *normal* development, as it is for understanding emotional disturbance (Hermans & Kempen, 1993; Ross, 1999).

My empirical objective in this project is to study self-plurality in midlife adults who have confronted or are confronting major identity issues, and who are capable of reflecting deeply on their experience. The key to method is to explore the person's narrative landscape in a systematic way. The methods developed to do this rely on the detection and juxtaposition of competing *narrative lines* or *narrative voices* in the person's construction of identity. In order to access these narrative structures, a method is required which will (a) uncover the symbolically-charged people, events and objects making up these structures, and (b) allow the individual to express relationships between those constituents. The rationale for this approach is explicated here using the concepts of *narrative voice* (a storied version of events), *symbolic attachment* (figureheads, emblems, myth, motif and iconography) and *positioning* (the culturally constituted components of identity, such as power, class or gender positioning). Each of these concepts is discussed in turn here.

Narrative voice and symbolic attachments

One sees in life narrative accounts, notably in biographies, a tendency to reductively impose a central story line, to find a monologic 'essence' or 'true' story locked inside the subject. On the contrary, I have proposed that the self is pluralistic, comprised of alternative narrative voices. But what is a 'voice' in the sense used here? It is fundamentally a *narrative* construct. The voice is that of a narrator telling a particular version of events, a particular plot line, which encompasses significant stretches of the life course. A voice is a thematic complex that tells a particular version of events about a life in time. It organises and makes sense out of experience, but it can also guide action. However, in a plural self there are other narrative voices telling other stories, and these voices compete to make sense of the world and to direct action.

How, then, can we gain access to this landscape of narratives? One route is via the person's symbolic and discursive behaviour, arising from their interactions with the world around them. Self-identity must be read at the level of symbol and metaphor, because that is the way that we make sense of our lives (Freeman, 1993; May, 1991). Ricoeur (1974) makes this clear when he says: 'there is no direct apprehension of the self by the self. No internal apperception or appropriation of the self's desire to exist through the shortcut of consciousness, but only by the long road of the interpretation of signs' (170).

Narrative, then, binds together the important emblematic attachments and symbols (people, objects, events, etc), that are, psychologically speaking, the stuff of our lives. But how might attachments be operationalised for research purposes? I shall propose a very broad definition – attachments include important people, critical events or nuclear scenes, places, objects and possessions, and one's body and/or body parts. Attachments are the important signposts in the narrative landscape of the self. The research objective is to sample the individual's important attachments in the social/interpersonal domain of people, the temporal/historical domain of events, the physical/environmental domain of objects and places, and the embodied domain, where the body or a body part acts as signifier (see Gilligan, Brown & Rogers (1990) for a discussion of embodiment). Once a list of attachments is generated, the objective is to have individuals group their attachments into clusters by strength of association. The glue that clusters attachments is *narrative voice*.

Let me turn now to the concept of positioning.

Positioning in the plural self

If the self is plural, polypsychic or polyphonic, by what processes are competing or alternative versions of narrative identity constructed? I shall approach this problem by using the concept of *positioning*, a concept which has emerged recently in 'critical' and 'postmodern' perspectives on the self and subjectivity (Davies & Harre, 1990; Harre & Van Langenhove, 1991; Hollway, 1984; Kvale, 1992). Taking the conversation as the proper object of analysis for the social sciences, Hollway (1984) and later Davies & Harre (1990) and Harre & Van Langenhove (1991) have used the concept of *positioning* (within dialogue) as an alternative to the concept of role. 'Positioning', according to Harre & Van Langenhoven, 'can be understood as the discursive construction of personal stories that make a person's actions intelligible ... as social acts, and within which the members of a conversation have specific locations' (395). Positioning is also defined as 'a metaphorical concept through reference to which a person's moral and personal attributes as a speaker are compendiously collected' (395). Hence one may be positioned as friend or foe, strong or weak, reliable or troublesome, comforting or threatening, and so on, depending on the flux and flow of conversational dialogue and the context in which it takes place.

But what of the 'internalised' dialogues (and narratives)? Can we apply the concept of *positioning* to the internal conversational exchanges theorised to take place in a 'dialogical' or pluralistic model of self? If positioning involves the construction of stories which make a person's actions intelligible, and which bring together their moral and personal attributes, then the answer should be yes. The narrative lines a person brings to the construction of an identity *position* that person in a matrix of social and moral relationships. Gregg (1991) has proposed that identity is constructed from a series of 'me' v 'not me' Gestalt-like oppositions. In order to make sense of the world, he says, we must define our lives by constructing narratives in the form of figure-ground contrasts. 'The self', Gregg says, 'is performed as a kind of contrapuntal dialogue of *voices* (that) ... debate and dispute among themselves the moral basis of the ... social order in which they find themselves *positioned*' (xiv). Gregg implies here that in the process of positioning within our internal dialogues, voices may be dominant or submissive. Hermans and his colleagues adopt a similar approach (Hermans, Rijks & Kempen, 1993), defining the 'dialogical self' as 'a multiplicity of relatively autonomous I-*positions* in an imaginal landscape' (p215). The narrating self moves dialogically from one position to another in a world of multiplicity.

If we regard the landscape of a person's internal talk as dialogical, then we can propose that the narrating of the self involves taking up different evaluative positions, such as 'strong person' or 'weak person', 'reliable person' or 'troublesome person', and so on, depending on the context of attachments to family, community, culture and so on. The self in this view is a dialogical exchange in which each of us explores conflicting ideas about what constitutes 'the good'. In other words, identity is constituted by a range of *good and bad stories* that are in dialogical relationship. The narrative voices of the self are positioned as moral-evaluative structures.

The immediate objectives for this project can be summarised as follows:

1. To empirically test a theory of *polypsychism* which posits conflicting or competing voices at the core of personality structure.
2. To combine quantitative and qualitative research practices in a method designed to test theory (called the *Personality Web* interview protocol).
3. To map the development of multiple narrative voices in adult individuals, focusing particularly on identity at midlife.
4. To write biographical case studies which illuminate the multi-voiced structure of the self, and which help to better understand processes leading to identity formation and change.

The personality web interview protocol

In this section a new method for mapping polypsychism is described. The *Personality Web* (PW) is an in-depth interview protocol designed to help explore the multiplicity of the self (Raggatt, 1998). It does this by eliciting the person's most enduring *attachments* in the domains of social, temporal-historical, physical-environmental and bodily or embodied understandings. In the first of two interviews, the person's life history and important life *attachments* are explored using four easily understood categories: people (including important associates and public figures), events (from childhood, adolescence and adulthood), objects-in-the-world (including important possessions, costumes, places and works-of-art), and body orientations (including strong and weak, and liked and disliked body parts). In all, 24 attachments from these four categories are explored in some detail. Table 1 presents a taxonomy of the attachments elicited in the PW protocol. The protocol was developed by the author and refined in pilot testing with graduate psychology students. The section on life events included adaptations from McAdam's *Life Story Questionnaire* (1993). Each attachment was explored using a semi-structured interview format, with the purpose of teasing out its context, history and significance for the person's experience of self. The first interview typically takes between two and three hours to complete. (A text of the protocol is available from the author on request.)

In the social domain the following questions and probes were used to explore important positive figures in the interviewee's life:

> ... I want you to identify two people who are positive figures in your life. Beyond merely being a role model, a positive figure is someone who has inspired you, occupied your thoughts, and guided your actions. The two figures must come from different dimensions of your experience: (1) A person you know, and (2): Either a public figure whom you have never met, or a fictional character from a story or other product of the imagination...
>
> Briefly describe your *relationship* to each of these figures (e.g., father, friend, my fantasy hero etc.).
>
> I would like you to relate a brief *story* about each of the figures which typifies the figures good qualities ...
>
> Imagine it were possible right now to have a *conversation* with each of the figures. What would you choose to talk about?
>
> I want you to summarise the qualities of each of the positive figures. One way to do this would be by identifying *trait* terms ...

Table 1 A Taxonomy of Attachments Comprising the *Personality Web*

People	Objects-in the-World	Life Events	Body Orientations
1 Liked Associate	1 Important Possession (i)	1 Childhood – Peak Experience	1 Like Body Part
2 Liked Public Figure	2 Important Possession (ii)	2 Childhood – Nadir Experience	2 Disliked Body Part
3 Disliked Associate	3 Symbolic Object	3 Adolescence – Peak Experience	3 Strong Body Part
4 Disliked Public Figure	4 Place-in-the-World (i)	4 Adolescence – Nadir Experience	4 Weak Body Part
5 Other Important Associate (i)	5 Place-in-the-World (ii)	5 Adulthood – Peak Experience	
6 Other Important Associate (ii)	6 Clothing, Costume (i)	6 Adulthood – Nadir Experience	
	7 Clothing, Costume (ii)		
	8 Work of Art or Imagination		

The same probes were used for negative figures. Negative figures were defined as 'more than mere stereotypes of evil or human weakness', and as 'people who have occupied your thoughts and influenced your actions, but with whom you associate strong negative thoughts and feelings'. Objects were defined very broadly as 'including your most private mementoes, and your most important material possessions ... but also objects to which you are attached psychologically ... (a flag, a logo, a public building, a national park ...)'. In the interview, objects were divided into a further series of sub-categories (see Table 1). Events were broken up into 'peak' and 'nadir' experiences, following the method of McAdams (1993). A peak experience was defined simply as 'a high point in your life; one of the most wonderful times in your life'. Nadir experiences were the opposite: 'a low point; a bad time in your life'. For objects and events the only structured interview probes were to (a) elicit temporal orientation, and (b) ask interviewees to 'reflect on the associations and connections you draw from the object (event etc.)'. Finally in the section under body orientations, interviewees were asked to 'think about particular body parts that mean different things to you'. They were then asked to discuss the meanings associated with four such parts (e.g. legs, stomach, eyes), which respectively were 'liked', 'disliked', 'strong' and 'weak'. The purpose here was to explore the importance of embodiment as a source of attachments for narrative voice (discussed later).

In a second session with informants, I have made use of a data reduction technique called multidimensional scaling (MDS) (Kruskal & Wish, 1978), in combination with a qualitative sorting task performed on the interviewees' list of attachments. As applied here, MDS is a useful statistical tool to assist the informant and the researcher to sort through and organise associations between the 24 *Web* attachments elicited in the initial interview. The procedure requires the informant to compare all pairwise combinations of the attachments elicited in the first interview, and assign proximity values on a 9-point rating scale to indicate 'for each pair, the degree of their association in your thoughts, feelings and experience'. Scores of 7 to 9 indicate strong association, 4 to 6, moderate association, and 1 to 3, a weak association. The resulting 'distances' between attachments can then be represented in an Euclidean space of 1, 2, 3 or more dimensions. Using this method, clusters of self-relevant attachments can be identified based on semantic judgements provided by the informant. The 'Scale' program from SPSS Version 6.1 was used for these analyses.[1]

When the ratings task was completed, informants were given a sorting task. They were asked to sort their attachments into groupings or clusters, and then provide a self-relevant label for each cluster. They were asked to try and limit the number of clusters they created to between two and six (in other words, larger clusters were encouraged rather than small, narrow ones). However, no restriction was placed on the number of attachment groupings that could be produced. Informants were told that they did not have to use all 24 attachments in the exercise, and that any one attachment could be included in more than one cluster, if this was appropriate. To elicit names for each cluster, the informants were asked to 'name the facet of self that is represented in each cluster', and to 'use a name which captures or identifies the qualities of the facet that you see as being *part of you*, or who you are'. Examples of the appropriate form for cluster labels were given, such as 'powerful self', 'religious self', 'activist', 'adventurer', and so on. Finally, distances between the informants new cluster labels and attachments were elicited in the same pairwise rating fashion, so that the cluster labels could also be mapped onto the MDS solution. This was important for *interpretation* of the MDS solution, which was guided by the informant's own efforts to sort through and label the clusters of attachments emerging in the *Web* interview. The work conducted to date suggests that MDS, when combined with more qualitative sorting tasks, can provide a powerful adjunct for helping to access and map the different narrative voices of the self. The following case example is provided to illustrate the method.

A case illustration: Sean – 'Lost Boy' / 'Good Guy' / 'Addict' / 'Magician'

The case example discussed in this paper is interesting on several fronts. It throws light on processes leading to addiction and recovery from addiction. Of more direct relevance to the present purposes, however, it illuminates complexities, contradictions and conflicts in the personality of a mature and intelligent adult at midlife.2 It is this plurality which will be the focus of concern here.

Sean is 43 years old. He has had, by any measure, an extraordinary life. He was born in Belfast to a working-class family who emigrated to Australia when he was 10 years old. His father was a highly skilled foundry worker, who played soccer for Ireland as a young man, but who subsequently became a violent and feared alcoholic. His mother suffered from prolonged bouts of depression, and the young Sean remembers being 'mothered' by his sister, some 11 years older than him.

Today Sean is tall, fine-featured, handsome, and gifted with a strong athletic body. He presents as warm, articulate and engaging. He describes himself as having 'the constitution of an ox'. As a youth he was a champion schoolboy footballer and, as a young man, a talented cricketer and (briefly) a rising star on the periphery of first class ranks (the national competition). He remains a member of the Wollongabba Cricket Club, and occasionally sits in the Members stand during Test (international) matches.

Sean's 'sporting life' is an important narrative line in the voice that he calls the 'Good Guy'. Like his father, Sean was a sporting champion both at school and in the adult world – 'I dominated everything in sporting achievement ... It was the way I built up my self-esteem'. At the same time he was 'not one who played the hero role, and that meant I was really well liked'. There is, of course, more to the voice of the Good Guy than these emblematic details of sports achievement combined with humility. However, the Good Guy has had to play a background role for long periods of Sean's life, while other, often more powerful voices, have taken centre stage. Table 2 shows Sean's attachments grouped into four clusters that he created and named in the qualitative sorting exercise. Figures 1 and 2 show the arrangement of attachments in the multidimensional scaling solution extracted from Sean's pairwise proximity ratings among attachments. Figure 1 shows dimensions 1 and 2. Figure 2 shows dimension 3. The four voices identified by Sean are

Table 2 Sean's Web of Attachments Grouped into Voices of the Self

1. ADDICT	2. MAGICIAN
HEROIN OVERDOSE (heart stopped; almost died; resuscitated with novocaine; hospitalised; happened several times) THE PARIAH OF DIXON'S CREEK (Binge on Ethyl Alcohol; didn't wash for 3 months; abscessed teeth; 'madman') TEETH (badly decayed teeth; symbol of a junkie; 'they are all about health – you wear them when you eat') CONJOINED EYEBROWS (joined at bridge of nose; 'The one brow is a killer; makes you feel like a psychopath') ARTHRITIC ANKLES (symbol for addictive 'weakness'; affects coordination)	JOINED ALCOHOLICS ANONYMOUS (Miracle; attended almost daily for 12 years; 'My life brought to me by others') FINGERS & THUMBS (long and curled: 'symbolise my powers of magic') STATUE of BUDDHA (The only object I have got from my youth; another power symbol; I have got nothing else) CAPE BYRON (favourite place; symbolises magical power in nature) NEW HOUSE (financial windfall; purchased beachside cottage; magic escape from the big bad city)
3. LOST BOY	4. GOOD GUY
FATHER (alcoholic, violent, explosive, sad, frightening, 'a brutal man') SISTER (M. was my mother. I slept with her. She cared for me till age 7. Then she let me down; enduring sense of betrayal) ABANDONED BY SISTER (Sister left Ireland for Australia; I was not told at time; traumatised) EX-FRIEND (dishonest, self-interested, frightened, charming; betrayed me) FAILED HIGH SCHOOL EXAMS (aged 16) (I kept up my self-esteem through sport; I was bored with classes)	TEACHER/CRICKET COACH (serious, nurturing; 'Taught me to respect others needs and abilities') ROBIN HOOD (exciting; strong; honest; physical; but he puts the needs of others first) FOOTBALL STAR (playing junior football in front of 40,000 spectators) PLAYING ELITE LEVEL CRICKET (National competition) WOLLONGABARRA CRICKET GROUND (Member of the Cricket Club – 'There, I can always meet people from my past') STOMACH (muscular; powerful)

Figure 1 Sean's Web of Attachments in the Multidimensional Scaling Solution: Dimensions 1 × 2

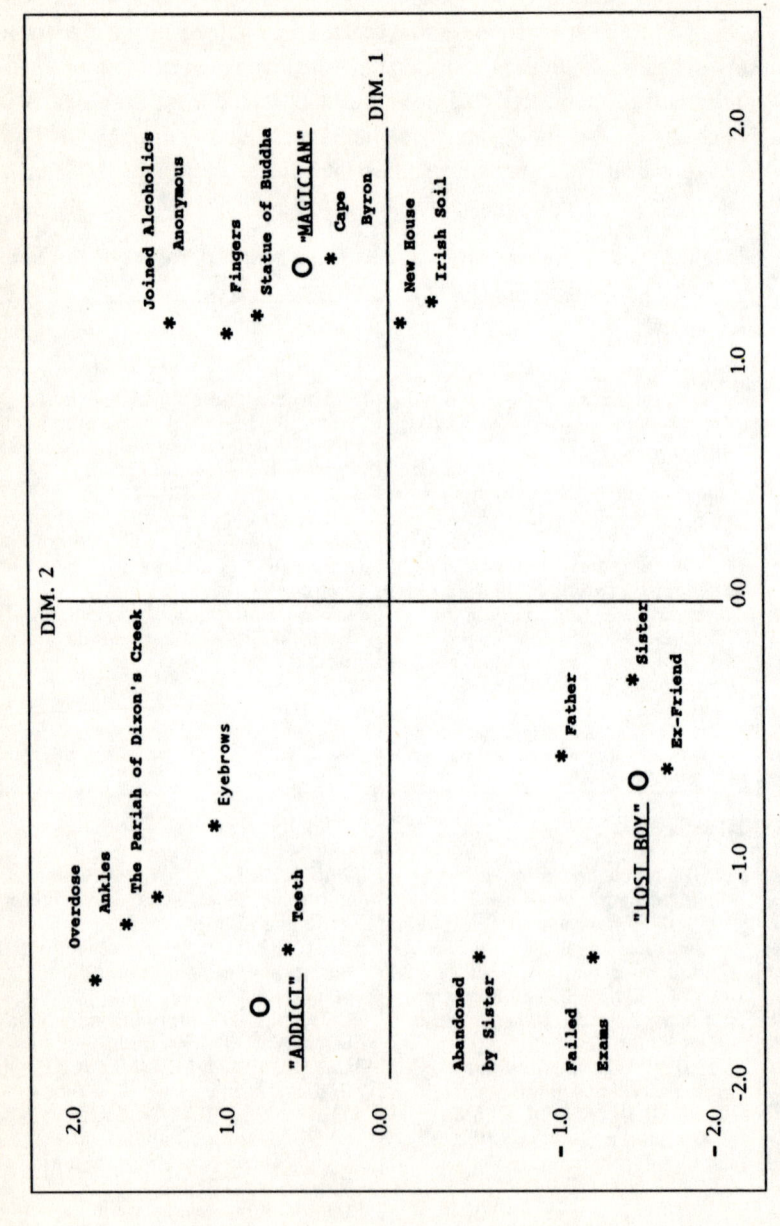

Note: Kruskall's Stress 1 = 0.14; Multiple R^2 = 0.68

Figure 2 Sean's Web Of Attachments in the Multidimensional Scaling Solution: Dimensions 1 × 3

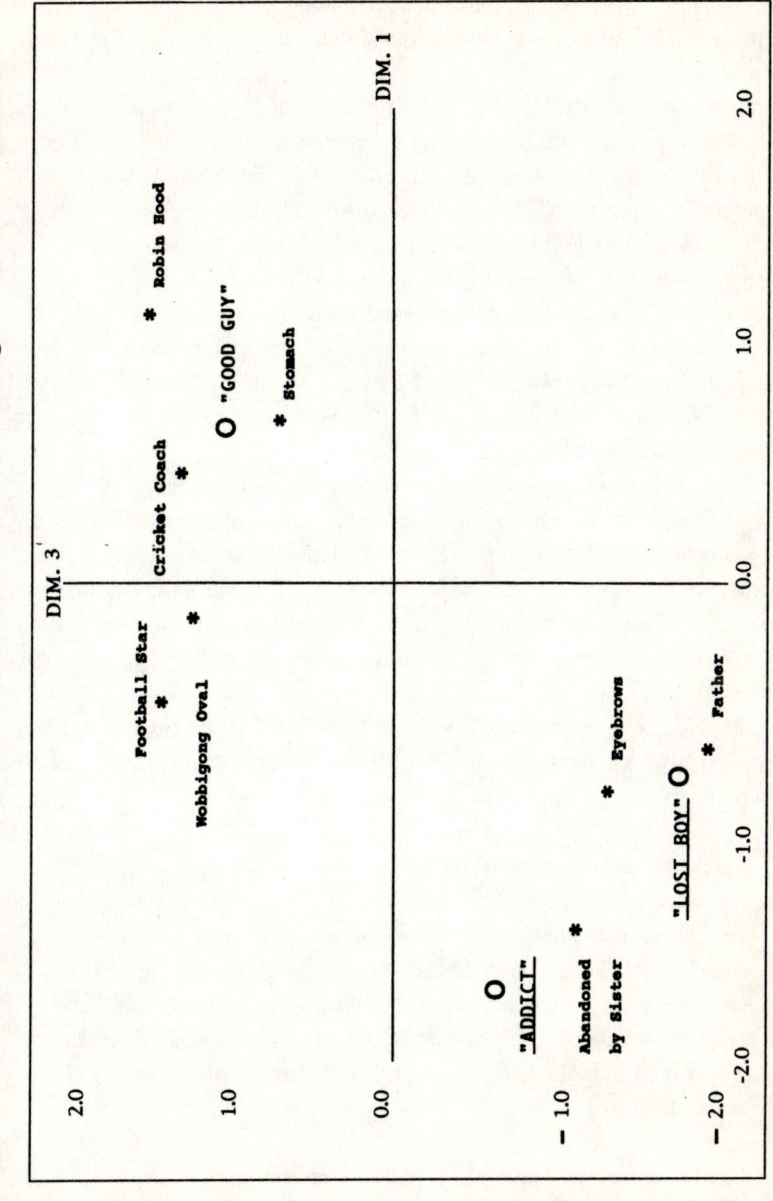

Note: Kruskall's Stress 1 = 0.14; Multiple R^2 = 0.68

a plurality of selves?

clearly represented as discrete clusters of attachments in the MDS solution. In addition to the 'Good Guy', Sean identifies voices that he calls the 'Lost Boy', the 'Addict', and the 'Magician'. The narrative lines that constitute these voices reveal profound contrasts and *multiple* trajectories in Sean's life.

Sean identifies the 'Lost Boy' as the oldest of his voices, dating back to infancy and his life in Ireland. There are many emblematic events embedded in the narrative line of the Lost Boy. Early in his life Sean is repeatedly abandoned – by an alcoholic father, and a clinically depressed mother, and later, by a sister who had been a powerful surrogate mother, but who disappeared abruptly from his life when she secretly emigrated to Australia (see Figure 1). The family kept the sister's emigration plans a closely guarded secret from the seven year old Sean, until after she had left Northern Ireland. This was clearly a time of great trauma for Sean. As he puts it: 'My sister *was* my mother. It was the first great absence in my life'.

Later in his life, the Lost Boy thema plays itself out in different ways. It is Sean who abruptly disappears, abandoning *others* with no warning – several lovers, a share farm and another relationship, and an entire cricket squad. (In the case of the latter, he abandons the team at an airport, goes on an alcoholic bender, blacks out for three days, 'comes to' in a strange city, and disappears from the cricket scene for two years.)

In 1975, at the age of 18, Sean's mother dies a lingering death from bowel cancer, an event that leads to the disintegration of the family. In Sean's words:

> My mother contracted bowel cancer...My sisters fell apart emotionally. My father fell apart emotionally ... So I didn't fall apart and took care of her ... I was there all the time for my mother, but I slipped out at night when she was asleep. And that is when I started drinking and taking heroin. It was ... emotional pain at a really big level and which I couldn't have other people see. Because they were in emotional pain, I literally had to hold myself together ... Early on I discovered the anaesthetic power of drugs.

At this juncture, the voice of the Addict, splitting away from the Lost Boy, becomes dominant in Sean's life. As Sean constructs it, the Addict is a coping response, a way of dealing with the powerful motif of the lost child – the boy abandoned by those around him. According to Sean, he took drugs in order to dull his pain:

> I picked up alcohol and I picked up heroin – and they were never there to ask girls out or to have fun – they were there to dampen my emotional pain.

This picture of the addict arguably does not match the stereotype of a youthful recreational pursuit that somehow got out of hand. From 1975 through to 1988 Sean succumbed both to alcoholism and to heroin addiction. His strong constitution (and perhaps his heroin use) allowed him to conceal his drinking, even when playing cricket at elite levels. Bleak and frightening narrative accounts of the Addict dominate the later period of this time in his life, culminating at the age of 31 in the story of 'The Pariah of Dixon's Creek' (see Table 2, Figure 1). This story symbolises Sean's ultimate descent into, as he puts it, 'abjection'. It is a significant nadir and turning point in his life. In his own words:

> I had gone back to [the city] ... I was living there in terrible physical condition using whatever drugs I could, and I had, yet again, a couple of overdoses. Then I had a suicide attempt and I decided that I had to get out of the city. I had known a lady who lived in the bush ... I phoned her up and as it turned out she was going [overseas] for some time and she said ... I could come and look after her place. Which is what I did. I went up there. [There] I discovered that, being a naturopath she had litres and litres of ethyl alcohol. So I had this supply of alcohol. I had no car, I had no licence, and I was on the dole. It took me an hour to walk from the house to the road, and then it would take me an hour to get into the nearest town hitchhiking. So I was really away from everybody and with no transport. So rather than carrying alcohol in and out I started drinking the ethyl alcohol up there and I lasted about three months with these concoctions of alcohol. And what I would do, strange enough, is buy big bags of oranges and I would carry those in and I would sit there thinking, 'Well at least I was getting some Vitamin C', as I squeezed the orange and then drank it up. So I would have one of those large glass decanters containing ethyl alcohol with a tap on it and I would drink that. And ... there was just absolute isolation. There was no power in this place ... I was totally isolated for a number of months until my health deteriorated terribly. My teeth started abscessing, so my face had blown up and I

started getting abscesses. I tried to stay there, but couldn't and came into the city looking for some pain relief. I went to a hospital. I remember coming into the city that day and, literally, people just parted in the street. I felt like a pariah, an absolute pariah, and seeing people part – walk away from you. Noticing that people diverge as you walk through the city. I mean that was a horrible feeling. My face was incredibly swollen; I must have been reeking of all sorts of concoctions. You can imagine, my hygiene had been terrible. I hadn't showered. I was isolated – I was just a madman in the bush. I went to a hospital, they gave me some painkillers, some antibiotics and then I suggested to them that I needed to be committed...

This was in 1988. For Sean it was a long way back from this painful place.

The last voice, the Magician (see Table 2 & Figure 1), is for Sean 'a kind of spiritual self'. In the role of saviour, it is the counterpoint to both the Addict and the Lost Boy. The Magician tells stories of salvation, miraculous escape, and of giving over to 'higher (moral) powers' – which is the third step in AA's 12 step abstinence programme. Whether by an act of will or by good fortune, or both, the pariah episode led indirectly to Sean's salvation. In hospital he befriended an AA support worker who had long experience of alcoholism in her family. In consequence of this meeting, Sean attended lunchtime AA meetings daily for five years, and then on a weekly basis for the past seven years. For Sean, the 'higher power' is not attributed to a God or deity. He was not 'converted' to the Church – nor does the church figure in the Magician's attachments. In Sean's terms, the 'higher power' is something that comes from the group of AA members themselves, an energy that is released in their daily, collective struggle against their own imminent abjection. Sean puts it simply: 'AA is my life brought to me by others. It is my consciousness expressed by other human beings'.

In the same way that the Lost Boy and the Addict repeat scenes of abandonment, isolation and anaesthesia, in the voice of the Magician there are recurring episodes and stories that repeat or rework a narrative line – in this case a fable of *magical rescue*. For example, Sean's second and present wife, who he met as a consequence of events set in train by the pariah episode, has been instrumental in facilitating a range of magical rescues – from addiction, from being lost or alone, and from poverty. The magician voice also contains other important symbolic elements. For a number of years Sean worked in children's theatre as a puppeteer, creating magic and illusion for classes of excited schoolchildren. Sean has very 'long and curled' fingers, an embodied quality that he associates with the mystical and powers of magic. Sean is also a qualified cook, with a 'magic touch' in the kitchen.

For Sean, the moral direction of his life is a cycle of abandonment and grief, followed by (addictive) anaesthesia, culminating in a magical rescue in which 'my life (is) brought to me by others'. Like most magicians it seems, there was always someone there to help him escape at the death. Sean has had many scrapes with potentially fatal overdoses, and as many chance meetings with individuals who gave him succour when suicide was an option. Sean feels he has cheated death.

In spite of the traumas and depredations of his life, Sean has survived – at 43 he is still in one piece, articulate and socially skilled. He is married to a professional woman and has a beach house. The Good Guy and the Magician seem to be the dominant voices in his life. But Sean has a history of periodic benders (the Addict), in which he lapses into binge drinking episodes for a few days (the most recent had been only months ago). And much to his partner's dismay, he occasionally disappears suddenly (like his sister) for days without warning or explanation (the Lost Boy). These episodes are revealing from the point of view of self-plurality or polypsychism. They show how voices that might appear to be dormant or even deceased can re-emerge or be reactivated in thought, feeling and action.

Conclusions

This case illustrates a number of important defining characteristics of a plural self. First, we learn that the landscape of identity contains contradictory elements – there are very good and very bad stories about the self, which in Sean, seem to be amplified, but which are not unique to Sean. A basic prediction of dialogical theories about the self is that the individual contends with opposing or alternative narrative voices. These certainly emerged in the landscape of Sean's life narratives.

Second, and related to the first point, we are dealing here with *moral concerns*. The individual is positioned in an evaluative landscape of action, and accordingly, there is a struggle to map the self into it. There are conflicting stories about identity. These voice-narratives are concerned with issues surrounding what it means to be living a good or a bad life, to be powerful or weak, virtuous or corrupted, and so on. These are moral issues.

Third, the plurality of voices synthesised from Sean's *Personality Web* has a developmental history. In Sean, the voices identified seem to correspond to several stages of splitting within his psyche, associated with traumatic episodes. First, and perhaps very early in development (cf Klein, 1948; Winnicott, 1975), there is a split between the narrative of the Good Guy, loved and nurtured by his older sister, and the Lost Boy, beaten by his father, and abandoned (eventually) by both of his 'mothers'. Later, the Lost Boy gives rise to the Addict, a response to the traumas of losing a mother. Later still, the narrative of the Magician becomes differentiated from the Good Guy as a response to the traumas of addiction. In this process of splitting, the life narrative branches into differently configured story lines.

Fourth, from the perspective of socio-cultural *positionings*, articulated earlier, it can be observed that Sean's narrative voices define a spectrum of class and power relationships. The Lost Boy is a refugee from working-class Belfast, and the Addict is a powerful symbol for the abject and downtrodden at the lowest stratum of society. Alternatively, the narratives of the Good Guy and the Magician are firmly in the domain of the privileged – Sean was an elite sportsman as a young man, and he is now living a relatively comfortable existence with a partner who is a well-paid professional. This is a long way from Dixon's Creek.

Fifth, in Sean's clustering of attachments, there is an embodied component to the narrative voices he has identified (see Table 2). For example, his conjoined eyebrows (which he manicures) and his rotting teeth both powerfully symbolise and embody the voice of the Addict as outcaste and pariah. This is how Sean puts it:

> ... the one (eye)brow is a killer – it makes you look like a psychopath

and

> ... the symbolic thing about my life that radiates my health more than anything is my teeth. They're all about health – you wear them when you eat ... mine are rotten.

On the other hand, Sean's long curled fingers, for him, embody his Magician voice, while his stomach (washboard flat) embodies the Good Guy. This suggests that the body can be a powerful symbolic vehicle for identity attachment. Parts of the body can be mapped onto different narrative voices in a model of self-plurality.

Finally, Sean's life narratives and the web of attachments underlying them can be read like a morality fable or saga. It is a saga narrated variously by a chorus of voices, *positioned* by relations of moral choice, social and class ties, and the exigencies of time. All of these voices remain active to varying degrees in Sean's life today. While he is in control of the Addict, he still goes on binges. While the 'magic' of his charm remains irresistible to both men and women, he still gets lost.

Sean was happy to discuss the ups and downs of his life, and for me to write about them under conditions of anonymity (as noted, all identifying details have been altered). It may be that getting closer in touch with the various voices that make up his lived experience will help him in the future. He thinks this might be the case. Indeed, the question of getting 'in touch' with voiced narratives raises a broader question – to what extent can individuals recognise their narrative voices? This is a moot point, insufficiently discussed in the literature (Rowan & Cooper, 1999). My impressions from working with the *Personality Web* (PW) suggest that this procedure helps to bring into focus, by a process of structured reflection, narrative voices of which the individual may only be dimly aware.

All the foregoing suggests that the PW methodology may have a contribution to make both to future research and clinical practice. First, in the growing area of narrative therapies, here is a method that has the potential to help individuals explore current identity issues, enabling them to 'map' and clarify the positive and the more threatening narrative voices that construct their lives. The PW may be useful both in assessment and exploration at the early stages of therapy, but also as a tool to promote change through the reorganisation of narrative structures. The Web clearly has potential as a clinical tool. (Clinicians may also note that the PW analysis can be performed without the MDS procedure, which is a statistical adjunct.) Second, there is a need for research which can focus more systematically and concertedly on what could be called the shadowland at the boundaries of the conscious and the unconscious. The PW procedure appears to set up conditions that allow (at least) partially repressed narrative material to rise into consciousness. The concepts of attachment and positioning are important in this process. Eliciting attachments gets at the symbolic substance, the signposts within narrative. The concept of positioning brings into the foreground the socially constructed conflicts and oppositions that give rise to splitting within the psyche. In Sean, we have seen how the process of splitting, mediated by a series of trauma of social origin, gave rise to two sets of opposing narrative voices: Good Guy vs. Lost Boy, and Addict vs. Magician. Whether this pattern of splitting can be demonstrated in other lives, i.e., whether dialogical narrative structures can be 'generalised' in any way, is a question that invites further inquiry. Future research needs to explore the unfolding of these complex narrative processes in the individual in detail, while also attending to the question of regularities of narrative structure across persons.

Notes
1. MDS relies on a Euclidean algorithm for deriving the co-ordinates of a set of points (the 24 attachments) in a space of r orthogonal dimensions, where the rank order of distances between each point in the space conforms to the rank order of distances between the points in the original proximity ratings data. See Kruskal & Wish (1978) for a readable and user-friendly introduction suitable for non-statisticians.
2 All names, places and other identifying details have been changed in this account to preserve anonymity.

Many thanks to Ben Bradley, Janet Pinto Correia, Aileen Sorohan and Deidre Mountjoy for support, advice and assistance. Thanks also to two anonymous reviewers of this paper, and thanks most of all to my informants. Preparation of this paper was supported in part by a Merit Research Grant from James Cook University. Requests for reprints should be sent to Peter Raggatt, School of Psychology, James Cook University, P.O. Douglas 4811, Queensland, Australia.

References
Bakhtin, M. M. (1929/1984) *Problems of Dostoevsky's poetics* (Ed. and trans. Caryl Emerson.). Minneapolis, MN: University of Minnesota Press.
Bradley, B. S. (1993) 'Questioning the researcher's existence: From deconstruction to practice', in H. J. Stam, L. P. Mos, W. Thorngate & B. Kaplan (eds), *Recent trends in theoretical psychology* 3: 153-161. New York: Springer-Verlag.
Barthes, R. (1966/1988) 'The death of the author', in D. Lodge (ed), *Modern Criticism and Theory* 166-72. London: Longman.
Davies, B. & Harre, R. (1990) 'Positioning: The discursive production of selves', *Journal for the Theory of Social Behaviour* 20: 43-63.
Erikson, E. H. (1959) *Identity and the life cycle*, New York: International Universities Press.

Foucault, M. (1969/1988) 'What is an author?', in D. Lodge (ed), *Modern criticism and theory* 196-210, London: Longman.

Freeman, M. (1993) *Rewriting the self: History, memory, narrative*, London: Routledge.

Gergen, K. J. (1991) *The saturated self*, Oxford: Basil Blackwell.

Gergen, K. (1994). 'Exploring the postmodern: Perils or potentials?' *American Psychologist* 49: 412-16.

Gergen, K. J. & Gergen, M. M. (1988) 'Narrative and the self as relationship', *Advances in Experimental Social Psychology* 21: 17 – 56.

Gilligan, C., Brown, L. M. & Rogers, A. G. (1990) *Psyche embedded: A place for body, relationships and culture in personality theory*, in A. Rabin, R. Zucker, R. Emmons, & S. Frank (eds), *Studying persons and lives* 86-147. New York: Springer.

Gregg, G. S. (1991) *Self-representation: Life narrative studies in identity and ideology*, New York: Greenwood Press.

Harre. R. & Van Langenhove, L. (1991) 'Varieties of positioning', *Journal for the Theory of Social Behaviour* 21: 393-407.

Henriques, J., Hollway, W., Urwin, C, Venn, C & Walkerdine, V. (1984) *Changing the subject: Psychology, social regulation and subjectivity*, London: Methuen.

Hermans, H. J. (1996) 'Voicing the self: From information processing to dialogical exchange', *Psychological Bulletin* 119: 31-50.

Hermans, H. J. & Kempen, H. J. (1993) *The dialogical self: Meaning as movement* San Diego: Academic Press.

Hermans, H. J., Kempen, H. J. & Van Loon, R. J. P. (1992) 'The dialogical self: Beyond individualism and rationalism', *American Psychologist* 47: 23-33.

Hermans, H. J., Rijks, T. I. & Kempen, R. J. P. (1993) 'Imaginal dialogues in the self: Theory and Method', *Journal of Personality* 61: 207-236.

Hollway, W. (1984) 'Gender differences and the production of subjectivity', in J. Henricks, W. Hollway, C. Urwin, L. Venn & V. Walkerdine (eds) *Changing the Subject: Psychology, Social Regulation and Subjectivity*, London: Methuen.

James, W. (1890) *The principles of psychology* (Vol. 1), London: MacMillan.

Klein, M. (1948) *Contributions to psychoanalysis*, London: Hogarth Press.

Kruskal, J. B. & Wish, M. (1978) *Multidimensional Scaling*, Beverly Hills, CA: Sage.

Kvale, S. (1992) 'Postmodern psychology: A contradiction in terms?', in S. Kvale (ed), *Psychology and postmodernism* 31-57. London: Sage.

Markus, H. & Nurius, P. (1986) 'Possible selves', *American Psychologist* 41: 954-69.

May, R. (1991) *The cry for myth*, New York: Norton.

McAdams, D. P. (1993) *The stories we live by: Personal myths and the making of identity*, New York: William Morrow.

Raggatt, P. T. F. (1998) *The personality web: An interview protocol for investigating the dialogical self*, Townsville: James Cook University.

Raggatt, P. T. F. (2000) 'Mapping the dialogical self: Towards a rationale and method of assessment', *European Journal of Personality* 14: 65-90.

Ricoeur, P. (1974) *The conflict of interpretations*, Evanston, Illinois: Northwestern University Press.

Ross, C. A. (1999) 'Subpersonalities and multiple personalities: A dissociative continuum?', in J. Rowan & M. Cooper (eds), *The plural self* 183-97. London: Sage.

Rowan, J. & Cooper, M. (1999) *The plural self: Multiplicity in everyday life*, London: Sage.

Sampson, E. E. (1985) 'The decentralization of identity: Toward a revised concept of personal and social order', *American Psychologist* 40: 1203-11.

Sampson, E. E. (1989) 'The deconstruction of the self', in J. Shotter & K. J. Gergen (eds), *Texts of identity* 1-19. London: Sage.

Shotter, J. (1993) 'Bakhtin and Vygotsky: Internalization as a boundary phenomenon', *New Ideas in Psychology* 11: 379-90.

Shotter, J. (1999) 'Life inside dialogically constructed mentalities: Bakhtin's and Voloshnikov's account of our mental activities as out there between us', in J. Rowan & M. Cooper (eds), *The plural self* 71-92. London: Sage.

Winnicott, D. W. (1975) *Collected papers*, London: Karnac Books.

The 'globalitarian' order to come?
11 September as event

Couze Venn

The bombing of New York has instantly become the exemplar of the historical event as disruption and dislocation, re-presented as an irruption on the surface of history, announcing a break with the taken-for-granted world. 11 September is thus already layered with the patina of myth, beckoning to other myths on the stage of history. Retroactively, such events play the part of new beginning and origin, which means that they oblige us to think anew the question of the present and who 'we' are, and thus the question of what is to come. This eschatological and messianic dimension is a matter that immediately drew attention: this is the end of the world as we knew it, a new order is in process. Of course, a similar assault, happening elsewhere, would have had nothing like the same historical meaning and impact. Indeed, in terms of the inhumanity of the assault, worse assaults have happened and are happening elsewhere: ethnicides, massacres, tortures and the kind of living death that existing exploitative systems inflict on countless people – though how can one callibrate suffering of this kind? Is it not enough that there be one proper name to stand for the many: Auschwitz, Mai Lai, Shatila, or Steve Biko, Martin Luther King, Victor Jara?

In the Western imaginary, the immediate response has tended to pull in two opposite directions that nevertheless are each located on the terrain of the exceptional. On the other hand, there has been the sliding of

11 September under the sign of the already-known trauma, namely, its re-presentation as repetition: this is Pearl Harbour again, or, the Taliban/Al Qaeda action is typical of Arabic brutality: a familiar stereotype. On the other hand, it has evoked the monstrous: this act defies understanding and must be cast outside normal human action. Both responses legitimated the call for the symmetrical action of countering excess with the force of other excesses. In the early days, the view that only such an excessive response could restore 'normality' appeared itself as 'normal'. Following the rapid collapse of the Taliban in subsequent events this attitude has become institutionalised, especially in the official discourse of the USA administration; other exceptional 'security' measures that have been put into place have acquired the reasonableness of common sense. The exceptional has become normalised.

Fortunately, the situation at the level of representation and imagination has cooled sufficiently to allow some space for dissent and for more measured analysis. For many, of course, this event was not entirely unexpected, not in its shocking actuality, but in terms of a possibility inherent in the excess of American power and domination. Baudrillard (2001), with typical rhetorical flourish that points to a hidden meaning, says as much in his reflections on the event: '... it is [this global superpower] which, because of its intolerable power, has stirred up all this violence in which the whole world is steeped, and thereby that terroristic imagination (without knowing it) which dwells inside all of us'. In the eyes of many, especially in the ex-Third World, neo-imperial/postcolonial world – take your pick – it was a matter of: 'well, what did they expect ?', meaning that the USA has for years now acted as world policeman, judge and executioner, mostly in its own interest, mostly fighting the cold war/'third world war' (Baudrillard, 2001) – witness Grenada, Chile, Vietnam, Guatemala, Cuba, the Philippines, and many more – and at some point someone was going to have a crack. It is ironic that the assault should have come from a source, Islamic fundamentalists, which has consistently fought the left, with not a little help from the USA, and which has been denounced and opposed by the left and by feminists everywhere for some years. What has stunned was the place and the scale and the implications.

The reality of globalisation took on a different meaning after 11 September, more threatening in the implication of the porous state of frontiers and borders, and the realisation that its viral character meant that 'contagion' from the outside is uncontainable. Furthermore, the intricate negotiations and the alliances being put into place have made visible the networks that usually operate in the background of globalisation, showing that these do not follow simple lines of dispersion from fixed centres, but look more like networks within networks, with complex interconnections, for instance between 'narcotrafico' (Castells, 1998) and military alliances in the Afghanistan war against Russia, and political networks in the 'middle-east'.[1] There are also those networks on the side of resistance and dissent, linking people globally in a web of information and solidarity, from the USA to the Middle East, from Latin America to the Far East. On a world scale, the decision by the USA administration – I say administration rather than people because one must acknowledge the bravery of the many Americans who do not support their government's policy – to characterise the aftermath in terms of a war between 'us' – freedom and democracy, liberal capitalism, the 'good guys' – versus 'them' – terrorists, despots, 'evil' – which has no place for anything in-between or neutral, and in which the USA will determine who the terrorists are, has forced states everywhere to make quick calculations of gains and losses in choosing sides. The opinion of dissenters and of those who refuse such options and what underlies them, has been marginalised or ridiculed as old left or naive, or branded as complicit with terrorists. Power has rarely been so visible as now, making the theoreticians of decenterings uneasy about their peripheral visions of the big picture. Sometimes, one could be forgiven for thinking that it has all become sadly feudal, for instance in the case of 'vassals' like the Philippine government. And, of course, there are pay-backs, with vast 'aid' and benefits packages for 'allies'.

For much of the media in the USA and Europe, one element of global visibility has been replayed precisely in terms of this reconstituted 'us' versus 'them' scenario, inflated on a world scale, sliding into the rhetoric of the 'clash of civilisations'. On the side of the 'Western' us – this is an inadequate representation, re-inscribing too much that needs problematising, especially the assumptions of unities and unitariness, but pointing to the visibility that the media has constructed – the 'big picture' has brought into consciousness aspects of the operation and apparatuses of globalisation that some people prefer to lose in the 'oubliette' of commodity and consumer culture, in particular concerning 'them', out there who labour in the sweat-shops, in the mines, on the plantations and so on to ensure that goods magically appear in the shops.[2]

'They' of course have been increasingly slipping across the borders in many guises, not content to remain at the gates of the rich or the free. But they were containable, as refugees or guest workers or illegals, and have their uses, as the casual workers who service the lifestyle of the more affluent. The brutal intrusion of this 'contagion' into the inner sanctum of sovereignty has thrown into turmoil the established lines of force. In the eyes of those who see the world in terms of the 'us' and 'them' divide, the army of the poor have become potential terrorists with their sights on the 'centres'. This is against the rules; 'they' are supposed to look exotic, work hard with a smile on their face, show respect and keep their 'uncivilised' behaviour to themselves. Terrorism is supposed to happen out there in the 'Third World' or the ex-USSR, the world of the 'losers', in Hardt and Negri's (2000) ironic terminology, in the war of appropriation and expropriation, where it has become a casual weapon of institutionalised violence. The fall-out includes a hypermodern fundamentalist counter-modernisation terror, as inflicted in Algeria and elsewhere. One could mention the use of terror by Christian fundamentalists against pro-choice activists in the USA, but that does not quite fit the dominant media imagination. Indeed, given the official definition of terrorism in the USA code – 'the calculated use of violence against civilians to intimidate, induce fear, often to kill, for some political, religious, or other end' – one could conclude that terrorism is often what the USA has done, and does, to 'them' in the course of the 'third world war'/cold war. Soon, the new 'security' laws introduced in many Western countries will globalise the territory of terrorism too, an interesting twist to the notion of de-centering. For de-centering at the same time de-territorialises, and opens all regions to multiple counter-flows with the result that vulnerability and risk are also globalised. The inside/outside line of demarcation, which has protected the 'centres' from the seriously destructive character of neo-liberal economic management and governmentality in the 'peripheries' – the latest case being Chile – has itself become breached and nomadic. One of the counter-flows concerns the return of political repression to the centres, increasingly in the form of the universalisation of the apparatus of political oppression. A new machinery of inquisition is being put into place, ready to operate should circumstances require it. The effects will surely erode the liberal democracies from within as hard-fought for freedoms and rights are curtailed; one can only hope that in time this development will become neo-liberalism's Achilles heel.

On the 'them' side, it has become apparent that when the gloves are off, the USA government and its allies (and global corporate capitalism, the forces of neo-liberalism) will select their friends and enemies, determine who is or is not a terrorist and decide their action irrespective of the cost to the other side. Everything now seems to depend on strategic calculations, as for example with the case of Pakistan, which before 11 September was regarded by the USA as fundamentalist, undemocratic. But, outside the citadels of bigotry within the 'West' and Arab countries, people are not taken in. Not everyone on the 'them' side constitutes themselves in the fantasy of repressed memory or knowledge, even if some factions on both sides are ready to assume that centuries of colonialism and modernism have had no effect on the cultures, European and otherwise, involved in the encounter. For these factions, it is as if all the work of critique and demystification undertaken by 'postcolonial' analyses, at the level of theory as much as in the whole range of the expressive arts, never happened. For instance, Soueif's (2001) report from Cairo about responses to 11 September shows clearly that the 'Islam versus the West' theory is dismissed as arrogance by the remarkably well-informed Egyptians he interviewed. Many reflect upon how much of western and modern culture – the music, the literature, the cinema, the fashion, the expectations, the knowledges – they have integrated into their own lives. Some of them pointed out that there are 12 million Egyptian Christians living in Egypt; and where, they asked, 'did Christianity come from in the first place? Bethlehem, Beit Sahour, Beit Jala, all essentially Christian Palestinian towns, bombarded by the Israelis every day'. The tie up between oil, politics and military action was not lost on them, for they were aware of plans being put into place for some time to secure the vast oil reserves around the Caspian Sea.[4] Commenting on the attitude to American and Western global plans, some of the informants alluded to the failure of USAID to deliver on its promises, and the devastation caused by the privatisation process, part of the model of economic 'reform' or 'new modernisation' that has been sold to them as the answer to their problems of poverty, but which has succeeded only in destroying what were already poor social provisions of health and so on. Their experience is confirmed in one of Edward Said's interrogations of American policy regarding the Palestinian struggle, where he castigates the arrogance of the attitude which dictates that conflict persists because some of the parties involved are so intransigent as to refuse the USA version of the solution.[5] The pressure (from the USA, the World Bank, IMG, etc) to reorganise in order to conform to a neo-liberal market-based socio-economic order is a common experience in the 'postcolonial' world, and now in the ex-USSR. It should surprise no one that the response of those at the receiving end of the grand plans instituting the 'new order' should be one of suspicion and opposition, including by military means. But what of the future? Will the scenario triggered by 11 September become a self-fulfilling prophesy?

Sovereignty, authority, exception

I would like to broaden the picture, going back to another world scenario, imagined before 11 September, and examine what lessons we can draw when other points of view are juxtaposed with it. I'm thinking of the theses in Hardt and Negri's (2000) book, *Empire*. As we know, they argue that a new form of power is appearing in the world, in the wake of globalisation and the end of the old imperialism, a power inscribed in a new type of rule that combines juridical categories and ethical values. Their analysis replaces the Marxist model of history, whereby class conflict, provoked by the inner logic of capitalist development, drives the process of unfolding of world history towards more 'mature' stages of the development of society – its forces and relations – until the final emergence of the communist form of sociality, in which capitalism and the state-centered form of power will have been superseded by collective and egalitarian forms of ownership, production and social relations. They examine the effects of the globalisation of capitalist production and of the process of decolonisation since the end of the second world war in terms of the construction of an order that breaks with the previous, modern (centered, territorialised) paradigm of authority and sovereignty. Global capitalism in its post-imperial form makes possible the integration of economic and political power into a single power that overdetermines them in a 'unitary way', uniting them in 'a new inscription of authority' (Hardt and Negri, 2000: 9) and a new model of the production of normative and juridical instruments that ensure pacification and a universal order: 'Empire is formed not on the basis of force itself but on the basis of the capacity to present force as being in the service of right and peace' (Hardt and Negri, 2000: 15). Its authority derives from this ethical claim to a just form of sociality. Besides, Empire is a deterritorialised and de-centered system; it is machinic in its operation, a totalising system for producing a new, self-referential, self-replicating and eternal order, including appropriate subjectivities for it. Empire, however, produces its counter-empire, the forces of the 'multitude' – the poor, the subaltern, the new knowledge-based worker – which resist incorporation.

Here is not the place to deal with the problems with these ideas or with their elaboration. What I want to highlight at this point are the arguments about sovereignty and authority. In their analysis, Hardt and Negri, developing the thoughts of Carl Schmitt, and of Agamben in *Homo Sacer: Sovereign Power and Bare Life*, argue that '(t)he juridical power to rule over the exception and the capacity to deploy police force are ... two initial coordinates that define the imperial model of authority' (Agamben, 1988: 17). For Agamben, the moment of exception is the moment when a sovereign authority, at a point of crisis or trauma for the state, suspends the rule of law in order to preserve the life of the state. In doing so, it 'does not limit itself to distinguishing what is inside from what is outside but instead traces a threshold (the state of exception) between the two, on the basis of which outside and inside, the normal situation and chaos, enter into those complex topological revelations that make the validity of the juridical order possible' (Agamben, 1988: 19). In the death camps in Nazi Germany, the state of exception became the rule. The Jews, according to the Nazis, could be judicially killed because they threatened the very foundation of German sovereignty, namely, the authenticity of the people/volk, and so placed themselves permanently outside the law. [The irony of the position of the Palestinians today in the imaginary of Zionism should not be lost.] As Santner (2001) indicates, when the state of exception becomes normalised or chronic – resonating with a Benjaminesque permanent state of emergency and with Kafka's parable about the law – the law is at once suspended and re-asserted as the sign of sovereignty: as the latter's excessive presence, for only the need for the assertion of sovereignty as such, its sacred character, legitimises the suspension of law. In the USA since 11 September, the suspension of law – inside the USA applying to anyone suspected of terrorism or of supporting it, and internationally: we want Osama bin Laden dead or alive, preferably dead – instantiates the state of exception and of sovereignty of the USA with respect to all other states. Exception here should be understood in two ways, that is, as indicating that these are exceptional times, and as referring to the USA as an exception. Support for this line of analysis is confirmed in the fact that the USA government has given itself the unilateral and messianic right to decide who is a terrorist, and what action is appropriate in pursuit of an almost divine or 'infinite' justice.[6] The performative relation between sovereignty and the right to decide the exception is further demonstrated in the strategy for invulnerability pursued through the obsession with the 'star wars' defence system. This strategy inscribes the desire of the USA to be the exceptional state, the only one which cannot be attacked militarily on its own soil, so that invulnerability can become the signifier of its sovereign status amongst the nations of the world. Clearly the bombing of the World Trade Centre challenged this fantasy of territorial invulnerability, and directly undermined American global sovereignty. No wonder anyone who criticises American policy or history is regarded as an intolerable threat.

The fact that the initial campaign was conducted in the name of 'infinite justice' reveals hidden layers of American self-understanding that would be worth further unpacking by reference to the analytical directions indicated in the texts I've mentioned, for they relay notions of justice, authority, sovereignty, ethics with ontological considerations that engage with the most pressing problems to do with the relation of the political with the emancipation of being. This is too large and complex an issue to be dealt with here.

However, the references to divine or 'infinite' justice, and to a messianic vocation in the discussion of the relation of sovereignty and authority reveal an important point, namely that authority works not on the basis of the juridical (a leaning in Hardt & Negri), or the juridical alone, but on the basis of a sacred dimension, that is, by reference to a secret and un(re)presentable dimension, as Derrida (1995) shows in his analysis of the ethical in *The Gift of Death*, and by reference to an invisible imperative – for example, the face, for Levinas, the divine Commandment, for Abraham – that inaugurates authority. The point is that the ground that founds authority cannot be presented as such, though one can name its (polysemic and transcendent) representatives: God, The People, The Prince, The Nation, The Aryan Race, The Party, The Market, the Great Leader. The signifier of authority reveals an imaginary construct around an undecidable and fugitive plenitude, thus betraying an invisible lack, so that, as Bourdieu has argued, the naming or vesting of authority relies on 'the performative magic of all institutions' (Bourdieu, 1991: 122). As we know from religion, the sacred keeps its ground secret as condition for its sacredness. Only faith covers over the lack, hence the attitude of abandonment to a sovereign power: one must consent to its ban for the magic to work, for sovereign power binds us to its ban, that is, 'to its proclaiming, to its convening, and to its sentencing ...' (Santner, 2001: 62, 63, citing Nancy). The wish to terminate the endless deferral of the place of the secret ends up revealing that the space of the 'Holy of Holies' conceals nothing/no-Thing, the non-place of desire or the empty place of lack, as some passages in Cixous and Derrida (2001) lead us to surmise. But this lack, when the whole imaginary which keeps it secret, thus sacred/inviolate, is threatened, becomes the trigger for a surplus of violence, an inhuman violence. Terror has been the instrument of that violence for an immemorial time, repeated in recent times in Northern Ireland, Palestine/Israel, Bosnia and many other places. One can detect its repetition in the symmetrical terror which the fundamentalists on both sides are ready to unleash.

Just/War

I would like to juxtapose another idea at this point since it hooks into the question of what Baudrillard calls the 'fourth world war' as well as extends the discussion of sovereignty. I will again focus on the USA because of its determining position in the new world order. I refer to Virilio's proposition of a relation of co-articulation between war, technology and the institution of the state. War is seen as the determining imperative. I suppose it would be useful to refer as well to Norbert Elias' (1982) idea that the monopolisation of violence by the state was a central feature of the civilising process in Europe, conditioning the emergence of forms of civility and a public sphere where disputes and disagreements could be settled without recourse to physical violence. If we look at the history of the USA since 1492, we find the coexistence of a permanent state of war alongside the development of a republican polity that appears, as Arendt (2000) has argued, as the ideal political arrangement to ensure that no particular force can prevail over all the others, that is, to ensure liberty. On the one side we encounter the example of, in principle, an open democracy of the people as sovereign authority, enshrined in the Constitution and the checks and balances which the elaborate system of representation is meant to ensure. On the other side, there is the history of a state of permanent war against a series of foes, at first the Native Americans, whose numbers are reduced over a century from over 100 million in 1492 to around 10 million, and whose lands are appropriated right into the nineteenth century in the name of civilisation, or of a Lockean rational efficiency and, finally, 'manifest destiny'. From the sixteenth century, a war of subjugation and containment is fought against African slaves, which does not diminish for centuries because of the need to quell the numerous, if localised, uprisings and to discipline the slaves ever resistant to subject(ifica)tion. In terms of the formation of the USA as a state, I need to add the numerous wars against the Spaniards, the Mexicans, the French in Canada, together with the War of Independence and the Civil War. Then, up to 1945, besides the colonial adventures of Theodore Roosevelt, sustained by the Monroe doctrine and the 'mission civilisatrice' (see Hardt and Negri, 2000: 175 for historical details), we have the two world wars. But it is in the period of the cold war that war on a global scale, and a generalised state of war, has become permanent. I will cite some names to recall the extent of military action: Korea, Vietnam, the Gulf War, to say nothing of military and para-military interventions in dozens of countries, as in the Congo leading to the murder of Patrice Lumumba, Chile, Nicaragua, Bolivia, Panama, Cuba and so on. No other state (outside colonised or subjugated countries) in modern times has experienced this permanent state of warfare, much of it, up to the Civil War, on its own soil. Since Yalta, warfare for the USA has taken the form of a permanent state of mobilisation, enacted in the military presence at bases throughout the world, legitimated in terms of the domino theory – not a single one (socialist reform/insurrection) must pass – or the 'we had to destroy it in order to save it' policy implemented in Vietnam. The homology between militarism, capitalism and imperialism is surprisingly uncanny when one thinks about them in terms of strategies of power and in terms of their genealogy in modern times.

If the cold war – and the proxy hot/murderous war which was its shadowy twin – has been the third world war fought between liberal capitalism and communism (and socialism), what is at stake in the 'fourth world war' that may have started? The representation in terms of a 'clash of civilisation', following Huntington (1991), will allow me to shift the discussion to a different terrain for a number of suggestions. One curious element of this rhetoric is that leaders in those 'civilisations' seen as 'other' or incompatible do not seem to see it that way, though some Islamic fundamentalists share that language with their foes, another interesting symmetry. The Russian and Chinese presidents have not been noted for describing the current situation in terms of civilisational conflicts. Most people in the postcolonial world have not conceptualised their conflicts or differences with the West in terms of a clash of civilisation. Furthermore, as far as I know, no one from outside the USA and the UK has spoken in terms of establishing a new world order. Indeed, for the Chinese or Indian or Japanese political leadership to speak in such terms would sound, to 'Western' ears, if not ludicrous, certainly like a provocation and a threat to 'world peace'. If the prime minister of Jamaica were to make a speech about inaugurating a new world order, he would quickly be institutionalised. So, what's going on? Is the conflict really about the emergence of a new totality – Empire – whether as understood by Hardt and Negri or not? Is it about the particular brand(s) of fundamentalism which will inaugurate this new temporality at the 'end of history', as the Fukuyamas of neo-liberalism envisage?

Back to the future: towards new totalitarianisms

For one thing, we need to take a closer look at fundamentalism. In the first place, it is worth noting that that there are several species of fundamentalism, notably, Christian, Islamic, Hindu, Zionist, Stalinist, neo-liberal, and that they have all been shaped by modernisation, so that, say, Islamic fundamentalism with kalashnikov and mobile phone is not a simple repetition of an older form of religious sectarian dogmatism, but more like a postmodern movement, and very much at odds with many interpretations of Islam. From this point of view, my questioning is directed at the fact that religious fundamentalism, well before 11 September, makes a demand for such a degree of abnegation and violence, directed at oneself and at anyone or anything perceived as a threat or inimical, and a demand for an excess of abjection and sacrifice in its promise of redemption, that one is led to allude to an 'inhuman' dimension in its make-up. I would set that idea of the inhuman against another equally inhuman reality: the invisibility and insignificance, and a future without hope to which the 'losers' in the game of 'Empire' are condemned. Today, the 'damned of the earth' – I prefer 'damned' to wretched in the translation of Fanon's *Damnes de la terre* – live their misery alongside the images of what is possible or available in the affluent world or the world of the rich, diffused by the media all round them, the source of an excess humiliation. The exploited have their faces ground daily in the dirt of the affluence which they make possible. For the 'damned', the abjection which they live is the spur for seeking, or being ready to believe in, fundamentalism as the promise of hope that they can nowhere else find, except of course in another promise: that of a socialist revolution. But the latter has been constantly under siege for generations, and is now subject to constant terror, instigated by USA policy.[7] On the one hand, the rejection of (occidentalist) modernity and of Western imperialism (and more confusedly capitalism) by Islamic fundamentalists expresses the perception of the selfish and 'alien' system which determines their oppression. On the other hand, fundamentalism elaborates the ground for recovering a sense of ontological security and a sense of worth, guaranteed in the, by definition, unimpeacheable truth of dogma. In any case, fundamentalism is not necessarily incompatible with capitalism or with feudal forms of oppression and exploitation. It is equally clear that, like capitalism, it attracts its fair share of criminal and psychopathic elements – witness the unspeakable brutality of massacres and punishments, as in Algeria.

The ideological symmetry between fundamentalism and neo-liberal capitalism can perhaps be extended a little further when we consider the correlation between modernity, capitalism and colonialism in the constitution of the hegemonic coordinates of the modern world, that is to say, a frame of intelligibility structured by occidentalism. The latter, as the space of becoming of a particular lifeworld and its affiliated subjectivity, a space already structured by a subjugating and universalising spirit (Venn, 2000), has increasingly taken a new form. It is no longer legitimated in terms of the humanist grand narratives of the Enlightenment, but has mutated into a semiotically closed space, colonised by the instrumental logic of capital, expressed in the language of managerialism. Capitalist occidentalist modernity has become operationalised in terms of performative practices that now institute a neo-liberal vision. The postmodern ordering of the world that is now proposed by the forces of oppressive power is determined by concepts like efficiency, flexibility, enterprise, modernisation, marketisation, choice and so on that are all self-referentially mapped into the neo-liberal frame of intelligibility. Accounting practice is becoming, for the promoters of this vision, the sole arbiter in determining value across all the activities that constitute the social, so that money appears as a new transcendent entity. The brave new order which 'third way' ideologues promise us is neo-liberal managerialism packaged in the united colours of a consumer culture which is fashioning a new totalising universalism through the colonisation of desire by consumer culture and the militarisation of the everyday. So, both religious fundamentalism and neo-liberal capitalism/occidentalism share elements of what one could properly call a totalitarianism.

The end of the cold war/'third world war' has released capitalism from needing to respond to calls for responsibility in the form of the rhetoric of 'capitalism with a human face'. It has lost the ability to respond to suffering (except by translating it into the language of accounting), and can only be thought of as an instantiation of the inhuman. 11 September as event has initiated a critique of the present which should be a principled opposition to this new order. The 'fourth world war' is about the soul of a transmodern, transcolonial humanity of the future.

Notes

1. See Arundathi Roy's (2001) response to 11 September, 'The Algebra of Infinite Justice', in the *Guardian*, 13.10.01, and in the magazine *Outlook*, October 2001, which points to CIA involvement in establishing a vast opium industry in Afghanistan and Pakistan to finance the war against the Russians.
2. The new cargo cult which the rhetoric of the 'service industries' has manufactured relies on making such boring details as production disappear from view.
3. See also Noam Chomsky: 'The Fifth Freedom', at http://www.guerillanews.com/counter_intelligence/206.html.
4. For details of the immense oil and gas reserves in the Caspian region, and the negotiations and plans that had been going on before 11 September, see the *Guardian*, Society Section, 24.10.01.
5. E. Said, (2001), 'Suicidal ignorance', at http://www.ahram.org.eg/weekly/2001/560/op2.htm
6. See also Francis Boyle's talk on the (il)legitimacy of the legislations rushed through Congress and the Senate in the USA, and the illegitimacy of the action taken with respect to international law: at http://msanews.mynet.net/Scholars/Boyle/nowar.html
7. The training in the USA of 'postcolonial' military personnel in the techniques of torture and subversion, at the School of America, is now well established.

References
Agamben, G. (1998) *Homo Sacer: Sovereign Power and Bare Life* (Trans. D. Heller-Roasen) Stanford: Stanford University Press.

Arendt, H. (2000) 'The social question', in *The Portable Hannah Arendt* (P. Baehr (Ed)) Harmondsworth: Penguin.

Bourdieu, P. (1991) *Language and Symbolic Power* (Trans. G. Raymond and M. Adamson) Cambridge: Harvard University Press.

Castells, M. (1998) *End of Millennium: Vol III of The Information Age* Oxford: Blackwell.

Cixous, H. & Derrida, J. (2001) *Veils* (Trans. G. Bennnington) Stanford: Stanford University Press.

Derrida, J. (1995) *The Gift of Death* (Trans. D. Wills.) Chicago: Chicago University Press.

Elias, N. (1982) *The Civilizing Process: State Formation and Civilization* (Trans. E. Jephcott) Oxford: Blackwell.

Hardt, M. & Negri, A. (2000) *Empire*, Cambridge: Harvard University Press.

Santner, E (2001) *On the Psychotheology of Everyday Life. Reflections on Freud and Rosenzweig*, Chicago: Chicago University Press.

Soueif, A. (2001) 'Nile blues', *Guardian*, 06.11.01.

Venn, C. (2000) *Occidentalism. Modernity and Subjectivity*, London: Sage.

Wading through quicksand
Between the philosophically desirable and the psychologically feasible

Dennis Fox and Isaac Prilleltensky

In times of relative peace we can afford to speculate on the psychological and sociological features of the *good society*. In times of all-out war we desperately try to stop our quick descent into the *worst society*. Neither is an ideal time for testing the strength and validity of our values – in the former we can idealise the human capacity for goodness, while in the latter we see nothing but the capacity for destruction. We are, paradoxically, in an ideal time to test our beliefs precisely because we now stand on quicksand. The earth and buildings shake, and so do our views about ethics, justice, peace, harmony, diversity, and meaning. It is under these conditions, just before the terror erases our collective ability to reflect, that we need to question unexamined assumptions and seek sustainable principles for action.

For some on both sides of the conflict, recent world developments justify latent or virulent fanaticism. For others, the ensuing chaos is evidence of their morally and politically superior stand – they could have predicted it! We, too, were not surprised that symbols of American power were attacked on 11 September. And we, too, share the emotional impulse to bring mass murderers to justice. But we choose, during this difficult time, to engage in self-reflection rather than give in to either self-righteousness or revenge. As critical psychologists who believe that human psychology is intertwined with political and social structures, we also reflect on the role that psychologists might play during the current situation and beyond.

How to proceed? We suggest three steps. First, an analysis of how our values and assumptions about power, oppression and well-being stand up in the current state of affairs. Second, a response to events in light of our examined precepts. And third, an assessment of mainstream psychology's approach to war and terror, as exemplified by a recent report of the American Psychological Association.

Values and assumptions

The well-being of individuals and communities depends on the balanced, simultaneous, and synergistic satisfaction of personal, relational, and collective needs. Values such as self-determination, health, growth, and spirituality foster personal wellness, whereas bonds of affection, social cohesion, and respect for diversity promote relational wellness. These types of well-being must be complemented by collective wellness values, such as social and economic justice, democracy, peace, and respect for the environment. In the absence of any one component, personal, regional, national and international well-being cannot be achieved. Hence, societies that extol self-determination at the expense of social cohesion promote individualism and alienation, while those that impose rigid norms foster conformity, homogeneity, and even tyranny. In either case, the lack of justice and democracy robs people of the chance to attain basic necessities and seek higher aspirations.

On the wellness formula, both Western and Eastern societies fail on many counts. Oppression and discrimination, subtle and overt, exist here as well as there, taking different forms under different circumstances. Despite continuing social and economic inequality, which hinders personal development and family well-being, women in the West experience liberties many in some Islamic countries merely dream of. Suicide bombers ready to kill thousands are not common in the West, but the urge to retaliate against the presumed perpetrators despite inevitable civilian deaths runs rampant, and Western publics have shown little interest in ending their own governments' long-time support for dictators and death squads. In terms of relational wellness, countries the world over have had colossal failures in establishing rules of conviviality, often reflecting the consequences of urban growth and economic dislocation. As for collective wellness, the economic powers have failed miserably to ameliorate the plight of poor countries, with ten million children under five dying of preventable diseases and malnutrition each year, often as a result of economic and environmental dynamics set in motion by Western colonialism and corporate policy. Unlike the case of Osama bin Laden, where the presumed chief culprit has not yet been found, in the case of infant mortality the enemy is known. Child poverty could be markedly reduced with a fraction of what the war in Afghanistan is costing developed and developing countries.

Until now the United States has not had to confront foreign terror on its soil in the way that so many people around the world do routinely. Nor did it have to contend with the risk of deadly bacteria, the way children in Sub-Saharan Africa do on a daily basis. What will this encounter with death mean for the national psyche, particularly if new atrocities arrive as predicted? Neither the escalation of right wing fervour nor blindness to the threat of suicide bombers will suffice.

Palpable threats test the validity of our idyllic notions. The closer we get to the lived experience of risk, the closer we are to understanding what others go through. We recognise the limitations of philosophically desirable states in the absence of structures that stretch the humanly possible. The problem: How do we stretch the humanly possible when planes crash into buildings, bombs drop, anthrax spreads, and refugees starve? How do we enact values of humanity when the real possibility remains of a descent into horror previously unknown to humanity? Utopian thinking helps push us toward the humanly possible and philosophically desirable, but can be risky if it blinds us to contemporary realities. So now – before mutual descent into mutual destruction makes consequences-be-damned blood lust irresistible – is the time to reflect upon possible principles to determine our course of action.

Reflection doesn't always lead to resolution. We too are torn by conflicting emotions, shaped by personal history as much as by philosophical musing. We each lived for a time in Israel, caught up in efforts to help create a better society. We left long ago, but today our Israeli friends and relatives routinely confront dangers only now reaching most of the West. Even as young Zionists we saw the Jewish tradition of social justice collide with the century-long search for national and personal safety, both the tradition and the search tested by the failure to create stable relationships among two peoples in one land.

Victims became oppressors and victims once again, the cycle ever harder to break as resentments and body counts grew, while political leaders on both sides became trapped in dehumanising policies, stumbling toward mutual oblivion.

Is it ever legitimate – in Afghanistan, the Middle East, the United States – to inflict death and destruction on innocents? To save our own? To delay, for a time, the next round of death? We know the urge to be even-handed, to be fair to all, to repair history's mistakes, but we know too the urge to protect those we love. On both sides, those seeking resolution find themselves pushed toward extremes. Even-handedness becomes a luxury of distance even as we push ourselves back toward our overriding concern with justice.

The attack on the World Trade Centre strikes many, certainly many Americans, as fundamentally different. It came out of nowhere, or so it seemed to a public too-long complacent about the nation's role in the world. Yet the terror came from somewhere, as did the widespread support for bin Laden by so many Muslims around the world, as shocking to many others as the horrendous attack itself. Both the terror and the support made obvious the clash of interpretations arising from wildly diverging lived experiences.

Toward a principled response

Under pressure of war and terror, too many people on both left and right succumb to one-sided reproach – calling for either action against Al Qaeda *or* the reversal of US actions, condemning either Palestinian attacks on Israeli civilians *or* oppressive Israeli policies – thus failing to oppose terror and injustice no matter where they arise. A more critical and sustainable response applies principles of justice wherever they fit, not only to those we oppose but also to ourselves and to those we support.

Oppression is dynamic and multifaceted, defying facile categorisation into heroes and villains. Critical justice, for us, begins with the acknowledgement that we are subject to the same propaganda as the rest of the world. We must be mindful that, in the wake of 11 September, some resonate with anti-Muslim or anti-Jewish sentiments. Critical justice implies that we apply the same stringent criteria to all.

Tentative principles emerge from our analysis of current events and invocations of good and evil:

First, terrorism is unacceptable regardless of the reason for it. The

September atrocity cannot be justified. Yet this principle raises complexities beyond easy condemnation. For example, our definition of terrorism is general: the knowing use or threat of violence against uninvolved civilians to achieve political or military aims. Importantly, we include violence by any group – state and non-state. Thus, while the media accept governmental definitions – focusing exclusively on groups such as Al Qaeda – we find it equally unacceptable when states bomb civilian populations, impose collective punishment, or destroy water systems and other components of civilian infrastructure. The predictable claim that such actions are merely unintended consequences of a justified assault on the enemy's military or an effort to foment popular rebellion against dictatorial regimes cannot be accepted. This is especially the case when alternative means of apprehending the targets have not been exhausted.

Second, the distinction between justifying and understanding is crucial, as is the link between understanding and policy-making. That we cannot justify terrorism does not mean we can ignore the reasons some people become terrorists and so many more applaud them. The power of terrorist leaders, built on a shifting foundation of real and imagined grievances, comes at the expense of their own disciples and their innocent victims. At the same time, Western power comes at the expense of those whose resources we have taken, economies we have controlled, values we have ignored. Domination of peoples by super-powers and super-terrorists alike must be decried.

Third, although we respect the views of committed pacifists, we believe that military action for self-defence or defence of human rights is sometimes justified. However, because war routinely causes far too many casualties, it must follow, not replace, less horrific measures. Strengthening international political and legal processes requires all nations to accept international jurisdiction. Refusal to do so – as the US does when its own actions are challenged – invalidates any claim that war is justified. Moreover, for war to be just, the likelihood of achieving its aims must be substantial. It cannot merely extend conflict while bringing to innocents brutality, death, and hardship.

Fourth, we need to challenge simplistic appeals to patriotism. Allegiance to nation can be as dangerous as allegiance to totalistic religion. We doubt that God, if he or she exists, favours any state that uses indiscriminate violence to impose its will on others, or approves of leaders who endanger their citizens for either celestial salutation or earthly grandeur. Our own primary allegiances are to our neighbours close to home and to the world community at large. National boundaries neither mandate nor limit our concern.

Principles lead to critique. Thus, we object to both exhortations to war and unsustainable peace agreements that lack historical, contextual, and personal knowledge of the circumstances leading to conflict. For example, most US citizens are oblivious to the CIA-sponsored coup that deposed Salvador Allende, the democratically elected president of Chile in the early 1970s. With US assistance, General Augusto Pinochet took over the government, imposed state terror, and proceeded to kill thousands of dissidents. Yet President George Bush wondered at a recent press conference why people hate America. Although Chile and too many similar examples cannot justify terrorism against uninvolved US civilians, they must be understood by anyone trying to transform US relations with aggrieved peoples throughout the world. Those who have suffered at US hands should receive not only compensation for past actions but also a clear indication that decision-makers are committed to just policies in the future.

Similarly, in the part of the world inextricably tied to Al Qaeda's battle to rid Muslim countries of US influence, history's complexity defies the easy tit-for-tat of isolated facts subject to shifting out-of-context interpretations. For example, supporters of Israel remember that the Mufti of Jerusalem, H'aj Amin-El-Husseini, colluded with Eichmann and Hitler to exterminate Hungarian Jewry towards the end of World War II; that in the aftermath of the Holocaust, in which six million Jews perished at Nazi hands, Israel accepted the partition of Palestine into two states, a 1948 United Nations recommendation rejected by Arab countries that attacked Israel; that Palestinian authorities rejected former Prime Minister Ehud Barak's offer to return close to 97% of the occupied territories. Yet supporters of Palestine recall that the arrival of Jews escaping European pogroms a century ago began the continuing displacement of Arabs, often by force, and created a Jewish State in which Arabs remain second-class citizens; that for more than three decades Israel's rule over occupied territories has imposed on uninvolved civilians mass punishments and other hardships; that even under liberal Israeli governments Jewish settlements on the West Bank and Gaza expanded while too many Palestinians remained in refugee camps. As we see it, in keeping with the principles we outlined above and regardless of the exchange of accusations and memories, Israel must take responsibility for displacing, oppressing, and too often killing Palestinians; the Jewish people's historically tenuous position throughout the world does not justify oppression in return. Yet Palestinians who kill uninvolved Israeli civilians are terrorists, not freedom fighters, and Arab governments and Palestinian leaders must take responsibility for their own part in fuelling the conflict.

We know that what we have to say will have little impact on decision-makers. The muddled effort to get bin Laden, to 'end terror', and – perhaps not a coincidence – to make the Middle East safe for Western resource and security interests, will continue. The shifting goals remain unclear, the methods potentially disastrous for all. Yet we choose to join with others seeking to find a way between doing nothing and doing too much. The more serious danger now is that we will go too far, not that we won't go far enough.

Psychology's role

In September 2001, the American Psychological Association's Board of Directors created a Subcommittee on Psychology's Response to Terrorism 'to help government agencies and Congress combat terrorism and deal with the psychological causes and consequences of the attacks' (Carpenter, 2001). In October, the Subcommittee issued a report outlining its approach to current events (see http://www.radpsynet.org/admin/response.html). Unfortunately, by narrowly describing the range of issues relevant to psychology and avoiding significant discussion of unavoidable values and politics, the APA's mainstream approach does little to advance the search for either safety or justice.

We have no objection to the APA's primary concern: responding to terrorism's impact by mobilising psychologists experienced in treating trauma, grief, stress and anxiety. Clinically trained psychologists have much to offer those who suffer from serious mental health difficulties caused by the September attacks. Yet surely that is not enough. Surely there is more that psychology organisations can suggest beyond a media campaign to 'encourage people to enroll in stress management training and support programs in their communities', to be 'followed up with local workshops and support groups'. Ironically, the APA calls upon 'the tremendous pro bono spirit of psychologists' to expand psychology's own turf: to 'help position psychology as a key national resource, perhaps as significant as the repositioning that occurred after WWII'.

The APA report's discussion about how to address the threat of terrorism notes psychology's traditional contribution to public policy, particularly during wartime. It calls on research psychologists to help end terrorism by reviewing existing research data and generating new data useful to 'mission critical governmental departments such as Defense, State, the FBI, etc'. The report adds that 'we now have requests for assistance from two of these agencies'.

Missing from the report is any request that psychologists apply their tools and expertise to assess United States actions that make terrorism more likely. No sympathy is expressed for the legitimate grievances of those who support attacks on the US. We can understand the temptation to choose sides and opt for protecting our own. Yet we can't help but notice the ease with which mainstream psychology's supposedly objective data-driven stance is shoved aside to advance the narrowly-defined war on terrorism. Also missing is any mention of the war in Afghanistan. Lacking a broader view of psychology's ability to address relevant issues, responses restricted to helping individuals function better – reflecting mainstream psychology's determinedly individualistic approach to human problems – and to helping governmental authorities avoid serious policy re-evaluation are unlikely to lead to fundamental solutions.

Other professional organisations have done better. For example, Psychologists for Social Responsibility's reminder to President Bush that 'The cure for terrorism must include social justice' (http://www.psysr.com/war letter.htm) should be kept in mind by all who seek to resolve the current crisis.

Conclusion

Bound by history and family, identity and community, we all may be forced by events to take sides in a battle between West and East. We would do so reluctantly, pained by the realisation that the survival of those we love might depend on the destruction of thousands or millions whose lives our own governments and their own tyrannical regimes have made far more desperate. This prospect appals us. So does the knowledge that so many civilians have already died in Afghanistan, in the US, and in the Middle East.

Will we strive to push the psychologically feasible toward the philosophically desirable? Will we pull back from the abyss before finding the ultimate commonality, one born not of peace and justice but of mutual destruction? We have no choice. Any alternative will assuredly pulverise the remains of what is still human and still humane.

Reference
Carpenter, Siri (1.11.01) 'Behavioral science gears up to combat terrorism', APA Monitor [http://www.apa.org/monitor/nov01/gearsup.html].

Personal response under attack

Ian Parker

Can more psychology help us to understand something more of the recent terrorist 'attack on democracy'? Or is psychology already too much around us, leading us in the wrong direction as we try to make sense of these 'strange times'? Psychology generally invites us to think about what people are thinking and why they do what they do – people as torn from social context; but psychological ways of thinking are also in the language we use when we articulate different ways of accounting for what is going on in the world. Some psychological theories are more tempting than others. A case in point is psychoanalysis, even when, or perhaps especially when, it seems to account for group psychology at times of war.

The search for a *personal* response to the World Trade Centre and Pentagon attacks is one of the easiest things to do in this culture, easier even than the search for the one person responsible; but both kinds of search are driven by an underlying assumption that the most important causes and effects of such an event are to be found deep inside individuals. And some kind of psychology is always already at hand here to help us target what we feel, and open it up for others to see. More difficult is an understanding of the material conditions which structure that search and make it seem as if the individual is source and destination of what has been going on since 11 September.

From where I am sitting here in Britain, for example, the kinds of psychological tools that come ready to hand – to describe personal responses to the dilemma of fight or flight, to find out how to forge alliances to combat terrorism, and how to find some reference point to guide us – might easily be found in the kinds of group analysis developed by Bion and his colleagues during the Second World War to rebuild army morale. But look a little more carefully at how our 'personal' and 'psychological' responses are structured and you start to see that those tools are so deeply embedded in the culture that they make it near impossible to find anything other than an individual check-in point or destination.

And the way these processes actually work gives lie to the idea that a group response is a genuinely collective alternative to what we feel welling up inside our individual selves. The way groups are constituted in this culture means that what will appear at the beginning and end of a social process will be a thoroughly individualised psychological subject.

Fight and flight, for instance, may look like a personal response to the attacks, but to see it like this is to lose sight of where it really comes from. There has already been a fairly successful sealing off of different ethnic communities in Britain by the media, the police and the main party politicians. 'Fight and flight' as a motif to describe images of Islam in Britain is now quite pertinent, with press hysteria over the numbers of asylum seekers 'flooding' in through the channel tunnel (a favourite focus of concern for every little Englander) homing in recently on refugees from Afghanistan. No matter that those waiting in Calais to come to Britain have fled from persecution by the Taliban, when they get here they will be attacked in the press and on the streets by racists. Asian communities have been virtually under siege in towns in the north of Britain over the last year or so, and the attacks on mosques in the wake of 11 September are only a continuation of the everyday racism that makes life for Britain's Muslims indeed a life of flight and flight.

And the forging of special relationships to combat an external reference point is nothing new. American readers will be surprised to learn, as will those in other countries perhaps, that the British public believe that the search and destroy mission against bin Laden and Co is being jointly led by Tony Blair and George Bush. It was at that moment when the second of the two trade towers was hit that we just 'knew' that a terrorist mastermind was behind the attacks; and now it is when an alliance of two world leaders is forged in a pairing that will save democracy that we think we are really going to see some action. But already long ago British readers were told that Blair gave much valuable advice to Clinton over when and where to bomb Milosevic and Saddam (and that most of the most smart bombs were British). The fantasy of the combined forces of one strong local leader and the leader of the most powerful nation state in the world is itself necessary to keep in place current economic and political alliances.

And now it is no surprise that we 'knew' so quickly who the real culprit was for these attacks. We have always been told, of course, that the most deadly attacks on the free world are conducted by madmen, and each mad man comes in turn to do his deadly work. And although the search for that single enemy is simple enough, it doesn't stop the puzzling about what is going on inside him that makes him want to hurt us. The spectacular headline during the Gulf War, when the oil installations were bombed (by American planes, it now turns out), leading to an environmental catastrophe – 'Saddam Attacks Earth' – is symptomatic, we might say: symptomatic of the image of a deadly malevolent mind directing the destruction of all of the rest of us. The speculation about the effects of the suicide of both Milosevic's parents on him as a child as the possible root cause of his hostility to everyone else is equally symptomatic. And now bin Laden is masterminding a 'network', and he erupts as the individual determining point of violence; he is no longer simply a multimillionaire head of a friendly building corporation, that was once invited to build CIA facilities during the righteous struggle with the Taliban, against the then government of Afghanistan.

We respond as individuals because we have been positioned as individual viewers of these events from day one. Look at how we saw what we saw on the day of the attacks and since. Something of the nature of the technological structuring of our vision renders what we are faced with as something powerfully individualised. When someone popped their head around my office door and told me that strange things, like planes dropping from the sky, were happening in America, I started searching and clicking on BBC news sites to try and find out what was going on. Notice that the internet as a site for information is organised in such a way that access and control necessarily lies at an individual sitting in front of a screen.

An unpleasant email appeared by the end of September, which also invited an individual sitting alone at a computer terminal to puzzle about the individual motivations of another who might have discovered this secret (or now, it transpires, to have fabricated it). Here one person opens a message from another that tells them that if they take the flight number, Q33NY, of one of the planes that crashed into the towers and turn it into Wingdings font they will find something very bizarre. Try it. It is. Not only does the linear sequence of this writing require us to run our eyes from left to right, not only does it lead us from the image of a plane through towers and death to a Star of David, but it also elicits an activity that can only be carried out by us at the terminal, by us one by one.

One by one is how psychology likes to see this played out, and one by one is how we already feel it to be. Against this, there are of course responses that make the struggle against our enclosed identities as individuals part of the struggle against state terrorism, responses which connect the activities of the anti-war movement in Britain with US Americans who see the real threat to democracy as coming from Bush and imperialist designs on secure oil routes through central Asia. There are responses that treat the coupling of leaders from Europe and America with the contempt it deserves, and which look to broader alliances with the opposition movements that will not opt for one leader against another, or one leader linked to the other. And there are responses which see fight and flight as part of the fabric of existence for minority communities in the West, and which refuse to make of them an enemy within to be fought, when they have sought asylum with us, from precisely the likes of bin Laden.

These are not primarily 'personal' responses, though they necessarily include a personal commitment as part of a political analysis. And that political analysis has to include an analysis of how it is that psychoanalysis functions so easily, too easily, as part of the popular psychology around us, in our groups and in us as individuals.

The other September 11: narratives and images

Ximena Tocornal and Isabel Piper

For Chilean people the date 11 September stirs powerful memories. It is largely remembered as a synonym of military government in Chile; as the end of a socialist project and the start of a new political order. As a collective remembering of that day, the following narrative relives three important moments: a speech, an image and a proclamation. Though the story has been told many times, each telling shares similar themes and impressions. 11 September 1973 is remembered as the day on which a deep scar was inflicted on our country.

It is the early morning of 11 September 1973, the capital city of Chile, Santiago, awakens to a strange atmosphere. It is an ordinary Tuesday, but people are not going to work, kids are not going to school, shops are closed, public offices close during the day and their workers go home, not knowing that they are unlikely ever to return.

The President[1] and his closest colleagues are at the government palace, La Moneda, from the earliest hours of the day. They have received a message from the Armed Forces. If they do not obey the message, it will be considered an act of rebellion and the government palace will be bombed by the Air Force. Disregarding the lives of those left inside the building, the Armed forces will not take any responsibility for the damage, since they have already tried, in their own words, 'everything possible to prevent larger loss'.

The president and some of his closer associates stay at La Moneda. He prepares a speech to thank his followers. His speech concerns the whole of Chilean society, and still has the power to do so even in 2002. The speech announces the temporary cessation of the socialist project, due to the prevailing conditions, yet expresses the hope that it may be taken up in the future.

Before noon, armed soldiers hide in buildings adjacent to the palace. Military aircraft from the south fly low over the city centre; they wait 'for instructions'. They are soon given and La Moneda is furiously attacked from the sky. While the planes drop bombs, the surrounding soldiers begin to attack. Within a few minutes the building is falling down. A fire, started in the rear, consumes many irreplaceable documents and artefacts. Columns of smoke and dust can be seen from all over the city. The president is dead and those who stayed with him until the end are taken prisoner, later to be murdered or to simply disappear. La Moneda is in ruins, a powerful *image* of violence and devastation.[2]

A new speech is made: the *proclamation* by the Military Junta.[3] The country is paralysed, in political and social terms, 'until new orders'. The Junta enacts the National Security Doctrine,[4] spreading fear and distrust.

These three things, speech, image and proclamation, contribute to the construction of a common discourse through which the Chilean people come to describe and understand themselves. It is a discourse of war, enemies, alarms, danger, damage, innocents, victims and loss.

The bombardment of la Moneda was captured on film. Those images now seem old and far away, but they still have a profound effect on how we construct narratives of the past. As Marita Sturken (1997) suggests, images such as these may be considered (from a Foucauldian point of view) as 'technologies of memory'. They are not simply passive containers of memory, but rather, 'objects through which memories are shared, produced and given meaning' (Sturken, 1997, p10). Thus narratives are articulated in an attempt to establish and negotiate the meanings of images. These narratives are supported by competing and contested versions of the past. These different versions produce a debate that attempts to bring closure to the events, and is undertaken in the context of broader narratives of history and identity. In this way the events become part of the past. As Andreas Huysen (1995) argues, the past is not just preserved in memory, but it must be organised and enunciated in a given form to become part of memory.

Initial reactions to the Chilean 11 September were 'this is not happening, it is a nightmare, this is not real'. Images of the event were 'unbelievable' because of their violence and unpredictability; and statements such as 'Chile will never be the same after this' became commonplace. Indeed, narratives about this day cannot avoid consideration of the distinction between the *before* and the *after* of those images. Thus, a powerful dynamic of constructing and giving meaning to the past has been established: history has to be rebuilt and Chilean society must face the prospect of inevitable and dramatic change.

Everybody knows that it was a Tuesday, even those who were born after that time. Accounts of that Tuesday are constructed in great detail: for instance, what the weather was like, or the 'exact' times of the bombings. Weather reports record that it was a pleasant sunny day, but memory constructs this day as cloudy and rainy (which would be unexpected during spring). By using these external and commonplace details, narratives are rooted in everyday life. In this way they can be more easily shared and believed, and have a deeper impact in terms of their communicability. Lived experiences are objectified in those special details and perceived as if they were common to everybody.

The ways in which the events of 11 September 1973 are constructed tell us about suffering, fear, pain and relief. Remembering is a difficult and painful exercise that takes us back to that experience. We smell the smoke and hear the shots. People feel fear and pain again. Yet remembering seems to be necessary in order not to forget, to keep memory alive. It is our duty to consider and honour those who died on this day. It is impossible to forget the day on which our history changed so abruptly and, therefore, we cannot underestimate the prevailing effects of this date on the present. Indeed, narrative constructions of this event make it appear as the day on which our country was divided into two antagonistic blocks, and a prevailing rhetoric of wars, enemies and victims was established. The effects of this rhetoric are indelible, and we refer to it as *the scar rhetoric* (Piper, 2001).

You are invited to substitute 1973 with 2001, and change the places from Santiago to New York. Beyond the obvious coincidences of the calendar – Tuesday 11 September – are there other parallels? Of course there are many differences, but let us focus on the rhetoric of the narratives attached to both events, and the ways in which images of them have been used.

It could be argued that narrative accounts of both events share a common central feature: the notion that one single event has changed a national identity and an historical process. Here, the distinction between the *before* and *after* of the event is important. Metaphors such as fracture, injury and damage *caused by the event* are used in the narratives through which a complex situation is articulated. When we talk about 'our 11 September', these metaphors introduce the idea that Chilean society was seriously injured, that we suffered deep transformations from the wounds inflicted on us, and that this interrupted the 'normal' course of history. It is in this way that *the scar rhetoric* is experienced as a narrative of victimisation; one that continues to work in the present. In so doing, narratives of the event have had significant influence on the construction of our identity, and given it a status of external reality outside of any human agency. In this context society is located in, and described through, the position of 'victim'.

It could also be argued that the images of both events have been produced and shown in similar ways, in 'documentary style', where the intent is to show the facts unfolding by themselves. We hear the bombs falling and see images of the buildings falling down, but what is missing, in comparison with the treatment of any other news, is the voice of the journalist explaining the situation. It is as if *the facts are talking for themselves* and that there is nothing to explain. For instance, we see the World Trade Centre collapsing in the frame of a moving camera. These images have been commonly used as self-explanatory texts, without need of an explanatory meta-text. There is no mediation, no contextualisation, *just the facts*. As a result, the audience is captured by the violence of the facts, as if the facts did not have an historical context through which it is possible to analyse the agencies responsible for the events.

We know that the past is not simply an accumulation of facts or events. And we know that memory provides us with interpretations of the past that are rooted in the present. In order to achieve that, we construct what Marita Sturken (1997) has described as 'technologies of memory', technologies through which memories are produced and discussed in a given context. In this instance we have tried to show, through reference to the ways in which images of two different events were constructed, how these technologies are used to produce narratives associated with what we have named *the scar rhetoric*. One of the most important effects of this narrative, and the use of metaphors of severe wounds or injuries, is the way in which collectives are positioned as victims. Such narratives position us as passive victims and diminish our capacity to recognise human agency in political conflicts.

Notes
1. The President was Salvatore Allende, a socialist democratically elected to lead the country in 1970 for a six year term. He represented a range of left-wing parties, including the Socialist Party and the Communist Party.
2. The devastation was not only produced on 11 September, but also because of all the crimes that followed this day: at least 3000 persons have been officially recognised as having been killed and a very large number of Chileans were tortured, exiled and persecuted because of their political opinions.
3. Augusto Pinochet led the Military Junta.
4. The National Security Doctrine was based on the idea that South America was in serious danger because of international intervention. The 'enemy' was conceived as persons from within our country, not foreign, who had adopted a socialist or left-wing political project inspired by Marxism and motivated by the Cuban Revolution. This made it possible to create a war between people from the same country on the basis of radical and ontological differences, 'we' and 'they" representing 'good' and 'bad'. This allowed the Military, in the name of the Nation, to do whatever was needed to 'pacify' the society to get rid of the communist evil.

References
Huyssen, A. (1995) *Twilight Memories: Marking Time in a Culture of Amnesia*, New York: Routledge.

Piper, I. (in press) *Trauma y Memoria: elementos de una retorica de la marca*. Paper presented at Seminario: Demandas y Respuestas de reparacion en el Chile de Hoy, Santiago, Enero de 2001.

Sturken, M. (1997) *Tangled Memories: the Vietnam War, the AIDS Epedemic and the Politics of Remembering*, Berkeley, University of California.

Reviews

Lisa Blackman, *Hearing voices: Embodiment and experience*
Free Association Books 2001

Rachel Joffe Falmagne

This book undertakes an ambitious project of considerable substantive interest, to provide a Foucauldian analysis of the manner in which the phenomenon of hearing voices has been constructed through history and through the development of the psychiatric profession, and to explore the interplay between discursive construction, situated practices and a (problematised) biology in producing embodied experience and meaning.

Lisa Blackman's perspective is that the 'turn to discourse', whose importance she does endorse and whose method she does employ, generally has been limited by its refusal to engage with biology. There are two strands to her contention, one critical the other substantive. From a critical angle, she argues in particular that by failing to engage with the biological, discursive approaches implicitly treat biology as a fixed, unchangeable entity, a substrate. Biology is to be viewed instead as '... a condition of possibility of certain kinds of experience, which becomes embodied and transformed through the strategies and practices people use to engage with somatic, bodily experiences' (p57). Substantively, she argues that to understand the embodied experience of hearing voices demands an approach that integrates the social, the psychological and the biological as inseparable and mutually transforming processes.

Within the 'turn to discourse', another limitation of Foucauldian approaches to the discursive production of subjectivity, approaches with which she otherwise concurs, has been their failing fully to incorporate situated practices in their analysis. Thus, in her study of the 'hearing voices' phenomenon, she examines both the historical and social construction of this phenomenon, and the manner in which particular agents negotiate their own understanding of their voices within the context of a supportive social service, the 'Hearing Voices Network'.

I find myself in strong agreement with Blackman's general metatheoretical stance on these issues. Too often is it the case that analytical approaches that are in fact complementary are constructed into an oppositional rhetoric, and that radical debate between extreme proposals unproductively forecloses the possibility of understanding a phenomenon in any depth, or of theorising the dialectic between processes at different levels of analysis and at different analytical angles.

The first two chapters in the book examine the manner in which the phenomena of hallucination and of hearing voices have been conceptualised by psychiatric and psychological discourses, and the constructs that have been developed to this end. One focus of critical attention in these chapters is on the manner in which the interplay of the social and the psychological is figured in various approaches to the problem of hearing voices, from the more cognitive approaches, to phenomenological approaches, to social psychological approaches, to transcultural psychiatry. Though these local critiques remain disparate and the discussion fails to build up to a clear standpoint, the chapters provide a useful space for reflection on theoretical issues about the psychological/social interplay. The discussion in the next chapter then turns to a critical appraisal of critical psychology, 'new paradigm research', social constructionism and Foucault's archaeological approach, as variants of alternative ways of conceptualising the psychological. While Blackman draws on a Foucauldian mode of analysis of societal discourses, she rejects '... the prioritisation of language as the primary site of subjectification' (p76) evidenced by some strands of discourse analysis and of critical psychology. Hers is a moderate phenomenological view, where experience is historically produced but embodied, and shaped by concrete practices while being also enabled by biological potentialities. This chapter also contains interesting discussions problematising the dualism between essentialism and constructionism, and a nuanced critique of some versions of constructionism.

The following three chapters examine the historical changes in the conceptualisations of the phenomenon of hearing voices from the seventeenth century through to the present, an examination intended to destabilise present understandings of voice-hearing and to open a space for fresh understandings. The discussion maps the transformations in the practice and discourses of psychiatry within broader cultural changes, such as the development of evolutionary theory and of neuroscience, with interesting discussions of how hearing voices has been alternatively linked to 'moral' definitions of human nature, to a biological disorder of the brain, or to an extension of normal functioning, within different historical contexts. The last two chapters, 'Techniques of the hallucinatory self' and 'Embodiment and experience' examine the construction of experience and meaning in 'hearing voices' people within the context of the Hearing Voices Network, drawing on Foucault's ideas about technologies of the self, on notions from cultural phenomenology, and on the author's prior discussions about the interplay of biology, situated practice and experience.

Lisa Blackman should be applauded for undertaking an integration with this kind of scope. She does not, however, achieve it convincingly in my view, partly because of some inconsistencies in her discussion, partly because of a loose thread of argument throughout, and partly because the different pieces of argument discussed through the various chapters never fully come together in the end. As one instance of inconsistency, it remains uncertain throughout the book whether she is arguing that social and psychological processes modulate and transform the workings of biological processes per se, or whether she is focusing instead on individuals' own *understandings* of biological processes, as illustrated when she states that her focus will be on '...how the biological and the psychological are processes which are made intelligible and embodied by individuals within a matrix of historical and social processes' (p9). There is a looseness in the discussion, which slides from one point to the other, and to points about the socially constructed nature of cultural understandings of biology, without acknowledging their distinctness. The chapter discussing the experiences of individuals within the Hearing Voices Network, a case study that is intended to provide a concrete synthesis of the various arguments in the book, does not resolve this ambiguity. My qualm is not with the validity of these points (all three are valid) but with their conceptual blurring.

The different threads of argument throughout the book also do not quite come together in the end. Lisa Blackman undertakes to show that the biological is transformed by social processes and embodied practices, and that it is in that light that we ought to consider the phenomenon of hearing voices; but she does not effectively show how this process is displayed in the individuals she discusses. More generally, the promise of using this case study to illustrate the interplay of societal discourses, embodied practices and biology is not really met. Blackman describes the practices of the network and the changes in meaning the individuals attribute to their voices, but it is not obvious how this description differs from other accounts of agency and empowerment now familiar in the feminist literature. Her comment that those experiences and practices are embodied remains a comment. So is her assertion that the experience of the voice-hearing people she describes shows how those new meanings are developed 'within the gaps and contradictions' of the psychiatric and psychological discourses about hallucinations; it is not obvious how the contradictions exposed in the historical chapters affect the emergence of those particular reformulations of meaning. The present critiques are not gratuitous. The extensive theoretical and discursive apparatus deployed in the book is important and I am in full accord with many of its tenets. But one needs to see it at work effectively when applied to concrete people and situations if it is to have substantive import.

Despite the substantive interest of its subject matter, of the ideas it highlights, and of the many threads of work upon which it draws, the book is an arduous read because of a loose thematic organisation overall and locally, a repetitious exposition, and an often muddled thread of argument. Digressions, redundancies, and frequent previews of future discussions undermine the cumulative development of the discussion throughout the book. The central tenets toward which the book is aimed are each stated a number of times but are not genuinely developed, including in the final chapter on embodiment and experience putatively devoted to this end.

The committed reader will, however, find in the book a wealth of interesting ideas and formulations, interesting connections with related lines of work, the outline of an integrative critical method for studying 'psychological' phenomena, and many thought-provoking explorations of the interplay between embodied experience, practice, biology and the social order. Its very attempt to bring together historical critique, practice, embodiment and biology within an integrated analysis of embodied and historicised experience is immensely valuable and maps the way for other attempts of this kind.

Lynne Layton, *Who's That Girl? Who's That Boy? Clinical Practice Meets Postmodern Gender Theory*
Jason Aronson, 1999

Tony Jefferson

Lynne Layton, a clinician 'trained in object relations and relational analytic theories' (p.ivx), an academic with a Ph.D. in comparative literature, and a feminist with strong interests in gender, has written an exceptional book. A mixture of old and new writings, it successfully brings together Layton's clinical, academic and political interests in a very engaging series of interconnected essays. Like Jessica Benjamin and Nancy Chodorow, two of the most influential of the highly talented feminist academics who are also analysts, Layton has a formidable grasp of object relations theory and its relationship to Lacanian-inspired work. Like them, her psychoanalytic theorising is always socially contextualised, most obviously in relation to gender inequality. But what gives her work its unique flavour is her ability to deconstruct popular culture as readily as the clinical case-study. The result is a mixture of fruitful theoretical dialogues, as postmodern gender theory is confronted with Anglo-American psychoanalytic feminism; of telling clinical case-studies, where the theory's clinical relevance is variously tested; and of illuminating deconstructions of popular culture, where novel gendered readings of Madonna and of Lynch's cult movie, *Blue Velvet*, are offered as further evidence of the utility of her specific take on gendered identity.

For a book covering such difficult terrain, it is remarkably accessible. Whether discussing Lacan, Judith Butler, popular culture or one of her clients, Layton makes it all seem easy, and her readings appear incontrovertible (no mean feat for such contested territories). Although her work is 'clearly indebted' (p35) to the work of Benjamin and Chodorow in particular (a point she is quick to acknowledge), it has its own unique emphases and, in consequence, ends in a novel place. How she manages that I will attempt (all too briefly) to spell out below.

Her Preface starts with a story about an individual, a male client of hers, and her Introduction with some memories of the cultural, namely, the social movements of the 1950s and 1960s. Both serve to show that where questions of identity are concerned, either starting point brings you up against the same theoretical concerns. In the former case, her client's self conception as bisexual to his 'core' provoked her postmodern suspiciousness about the fixity of identity even as her clinical experiences could identify with it and lead her to question whether the fluidity of identity espoused by postmodernism was not better conceptualised, psychologically, in terms of trauma and defensive splitting. In the latter case, postmodern theorising about the multiple, conflicting and changing nature of identity comes up against the fixed and coherent identifications (of women, blacks, gays, etc) that structure (and often divide) social movement politics. In either case, from either end of the individual-cultural spectrum, the tension between the fluidity and fixity of identity, between Layton's 'growing [postmodern] awareness of the fictional status of gender, sexual and racial categories' and her [clinically-based] 'awareness of how these categories are experienced psychologically' (p4) provides the 'impetus' for writing the book – and its recurrent theme.

Perhaps the most helpful thing Layton does in her introduction is to spell out the sources of tension between the language of postmodernism and theorising inspired broadly by object relations and similar work (what she calls 'relational'). These include: the different ways terms like self, individual, ego and subject are used; the assumptions about the place of culture in the construction of the subject; the extent of culture's coercive character; the nature of narcissism and its relation to subjectivity; how to understand agency and the role of attachment and loss; the way categories like masculinity and femininity are used and their assumed degree of fluidity and fixity. Given all these differences, Layton asks whether it is possible 'to conceptualise a notion of the subject that is informed by the postmodern emphasis on the general constituents of subject formation and by the Anglo-American emphasis on its specific, individual relational constituents' (p26). Her answer is to maintain that '"the subject" is both a position in discourse (sub-jected to the multiple and contradictory discourses of culture, including family) and a multiple and contradictory being whose negotiation of early relationships will shape the meaning that these discourses take on and so shape the discourses themselves' (p26) – a position which makes 'the self/subject/individual ... neither a true self nor fully determined by existent discursive positions but rather ... a continuously evolving negotiator between relationally constructed multiple and contradictory internal and external worlds' (p26). It is the relational patterns, and their meaning to the subject, not language, which accounts for the fluidity of the subject; it is their stability 'as they repeat over time' which 'accounts for the subject's coherence' (p27). This stability of relational patterns can be both coercive, in that they will inevitably suffer the imprint of 'gender inequality and other cultural and familial constraints', and non-coercive, insofar as 'the stability of internalised attachments can be the very thing that opens one to creative and emancipatory possibilities' (p27). As against the postmodern suggestion that 'oppression and hierarchies of all kinds are created and sustained by defences against uncertainty or against existential lack', Layton assumes that 'they are created and sustained by defences against relationally inflicted pain, that binaries in hierarchic relation are the sequelae of trauma, and that the capacity to go beyond binaries is a developmental achievement' (p27).

The following chapters each take up a particular aspect of this attempted integration of theory, mediating between the individual and the social while investigating the relationship between modern (binary) and postmodern (more fluid) aspects of the subject. The particular aspect that Chapter 2 develops is the question of how to conceptualise narcissism and its relation to identity. Since this serves to justify the position she has staked out in the Introduction, and to spell out its differences from other relational analysts, it is arguably the book's theoretical 'core'. Though clearly and persuasively expounded, it is not easy to summarise briefly. But, given its centrality to the text, I shall try to. Her starting point is the interesting suggestion that the underlying project of feminists interested in gender identity formation is how 'to ground the possibility of a fluid, agentic, heterogeneous self that recognises its own multiplicity (gendered and otherwise), that does not defensively foreclose on its own (or another's) multiplicity, and that can recognise and be recognised by an other like and different from the self' (p32). Implicit in such a project is a search for an exit from the pathologically narcissistic 'ties that bind'. Her first move is to agree with Kohut that pathological narcissism ('the incapacity to experience self and other as separate centres of awareness', p32) is a product of trauma and not an inevitable part of the human condition. However, she wishes to extend an understanding of the developmental origins of trauma from the conventional familial ones of Kohut (and others), 'to include sexism, racism, homophobia, and class inequality' (p32). This extension enables her to call on Chodorow and Benjamin and their understandings of the ways in which inequalities produce 'interferences with the negotiation of connection and differentiation that reproduce hegemonic or normative femininity and other kinds that reproduce hegemonic masculinity' (pp32-3), interferences that Layton calls 'narcissistic wounds'. These, she says, in typically clear and concise fashion, 'are caused when cultural and familial gender expectations restrict the many ways that one can be agentic and relational to two ways: those that define hegemonic masculinity and femininity' (p33). The nature of these narcissistic wounds, the defensive splitting off of dependency needs (and the ensuing problems of connecting) characteristic of hegemonic masculinity, and the splitting off of autonomy needs (and the ensuing problems of differentiation) characteristic of femininity, will not be unfamiliar to those acquainted with the work of Chodorow and Benjamin, as she accepts. But, despite the criticisms of this work for its essentialising and universalising tendencies, Layton wants to insist on the continuing social and clinical importance of the gender binary, and the inability of the postmodern stress on fluidity to be psychologically convincing. 'Translated into clinical terms', she neatly summarises, 'normative masculinity looks like phallic narcissism, where only the self and not the other is experienced as a subject, and normative femininity looks like a self-effacing narcissism, where only the other and not the self is perceived as a subject' (p42).

The route 'beyond narcissism' involves a return to Benjamin's take up of Stern's observation that 'babies assert some form of self from the beginning' (p42), a notion that 'gives Benjamin a developmental rationale for the possibility of non-narcissistic relating' (p43). However, because of gender inequality, this early possibility of 'mutual recognition of self and other as separate but related centres of awareness' (p43) breaks down. In her early work Benjamin argued this was because mothers are ill-equipped, culturally and psychically, to offer a model of independence to their daughters, and fathers failed to recognise a daughter's attempt to identify with his autonomy – a process which resulted in the reproduction of normative femininity, where agency can only be expressed indirectly, 'by gaining the love of an idealised male' (p43). For boys, the concomitant loss is the relational capacities that mothers disallow as sources of identification and fathers are unable to offer. The result is the reproduction of normative masculinity as 'pure assertion, omnipotence, individualism' (p43). Despite this violent cultural imposition of the gender binary, 'both sides of the split [autonomy/relationship] continue to operate psychically' (p44).

The way out, for Benjamin, is to use 'Stern's and Winnicott's developmental theories to show what must happen to achieve non-narcissistic relating' (p50), and, following Fast, to look to 'preoedipal identificatory processes to ground gender fluidity' (p51). In the former case, the mother has to be differentiated enough to be able to withstand the imperious demands of the baby 'without retaliating [the omnipotent response] or withering [the submissive response]' (p51); in the latter case, the bisexuality and cross-gendered identifications argued to be characteristic of the preoedipal period remain available, in the postoedipal phase, to counter oedipal, gendered 'realities'. Layton suggests two problems with this basis for gender fluidity: (i) 'grounding gender ambiguity in early cross-gender identifications suggests that the child does not feel the effects of culture until a later age ... which does not seem plausible' (p53); (ii) it continues to work 'within the cultural confines of male and female, with identifications with father defined as male and those with mother as female' (p52). This critique of a stage-based theory of development, and of the notion that gendered identifications need be sex-specific, provides the basis for Layton's proposed way forward, namely a 'negotiation model of gender identity' (p54). The essence of this is that gender internalisations, in which issues of dependence and independence are always implicated, are 'multiple and competing' (p55), always contingent, and may or may not eventuate in narcissistic relating. In sum:

> '[n]arcissistic gender disturbance is a matter of degree; no one escapes it, but not everyone is incapacitated by it. Gender, identity, agency and relationship involve ongoing processes of negotiation between outcomes of narcissistic relating and outcomes of non-narcissistic relating,

between products of gender inequality and possibilities that counter gender inequality' (p55).

The apparent simplicity of this conclusion should fool no-one; it is a conclusion that has been scrupulously argued for at each step of the way, an argument that I have only barely hinted at here, unfortunately. Typically, she ends with an engaging example, in this case her own turn to feminism as a defensive response to her mother's mediation of gender inequality by 'clearly preferring' her brother. It nicely, and movingly, demonstrates the value of her model.

The next few chapters variously demonstrate the value of the approach in making sense of manifestations of popular culture. Normative versions of masculinity and femininity can be endorsed, as is the case with characters from 'classic romance and hard-boiled detective fiction' – the 'gender binding' subject of Chapter 3 – or challenged – as in the 'gender bending' case of Madonna, the subject of Chapter 4. In either case, Layton is concerned to show how only by integrating postmodern feminist and relational feminist approaches to psychoanalysis is it possible to 'understand fully what each of these strands of popular culture tells us about contemporary issues of gender identity, agency and relationship' (p68). In the gender binding example:

> ... attempts to live out one side of the gender binary are threatened and undermined by the internalised other side of the binary, by what has been split off. The impossibility of banishing what is split off is manifest in the repetition that is the essence of formula fiction, a repetition compulsion meant to heal the wounds of dichotomised gender socialisation and gender inequality (p67).

In the gender bending case of Madonna, the reverse is true: her attempt to live out postmodern, gender bending fluidity is constantly contradicted and undermined by her masculine insistence on being in control (of her work/life/image). It is a contradiction which has proved fruitful for Madonna since, as Layton argues, it is probably the basis of her extraordinary popularity. But it has not come without cost, as is persuasively revealed through the tracing of Madonna's obsessive pursuit of control to early losses, and the masculine abjuring of dependency needs this gave rise to.

The chapters that follow explore: the relationship between trauma and fragmentation (5); *Blue Velvet* as 'A Parable of Male Development' (6); clinical examples that challenge the normative masculinity exemplified in the David Lynch film (7); Kohut's concept of self (8); and the evolution of Judith Butler's concept of performativity, particularly its shift away from the Lacanian tradition and towards object relations theory (9). Is to be fragmented our universal fate, as Lacanians would have it, or a cause of celebration, as some postmodern theory suggests, or the specific result of developmental traumas, as Kohut, and others, have argued? How can *Blue Velvet* help us understand contemporary gender relations? What can male narratives of men who identify with femininity tell us about contemporary masculinity? What have Kohut's writings on narcissism contributed to relational theory? How has Judith Butler's theorising about gender and subjectivity differed from that of feminist psychoanalytic relational theorists? These, and a host of related questions, are felicitously dissected, through constantly comparing and reworking theories, and providing thoughtful examples, in the light of her overriding interest in understanding gendered subjectivity as the contingent and contested outcome of intrapsychic, intersubjective and cultural dynamics.

It is, to repeat, an impressive achievement. For anyone interested in questions of gender, as clinical practitioner or theorist, it is a valuable addition to the literature. As someone whose approach to gender covers a very similar theoretical terrain, albeit as a non-clinician, I found the discussions of Benjamin, Kohut and Butler, in particular, exceedingly useful and illuminating, providing plenty of food for further thought. As a reviewer, however, I feel I should end with at least one point of criticism. Finding nothing of substance with which to disagree, I can only resort to pedantry. According to Bob Connell, we can talk of hegemonic masculinity but only 'emphasised femininity' since '[T]here is no femininity that is hegemonic in the sense that the dominant form of masculinity is hegemonic among men' (1987: 183). Perhaps Layton disagrees with Connell on that point, but, in the absence of some clarification, it jarred slightly whenever I came across the term 'hegemonic femininity'. Would that this were the extent of my disagreement with all the books I read.

References
Connell, R. W. (1987) *Gender and Power*, Cambridge: Polity

Brent Slife, Richard Williams & Sally Barlow (eds), *Critical issues in psychotherapy: Translating new ideas into practice*
Sage, 2001

Tom Strong

Trying to follow developments within psychology and psychotherapy can be dizzying and, at times, infuriating. The progression has been far from linear, and, increasingly, psychology has had to make its 'big tent' bigger, to be more representative and accepting of new methods and ideas in areas such as research and psychotherapy. Each development, however, seems to spawn its own controversies, some at odds with mainstream psychological practice. While it may feel reassuring to stay ensconced within particular models of practice, the breadth of the changes that have been occurring leaves virtually no domain within psychology unaffected. The authors suggest we need ways to reflect upon these changes for what they mean to frontline and mainstream practice.

The writers in this collection wade into these controversies. They offer an intriguing, opinionated and well-informed walk-through of our discipline's minefield of challenging issues. For starters, the editors describe themselves as being on a quest to illuminate 'overlooked problems that cannot ultimately be decided by empirical criteria alone', finding significance in 'investigating the "sacred cows" of the discipline as well as rethinking its familiar and seemingly settled elements'. With chapters that explore such issues as empirically supported treatments, assessment, the biologisation of psychotherapy, spirituality, culture, managed care, individualism, the scientist-practitioner model, free will/determinism, eclecticism, postmodernism, multiculturalism, diagnosis and feminism, it is clear that these authors are willing to address some of our discipline's most contentious concerns. And, for each author on a particular issue, the editors have found a less-than-agreeable responder to exemplify the discussions these issues provoke in contemporary psychological discourse. It is hard not to take positions on such issues as practitioners, and these authors invite us to draw from their reflections to better inform how we might take up our own positions on these issues.

Each of the chapters merits greater attention than can be provided in a review of this size, so I will selectively highlight a few to convey a sense of the rich contributions to be found here. The chapter on the biologisation of psychotherapy, by Richard Williams, serves as a case in point. Starting from two case examples, Williams confronts readers with the 'reductionist challenge' of biologising the complicated presenting issues of both clients. Since each client could be seen as also presenting social and moral issues, Williams takes his view of their issues as a jump-off point to trace the history of biologisation, and his concerns about where it could take psychotherapy if left unchallenged. Calling into question the 'supervenience thesis' ('one realm of phenomena (the mental) depends entirely on another (the biological) even though explicit and evident relations between the two are lacking'), he goes after hidden materialistic assumptions that undergird our clinical theories and practices. While he doesn't write off biologisation as one valid way of conceptualising psychological concerns, he is concerned about its alleged primacy, as causal mechanisms are increasingly imputed to genes, neurological deficits or impairments and biochemistry. For him, there is more than biology behind the causes and cures in what clients bring to therapy. The chapter is quite strong (as is the more balanced rejoinder by psychiatrist Louis Moench), though it ends with a weak exhortation that the biologisation of psychotherapy must be resisted because 'the moral integrity of the enterprise hangs in the balance'.

As someone who has had concerns about the manualisation and standardisation of therapy, the chapters on empirically supported treatments (ESTs) and diagnosis were of particular interest. Each chapter tackles dilemmas posed by the strong push, primarily from researchers, to model psychotherapy on the medical model and thereby reduce the practice of therapy to a protocol-driven enterprise. It is what is excluded by these approaches to therapy that concerns the authors. If therapy were to be reduced to manualised ESTs, because they best lend themselves to quantitative analyses and lock-step protocols, they ask what then will become of psychodynamic, experiential and other forms of therapy that have been part of therapy's offerings. Similarly, the diagnostic scheme of the DSM-IV, while focused on symptoms, promotes psychotherapy as a symptom-reducing exercise. This can disregard clients' aspirations in their 'treatment', an approach critical psychologists equate with serving the cultural status quo. ESTs and diagnostic schemes are, in the views of the contributors, part of an excessive drive to shoehorn psychology into narrow tracks that, while being researchable and clear to articulate, fail to capture other complexities of adequately conceptualising and responding to clients' presenting concerns. Again, these viewpoints find their counters in respondents who extend or challenge the writers' views.

The other chapters in this book offer much in areas that have to do with psychology's apparent exclusivity of focus (feminism, culturalism, spirituality, or its unwavering attachment to individualism). Other chapters challenge postmodern excesses by giving a balanced look at issues like the scientist-practitioner orientation of our discipline, and eclecticism. The chapter on 'Managed Care' gives us a glimpse (among other things) of how psychology's standardisation inadvertently became the handmaiden to health delivery systems hell-bent on 'rationalising' the costs of psychotherapy, a fact most American practitioners have to live with.

Count on this book to challenge you in more than a few places. You will find a primary undercurrent of concern about psychotherapy becoming too tied to scientific practices bereft of moral judgements or concerns that make us relevant to our clients. The editors intended this book to be directed to seasoned clinicians and advanced graduate students. That seems right by me, and you need to be up for some occasionally steep philosophising along the way. The issues to which the editors and contributors invite our consideration are some of the greatest facing the practice of psychotherapy today. There will be a lot to agree and disagree with, for most readers, but the greatest service of this book is the way it draws us into forming our own conclusions about issues on which we need to take positions.

Notes on contributors

Rachel Joffe Falmagne is Professor of Psychology and former Director of Women's Studies at Clark University, Worcester, USA.

Dennis Fox is Associate Professor of Legal Studies and Psychology at the University of Illinois at Springfield, USA.

Janie Conway Herron lectures in writing at Southern Cross University, Australia.

Tony Jefferson is a Professor of Criminology in the Department of Criminology, University of Keele, Staffordshire, UK.

Lorraine Johnson-Riordan has taught in Universities in New York City and Australia and is currently working on several books.

Pam Johnston is a practising visual artist whose works are represented in private and public collections in Australia and internationally. She is also a lecturer in visual arts and Indigenous Art and Culture.

Catriona McLeod is a Senior Lecturer in the Psychology Department at Rhodes University (East London), South Africa.

Brendan Maloney has been studying and working at the Institute of Philosophy in Louvain, Belgium, since 1992.

Maritza Montero is Professor of Social Psychology at Central University of Venezuela.

Desmond Painter is a Lecturer in the Department of Psychology at Rhodes University (East London), South Africa.

Dimitris Papadopoulos is an Assistant Professor of Theoretical and Developmental Psychology at the Free University of Berlin, Germany.

Ian Parker is Professor of Psychology in the Discourse Unit at Manchester Metropolitan University, where he is managing editor of *Annual Review of Critical Psychology*.

Isabel Piper is Director of the Master Program in Social Psychology at ARCIS University (Art and Social Sciences University) Santiago, Chile, and a researcher at the Latin American Institute of Mental Health and Human Rights, Santiago, Chile.

Isaac Prilleltensky is Professor of Psychology at Victoria University, Melbourne, Australia.

Peter Raggatt is a senior lecturer in the School of Psychology at James Cook University in Townsville, North Queensland, Australia.

Tom Strong is an Assistant Professor at the University of Calgary where he trains graduate students in counselling and applied psychology.

Ximena Tocornal is a PhD Researcher at Loughborough University, England and a researcher at the Latin American Institute of Mental Health and Human Rights, Santiago, Chile.

Couze Venn is a Reader in Cultural Theory at the Theory, Culture & Society Centre at Nottingham Trent University, UK.

SPECIAL OFFER

Take out a subscription NOW and get
4 issues for the price of 3

These are the planned issues of **The International Journal of Critical Psychology**

Issue 1:	**Launch Issue**	Edited by Valerie Walkerdine
Issue 2:	**Critical Theory, Critical Practice**	Edited by Valerie Walkerdine
Issue 3:	**Sex and Sexualities**	Edited by Valerie Walkerdine
Issue 4:	**Discursive Politics of Counter Stories**	Edited by M. Fine and A. Harris
Issue 5:	**Embodiment**	Edited by Valerie Walkerdine
Issue 6:	**Political Subject**	Edited by Valerie Walkerdine
Issue 7:	**Therapy/Counselling**	Edited by Lisa Blackman
Issue 8:	**Spirituality**	Edited by Valerie Walkerdine
Issue 9:	**Subjectivity**	Edited by Valerie Walkerdine
Issue 10:	**General Issue**	Edited by Valerie Walkerdine

Subscription rates: Individual subscription: £ 40.00 (US $ 65.00)
                                        Institutional subscription: £120.00 (US $190.00)

Normally for 3 issues but, with a copy of this ad (photocopy will suffice), we will extend the subscription to cover 4 issues.

To subscribe, send your name, address and payment (cheque, Visa or MasterCard), stating which issue you want to commence with.

IJCP, Lawrence & Wishart, 99a Wallis Rd, London, E9 5LN
www.l-w-bks.co.uk